The Forgotten Prophet

The Forgotten Prophet

Tāmati Te Ito and His Kaingārara Movement

Jeffrey Sissons

BRIDGET WILLIAMS BOOKS

First published in 2023 by Bridget Williams Books Ltd,
PO Box 12474, Wellington 6144, New Zealand, www.bwb.co.nz

© Jeffrey Sissons 2023

This book is copyright. Apart from fair dealing for the purpose of private study, research, criticism, or review, as permitted under the Copyright Act, no part may be reproduced by any process without prior permission of the publishers.

ISBN 9781991033482 (Paperback), ISBN 9781991033499 (EPUB), ISBN 9781991033505 (Kindle), ISBN 9781991033512 (PDF)
DOI: https://doi.org/10.7810/9781991033482

The support of the BWB Publishing Trust is integral to all books produced by BWB, and the publishers gratefully acknowledge this support. The commitment of Creative New Zealand to good New Zealand publishing is also warmly acknowledged, and its support for this publication is appreciated.

A catalogue record for this book is available from the National Library of New Zealand. Kei te pātengi raraunga o Te Puna Mātauranga o Aotearoa te whakarārangi o tēnei pukapuka.

Edited by Nancy Swarbrick
Cover design by Chloë Reweti
Internal design and layout by Katrina Duncan
Index by Ross Armstrong
Printed by Blue Star, Wellington

Contents

Foreword by Dennis Ngāwhare-Pounamu   vii

Chapter One	Origins	1
Chapter Two	The Mounted Tohunga and His Horsemen	19
Chapter Three	From Tohunga to Prophet	38
Chapter Four	Mana Trouble	60
Chapter Five	Living with Atua: The Kaingārara Letters	79
Chapter Six	Prophet and Rangatira	98
Chapter Seven	Mataitawa Years: 1860–1864	116
Chapter Eight	A Gun Broken: The Path to Parihaka	135

Acknowledgements	159
Editorial Note	161
Notes	162
Index	183

Foreword

Tērā te whetu ka ara ake,
I tōna whitianga o te paerangi.
Tukua mai te haeata,
Kia tau ki runga i te Kāhui Tupua,
Ko ngā maunga koroheke o Taranaki.
Kei ngaro i te wareware,
Ko ngā tūpuna mā kua wheturangihia,
Whitikia rā ngā tātai arorangi o te pō!
Tangihia mai e ngā manu mōhio,
Ohooho ake ai te hunga ora i te atakura nei.
Tihei mauri ora!

Te Whiti o Rongomai of Parihaka Pā once said we need to ask the mountain, as only the maunga had seen it all.

Perhaps only the mountains hold the truth of the past?

Human lives are brief, and for most of human habitation on these islands the memories of the old people were retained only as the murmur of flowing water, as footprints in earth, in graven stone images, on carved wooden surfaces; or as the echoes of voices in the ngahere as the spoken retelling of the past through generations.

Towering above the Taranaki landscape are the mountains Taranaki, Pouākai and Te Iringanui, silent witnesses holding the secrets of a bygone era. The old people said that Tahurangi was the first human to climb to the peak of the mountain once known as Pukeonaki. Upon reaching the summit he lit a ceremonial fire and proclaimed his father's name upon the mountaintop, thereby naming and claiming the maunga and all of the land within its shadow.

Rua Taranaki, the eponymous ancestor of the Kāhui Maunga, thus had his name, mana and bones intertwined within Taranaki maunga.

Ancient narratives relate that both the man and the mountain were led to the west coast by Rauhoto Tapairu. Rauhoto married Rua Taranaki, and her mauri and memory were inscribed on the stone Te Toka a Rauhoto, the revered carved rock of Pūniho Pā. It was the karakia of her father, Maruwhakatare, a tohunga of the highest order, that gave spiritual protection to his grandson as Tahurangi made the dangerous climb to the peak of the maunga. Those ancestors were amongst the earliest inhabitants of the Taranaki region known as the Kāhui Maunga, the original tāngata whenua. Their memory was retained in names carved into the landscape through the many generations of their descendants.

This book tells the story of how another of our ancestors, Tāmati Te Ito, sought to sculpt his name into history during a time of great change in Taranaki and Aotearoa. In the 1850s and early 1860s Te Ito's name and reputation were on fire. He strode across tribal boundaries and news of his work clearing the land of dangerous influences and desecrated places resounded across the whenua.

Yet it seems that his deeds, in time, became mere footnotes in the stories of other great leaders whose fame would eclipse that of Tāmati Te Ito, both regionally and nationally. Te Ito began his mahi at a truly fascinating time in Taranaki history, during which the mountains witnessed a bonfire of new ideas, amidst a swirling mixture of people including refugees returning home and a deluge of British settlers.

Amidst this turmoil, the old people continued to tend the ahikāroa, the long burning fires signifying occupation and mana whenua. Naming and claiming through karakia, like the lighting of ritual fires, wove together the physical and the spiritual, the human and the environment. Ancient prayers and incantations like the karakia uruuruwhenua that were performed when migration waka landed on new shores, secured the land and made it safe for inhabitation.

Many of these karakia were performed and ahikāroa lit when the migration waka landed along the rocky Taranaki coastline. Called the Uruwaka, the crews and descendants of the settlers from Hawaiki joined with the tāngata whenua, the Kāhui Maunga peoples, both peacefully and violently. The three greatest and last waka to arrive in the region were the *Kurahaupō*, *Aotea*, and *Tokomaru*. From these waka all iwi in the shadow of Taranaki can claim descent, including Ngāti Tama, Ngāti Mutunga, Ngāti Maru, Te Ātiawa, Taranaki Iwi, Ngā Ruahinerangi, Ngāti Ruanui and Ngā Rauru. Like streams that flow from the maunga are the many hapū affiliated with the iwi of the region: hapū who still hold fast to their mana whenua. Of course, each iwi and hapū has its own kōrero tuku iho, upholding its own mana tūpuna, and this book does not delve into those histories, because the mana of those narratives belongs to iwi and hapū.

Nonetheless, they were present when Captain James Cook sailed around the coastline and renamed the maunga 'Mount Egmont'. But unlike the Uruwaka, Cook didn't stop, greet the locals, or climb the maunga before granting his own nomenclature to the landmark. What followed Cook's voyage in 1769 was a century of change that would rip through the land, as a storm tide scours the sand from the beaches.

Within fifty years of the first European encounters, an arms race to acquire guns caused a maelstrom of death, violence and misery that became known as the musket wars, ngā pakanga o te pū; the intertribal wars that enveloped Aotearoa in flame and destruction, shifting the balances of power with the barrel of a gun.

In Taranaki, war parties from the north destroyed many settlements, killing thousands of people and enslaving hundreds more. The ripple effect caused a flood of refugees to travel south, thereby displacing other tribal groupings throughout the lower North Island, the top of the South Island and the Chatham Islands. When an uneasy peace returned to Taranaki, it was like a boiling pot that would soon overflow into the fire, undermining established hierarchies and infecting forgotten places. Adding fuel to the fires of this shifting political, spiritual and cultural landscape was an influx of British settlers with a burning desire for land on which to build for their families. This foreword cannot delve further into the often sad and painful history of that era, but it must be acknowledged for its contribution to later events in the region and the rise of Tāmati Te Ito.

This book explores the life and times of Tāmati Te Ito, and how his narrative is interwoven with the events of the second half of the nineteenth century as outlined here by Jeff Sissons. I first met Jeff in 2018 at the beginning of his research into the Kaingārara movement led by Tāmati Te Ito. Over time and many conversations in Taranaki and Te Whanganui a Tara, his project to discover more about the Kaingārara movement, and the nature of iconoclasm in Taranaki, became a search for understanding of Tāmati Te Ito, a person whose historical significance was far greater than commonly recognised.

With any narrative depicting and describing tūpuna Māori there can be alternative versions, and Tāmati Te Ito's will be no exception. However, Jeff Sissons has researched, theorised, described and written as much as is currently possible about Tāmati Te Ito. He has pieced together the meagre resources available on Tāmati's life into a narrative that places him in the middle of dramatic events in the middle and late decades of the nineteenth century.

Further kōrero and whakapapa belongs with whānau, hapū and iwi and these may come forth when the time is right. Mātauranga Māori and kōrero tuku iho are by their very nature whānau-, hapū- and iwi-centric. But at least for this time, through this book, the mana of Tāmati Te Ito is elevated back into common knowledge, his deeds no longer forgotten, his fires destined to burn again in our collective memory.

Nā Dennis Ngāwhare-Pounamu (Taranaki Tūturu)

CHAPTER ONE

Origins

On 28 April 1906, two former government surveyors, local Pākehā with a deep interest in Taranaki tribal history, approached a small cluster of houses on the northern outskirts of New Plymouth. Here, they were greeted by an old man whom they thought to be 'probably not less' than ninety years of age. The visitors were S. Percy Smith and W.H. Skinner, foundation members of the recently formed Polynesian Society and early editors of its journal. The old man was Tāmati Te Ito Ngāmoke. The surveyors greeted him and outlined their kaupapa: they had come on the train from New Plymouth to Paraiti in the hope of learning more about Taranaki tribal history and the Kaingārara movement that Te Ito had formed in the mid-1850s. There was a brief interview, but it quickly became apparent to his visitors that Te Ito did not want to talk to them. The page for 28 April 1906 in Smith's diary is blank.[1] Skinner, however, did describe the visit:

> Mr Percy Smith and self went by the 10 to 1 train to Bell Block to see the old natives at Paraiti with a view of getting information from them connecting with the history of this West Coast. Visit unsatisfactory as one did not know much and the other would not talk; this one, Tamiti Teito [sic], was a man of knowledge in old times but unfortunately he would not parl[ey]. We walked back as it would be too long to wait for the train.[2]

But before his visitors departed for their comfortable homes in New Plymouth, Te Ito did make them, and us, a small but valuable offering: a succinct summary of his vision and work during the 1850s. Smith later recalled:

> He told us he was the man who went round the country to *whakanoa* [remove the tapu from] the *pas*, and said, 'we wanted to combine all the Maori people from Mokau [in the north] to Patea [in the south] in one body, and remove the tapu from the old *pas* as it was harmful to people'.[3]

In this very brief statement, Te Ito was recalling a grand vision of pan-tribal unity and independence for the whole of Taranaki, at a time when deadly epidemics were assailing his people and the colonial government was creating deep divisions within and between tribes through its efforts to acquire land for Pākehā settlement. The fulfilment of this vision would require a massive collective effort to free the land and people, most of whom were baptised Christians, from the malignant influences of pre-Christian atua (ancestral spirits or demons). These atua took the form of ngārara (lizards and insects) and were concentrated in tapu places such as old pā and groves where pre-Christian rites had been performed by tohunga.[4]

Te Ito had begun his ritual work as a young man in the early 1850s, conducting cleansing ceremonies in tapu groves, and later leading a troop of horsemen dedicated to expelling atua from pā throughout Taranaki. By the mid-1850s he had emerged as the prophetic leader of Kaingārara, the Taranaki-wide movement that sought not only to combat sickness but also to bring about greater pan-tribal unity and prepare the way for God to be more present in a land free from demons. To this end, the prophet had organised the building of great fires north of New Plymouth and in settlements all down the west coast as far as Pātea. Entire Christian communities had gathered around these fires, in which tapu items were burned. In addition to staging these dramatic spectacles, Te Ito had also provided his followers with more personal advice, in some cases via letters, on dealing with sickness and conflict resulting from the influence of atua.

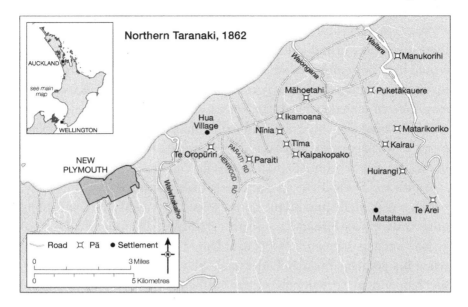

This map of the northern Taranaki area around New Plymouth shows Te Ito's home pā, Paraiti, and the neighbouring pā, Oropūriri. It was from this locality that Te Ito began his work of tapu clearance. *Source: Based on a map by Octavius Carrington, 'Province of Taranaki from Waitara to Oeo', 1862, Puke Ariki, ARC2004-306. Carrington's map is reproduced in full colour in the first set of images.*

The first Taranaki war, which began in March 1860 with the invasion of Waitara by government troops, had resulted in a militarisation of the Kaingārara. Its tribally based councils mobilised strong support for Te Ito and the Te Ātiawa chief Wiremu Kīngi Te Rangitāke, both of whom were then living at Waitara. During the military resistance that ensued, Te Ito had initiated and led a new type of incendiary campaign, setting fire to settler farmsteads on the outskirts of New Plymouth. He also kept his people safe at his well-organised inland settlement, Mataitawa, situated near present-day Lepperton. When this too was invaded in 1864, he took his people further inland for the remainder of the war.

Smith put Te Ito's reluctance to talk about these events down to the fact that after the fighting had ended he had become a 'convert' to the pacifist teachings of the Parihaka prophet Te Whiti. It is true that the old man had joined Tohu Kākahi's and Te Whiti-o-Rongomai's religious community at Parihaka south of New Plymouth in the early

1870s, and his visitors should have known that he had been arrested there during the brutal military invasion of November 1881. But there would have been more to it than this: his visitors had apparently turned up uninvited and, without any prior relationship, had expected information from someone they treated as a resource. Te Ito's reticence might also have been due to extreme ill-health. Smith recalled that the former prophet was probably at least ninety years old at the time of his visit. In fact, he was seventy-seven, and dying.[5]

Smith and Skinner would make no further visits to Paraiti and sadly, within a year, Te Ito and his memories would pass away, his death going unrecorded: no obituary, no death certificate. The only evidence of Te Ito's passing is a record of a Native Land Court hearing in June 1908, when his younger brother Paramena, who lived with him at Paraiti, succeeded to his land interests there.[6] When Paramena died four years later, Te Ito's daughter Maiterangi, who also lived with him at Paraiti, inherited her father's shares.[7] But by 1975 the entire Paraiti reserve had passed out of Māori ownership.[8] 'Paraiti' has since become 'Paraite', and the name of its once famous resident, Tāmati Te Ito, has all but been forgotten. This is the story of his life. It is also a story of intense colonial struggle over three decades between 1851 and 1881 – watershed years in the history of New Zealand – during which chiefly authority and control over land were wrested from Māori leaders. Te Ito's life affords us a new perspective on these years, so deepening our understanding of the ways in which the colonial campaign unfolded in Taranaki and beyond.

Returning to Paraiti

Tāmati Te Ito Ngāmoke was born in 1829, the son of Te Manu Karaitoa of Ngāti Ruanui and his wife Miriama (or Maiterangi) of the Puketapu hapū of Te Ātiawa. He probably moved to Paraiti with his first wife, Huihana of Ngāti Maniapoto, in the mid-1840s. Around this time, possibly before their move to Taranaki, the couple's son, Te Oneroa Tapeka, was born.[9] As a youth of sixteen or seventeen Te Ito would have been living at Paraiti with his maternal grandmother Hine Tiere, his mother Miriama, his brother Paramena and two older brothers, as well as his wife and child.[10] Te Ito's uncle, Te Tahana Papawaka, and his cousins, Rāniera Ngaere and Matiu, were living some two kilometres away, nearer the coast, in the neighbouring settlement of Te Oropūriri.[11]

Both Paraiti and Te Oropūriri (sometimes written as Horopūriri) were Puketapu settlements; that is, they comprised members of Puketapu and others who had married into the hapū. During the 1820s and 1830s these settlements had been almost completely abandoned when, threatened by better-armed tribes to the north, Puketapu, along with all other Te Ātiawa hapū, migrated south to the Kāpiti coast and the Marlborough Sounds. Hundreds of Te Ātiawa were also captured by northern Ngāti Maniapoto and Waikato forces in the early years of this period of disruption. From 1840 onwards however, Puketapu, along with other Taranaki people, began returning to their lands. Among the first people to return were the northern captives released by Waikato and Maniapoto chiefs after they had converted to Christianity. In June 1840, some two hundred left Kāwhia accompanied by the Reverend Samuel Ironside and two other Wesleyan missionaries.[12] Hundreds more followed soon after.[13]

The Wesleyan missionary stationed at Kāwhia, the Reverend John Whiteley, was particularly influential in encouraging local chiefs to release their Taranaki captives. In 1844, he noted that before the arrival of settlers in New Plymouth in 1841, 'many natives had returned from captivity to their original possessions and the number has been constantly augmenting. More lately the banished ones have taken courage and have also returned in considerable numbers to claim their lands.'[14] Settler John Cooke, who began farming near Te Oropūriri in 1843, recalled that the Puketapu population was then already about three hundred and new groups were constantly arriving.[15] Te Ito and his wife Huihana were probably among the returning captives, but in the absence of a baptism record for either of them we cannot be certain.[16]

Perhaps Te Ito had moved to Paraiti from the south. Among those who did so was his cousin, the Te Oropūriri leader Rāniera, who had been living in a Puketapu community in the Marlborough Sounds under the leadership of Te Manutoheroa.[17] A very large southern migration of Puketapu people had taken place around the year 1824, when Te Manutoheroa and some four hundred others left Taranaki to settle just south of Waikanae. The migration, termed 'Te Heke Niho Puta' also included many of the Te Ātiawa people who had been living north of Te Oropūriri and Paraiti.[18] In the early 1830s, a number of Puketapu people moved again with Te Manutoheroa from Waikanae to the Marlborough Sounds, and after 1834 there was a 'major redistribution' of the Te Ātiawa, including Puketapu, as they crossed Cook Strait from the Waikanae district to join relatives already living in the Sounds. By 1840, they had become widely dispersed, although most of the communities were concentrated in Queen Charlotte and Pelorus Sounds.[19]

In 1846 Te Ito's cousin Rāniera wrote to Donald McLean, Sub-Protector of Aborigines stationed in New Plymouth, requesting transport to New Plymouth for himself and a large group that needed to be picked up from Te Awaiti, a whaling station in the Sounds:

17 Pepuere 1846

Te Awaiti

E tama, e Te Makarini, Tena koe. Tena taku korero ki a koe. Ka tae atu ha Wikitoria ki kona, kei a koe te whakaaro, ka korero e koe ki te rangatira o Wikitoria, kia nui to korero ki a ia ki rongo tonu ia ki a koe. Mau e korero kia haere mai ha Wikitoria ki Te Awaiti nei, ki te tiki mai i a matou, ki te uta atu ki Ngamotu ... Kei wareware koe ki au, kua kite koe i au, nau i korero i haere mai ai i runga i a Wikitoria, nau i tuhituhi te ra moku. Tokomaha matou ki te haere atu.

Na tou tamaiti aroha, na Raniera

17 February 1846

Te Awaiti

Young Man, McLean,

Greetings. This is my message for you. Its about the Wikitoria coming here. Its up to you, but could you speak to the captain of the Wikitoria, and speak of the importance of him listening to you. Tell him to have the

Wikitoria come here to Te Awaiti to fetch us and take us to Nga Motu [New Plymouth] ... Don't forget me and that when you saw me you said to come on the Wikitoria and you wrote down the day for me. Many of us will be going there.

From your loving son, Raniera[20]

Rāniera must have earlier returned to Taranaki ahead of his Marlborough kin to organise the clearing of the land and re-establish Oropūriri, because he had been living in this pā in 1844 when McLean, having just taken up his position as Sub-Protector, wrote to him requesting the names of the people belonging to his hapū.[21] Rāniera's letter suggests that he later met with McLean to discuss his plans for returning his people to Taranaki from Te Awaiti.

Rāniera shared the leadership at Te Oropūriri (and possibly Paraiti) with his and Te Ito's uncle, Te Tahana Papawaka, the younger brother of Rāniera's father.[22] It is not clear when Te Tahana returned to his land, nor where he had been living prior to this, but in March 1847 he requested a thresher for his wheat from McLean.[23] The timing of the request suggests he may have returned with the group that Rāniera escorted back from the Marlborough Sounds. It is possible that Te Ito and his wife also moved to Paraiti with this group, but given Huihana's tribal affiliations (to Ngāti Matakore, a hapū of Ngāti Maniapoto), it is more likely that they had arrived earlier from the north.[24]

There is also a remote possibility that Te Ito moved to Taranaki from Waikanae with Wiremu Kīngi Te Rangitāke, the great Te Ātiawa chief. Te Rangitāke had shocked a meeting of Taranaki leaders and Governor George Grey in March 1847 when he publicly and unexpectedly announced that there should be no land sales north of the New Plymouth settlement, thus supporting a proposal that had been advanced by the Puketapu leaders, Rāniera, Waitere Kātātore and Rāwiri Waiaua. Adding insult to injury, he further announced that he and his people would be returning from Waikanae to reoccupy their lands at Waitara, and rejected outright a proposal by Grey that the government assist him in establishing a model village there on the north side of the river.[25] As reported by the Wesleyan missionary,

Henry Turton, '[He] told the Governor at once that he did not need his assistance. He would erect his Pa himself and moreover he would build it where he pleased and when he pleased without asking permission from anyone.'[26] Grey responded angrily, threatening to arrest Te Rangitāke and smash his canoes if he attempted to leave Waikanae. This was a turning point in the relationship between the two men: Te Rangitāke, a former government ally who had supported its military campaigns in the Hutt Valley and who had travelled with the Governor to New Plymouth for the meeting, would never bow to threats such as these. Grey, in turn, felt betrayed.[27]

Te Rangitāke's return migration from Waikanae to the mouth of the Waitara River (on the *south* side) took place over a period of seven months between April and November 1848; some of his people travelled by canoe, others drove stock overland.[28] As they passed through Whanganui in June, the Church Missionary Society (CMS) missionary, the Reverend Richard Taylor, took a census of those travelling: there were 587 men, women and children, 44 canoes, 5 boats and about 60 horses. Fifty of the migrants belonged to Puketapu and they intended to settle in the neighbourhood of Te Oropūriri and Paraiti.[29] Rāwiri Waiaua, whose boat was named *Louisa*, and Rāniera, whose waka was named *Tamakaihou*, were among them. Rāniera had probably travelled from Te Oropūriri to lead the return migration of his relatives, as he had done earlier with the group from Te Awaiti.[30] It is possible that Tāmati Te Ito was among the Puketapu returnees (he would have been around nineteen years of age at the time), but again, because his wife was of Ngāti Maniapoto descent, it remains most likely that he had earlier moved to Paraiti from the north.

Te Ito emerged as a ritual leader at Paraiti in the context of increasing political rivalries among his Te Ātiawa relatives, especially within his Puketapu hapū, but also between Te Ātiawa and the tribes to the south: Taranaki Iwi, Ngā Ruahine and Ngāti Ruanui. In the following account, this rapidly shifting political context is briefly sketched. We begin with his mother's people, Puketapu, and then travel to southern Taranaki to introduce the political and religious concerns of his father's people, Ngāti Ruanui.

Te Ito's Puketapu Kin

By the late 1840s Te Ito's Puketapu kin were living in a number of lightly palisaded settlements or pā north of New Plymouth, between the Waiwhakaiho and Waiongana rivers. The general area was often referred to as 'the Hua' in official reports, and Te Oropūriri, the main pā where Te Tahana and Rāniera lived, was frequently referred to as 'Hua Pa'.[31] A portion of Te Tahana's settlement at Oropūriri was excavated by archaeologists from the University of Auckland in 2002 and 2004, and on the basis of these excavations, archaeologists Simon Holdaway and Rod Wallace were able to reconstruct the layout of its dwellings and gardens. Their drawing of the settlement in the late 1840s and early 1850s shows six or seven thatched whare pūni (sleeping houses), each in a fenced compound within a lightly palisaded enclosure, beyond which are three fenced vegetable gardens and a number of paddocks.[32] Te Ito's nearby settlement at Paraiti would have been similar, although the smaller enclosure probably contained fewer houses. Gardens and paddocks would have been located outside a palisade.

Te Tahana was a strong supporter of the government, at a time when most of Te Ito's relatives at Paraiti and Te Oropūriri were opposed to colonial dealings in Taranaki.[33] At the New Plymouth meeting in 1847, during which Te Rangitāke announced his planned return to Waitara, Te Tahana met with Grey. He arranged a separate meeting between the Governor and, as he described them, his 'bad' Puketapu people, who were strongly opposed to any selling of their land. An award of some 60,000 acres in north Taranaki to the New Zealand Company in 1844 had recently been declared invalid by Grey's predecessor, William FitzRoy, and Grey had come to New Plymouth in February 1847 to discuss alternative prospects for settlement.[34] But if he and Te Tahana had expected a softening of the Puketapu position regarding the selling of land they were to be sorely disappointed. Grey expressed particular annoyance at the reception he received from Rāniera and two other Puketapu leaders, Waitere (Whiteley) Kātātore and Rāwiri Waiaua. The Governor's subsequent 'high tone' and bullying did not go down well. McLean recalled:

The next meeting was that of the Puketapus. About 40 or 60 attended, and offered the most determined opposition to part with an inch of land. The parties who spoke were Raniera, Katatore, Waiaua and two or three more unimportant fellows. The Governor told them that unless they were inclined to come to his arrangements he would doubt the validity of their claims ... that they ought to remember that they were once driven from their land and they better not run the risk of its being repeated ... The natives did not much relish the Governor's speech and set off home.[35]

While there was united opposition to land sales at this meeting, tensions between the Puketapu leaders, particularly between Waiaua and Kātātore, would soon increase significantly. When Waiaua and others offered some land, now known as Bell Block, in March 1848, Kātātore and his relatives erected a tall, carved pole (pou whenua) on the north bank of the Waiwhakaiho River (between New Plymouth and Bell Block) to mark the limit of land sales.[36] The sale was mostly completed in November, but Kātātore refused to accept payment and, largely due to his threats, Pākehā settlers were unable to move onto the land until 1853.[37] Te Tahana was appointed as a native assessor in 1850 to work with the resident magistrate in 'settling disputes between persons of the native race'.[38] However, as we will see in the next chapter, his efforts to mediate between Rāwiri Waiaua and Waitere Kātātore would be spectacularly unsuccessful.

By 1852, tensions were also increasing between members of Te Ito's Puketapu community at Paraiti and their Puketapu neighbours a little to the north, led by Rāwiri Waiaua. This strain, combined with the hostilities between Waiaua and Kātātore, would erupt into deadly warfare in the mid-1850s. It started with the killing of a horse. Police inspector Henry Halse reported in 1852:

Jan 2. Rawiri Waiaua came to Barracks. Told me his father's horse had been killed by Paraiti natives for trespass. Payment having been refused, hostilities were proposed and his people were under arms awaiting his return. He left me to call on the Reverend H.H. Turton ...

[Jan] 3. At daylight Hakopa [an assessor] left for Puketapu to watch the movements of the natives there assembled. 10.am Native information. Thirty pounds had been offered and refused. The sum required is fifty – the chance of an outbreak unlikely.[39]

Waiaua's father's horse, Miriona (Million), had been part of the payment for the Bell Block. The animal had clearly been speared, but Halse was unable to determine who the killer was. Nonetheless, Te Tahana proposed that a payment of £30, the average price of a horse at that time, be made to Waiaua by Te Ito and the inhabitants of Paraiti to settle the issue.[40] Waiaua rejected the offer, demanded £50 to compensate for the loss and insult, and threatened bloodshed if the money was not paid.[41] Te Tahana, Rāniera and others at Oropūriri wrote angrily to McLean, requesting that their letter be published widely:

Ka karangatia e [Rāwiri Waiaua] kia piro te ao katoa, ka mau tona ringa ki te pu, ki te hamanu. Ka tu ki runga ka korero, ka whakakaha i ona tuakana kia maia ratou ki te whawhai. He inati, e hoa ma, te he o te whakaaro o tenei kaiwhakawa, o Rawiri Waiaua. Tenei ano te kupu o te rongo pai ara o te Karaipiture hei whakarite i tona he, 'ko waho e tika ana ki ta te tangata titiro, ko roto ia i toki ana i te kino, te paru i te whakarite kau'.

[Rāwiri Waiaua] announced that the whole world was rotten, and grabbed his gun and ammunition. He stood up and made a speech encouraging his elder relatives to be brave for the fight, its appalling, friends, how wrong this assessor, Rawiri Waiaua, is in his thinking. This is the word of the Gospel, that is, of the Scriptures, which equates with his wrongdoing: 'on the outside he looks righteous, but inside he is altogether evil and defilement without equal' [Matthew 24:28].[42]

It was in the midst of these heightened tensions involving the people of Paraiti and neighbouring Oropūriri that Te Ito began his work as a tohunga, aiming to expel the malevolent atua that had been causing much conflict, sickness and death, and thus hopefully enabling his people to live more freely upon the lands to which they had recently returned.

Te Ito's Ngāti Ruanui Kin

But if Te Ito's project of spiritually inspired unification had its immediate origins in conflict amongst his mother's people, it also drew upon a deep desire for unity and self-determination among his father's people, Ngāti Ruanui, living in southern Taranaki.[43] Te Ito was identified as belonging to Ngāti Ruanui on the death certificate of his son, Te Oneroa, signed by a Methodist (Wesleyan) minister in Ōtorohanga in 1918. This iwi identification is further supported by letters written to Te Ito in 1858 by Tāmati Reina Ngāwhare, a Ngāti Ruanui chief and Wesleyan teacher who was then a strong Kaingārara supporter. In a letter sent in September 1858, for example, Reina addressed Te Ito as 'taku tamaiti' (my son) and, even more significantly, he signed himself endearingly as 'tou papa kuare' (your foolish father), strongly suggesting that he was his adoptive father, his uncle, or both.[44]

The Reverend William Woon, the Wesleyan missionary living at Waimate in the 1840s, described Reina as 'a charming man', 'a very superior man and very conversant with the Scriptures'.[45] He added, 'I have been frequently delighted while listening to his addresses and prayers and he considers no journey too long in going place to place preaching "the truth it is Jesus" though of a weakly constitution.'[46] Tāmati Reina was one of Woon's two main teachers and he assumed a leading role in the organisation of church services and other large Christian gatherings in the south.[47] In September 1846, for example, he organised the building of a large church, 90 feet long and 45 feet wide, for the baptism of a local chief, Hōri Kīngi Pākeke. For this service, which lasted all night, Woon recalled some 1,200 people were seated in the building:

> The teachers were preaching till break of day after the sabbath exhorting those who have not repented to repent etc. and with singing

and prayer did not break up till we left them to return home … Religion engrosses their attention wherever they go. At the sacrament on the Sabbath referred to, when closing the services, the two teachers [one of whom was Reina] prayed and there was general weeping throughout the congregation. Such a scene I have never before witnessed in New Zealand.[48]

The religious fervour witnessed by Woon and encouraged by Reina had been building among Ngāti Ruanui communities for at least a year. In October 1845, as he journeyed down the coast, Donald McLean learned of a 'new doctrine' that had just 'sprung up'. Some people had seen the Almighty and his angels, and they were able to baptise with the Holy Spirit.[49] Revd Richard Taylor at Whanganui learned more about this movement, which he termed 'tikanga hou' (new practices), in January the following year:

I learned some fresh particulars from them relative to the strange delusion which has seized some Taranaki natives. It is now principally at Haurangi and Warea, they have given up all prayer and observance of the Sabbath they no longer read God's word, this native said he brought away a basketful of books as they did not care for them and he could not bear to see sacred books neglected, still they acknowledge God and Xt [Christ] but they say that he has himself appeared and entered into them and therefore have no further need of prayer to him. When any one comes to their pa they stroke him all over with their hands saying they do that to rub out his sins, all the time drawling out Amine.[50]

As we will see, throughout the 1850s Tāmati Te Ito was continually moving back and forth between Paraiti in the north and Ngāti Ruanui communities in the south, and it is likely that he had also been doing so in the 1840s. If so, he would undoubtedly have encountered this heightened religious fervour amongst his father's people, zeal that would find new expression in his Kaingārara movement a decade later.

Similarly, Te Ito's brother Paramena appears to have also moved freely between Paraiti and the Ngāti Ruanui community of Ketemarae,

Tāmati Reina's settlement. In 1858, for example, while living at Paraiti, Paramena had received a police warning that by carrying a pistol he was in violation of a proclamation prohibiting the carrying of weapons.[51] Te Ito or Te Tahana must have sent him to live with Reina soon after this, because four months later, in September, Te Ito's 'foolish father' wanted to send him back. Reina wrote: 'Tenei hoki tetehi. Ko to teina, Paramena, kia riro atu i a koe ki kona. Kei a koe he tikanga mona. Ka kite koe i te marama mona, e pai ana. Ka Mutu. Na tou papa kuare, na Tamati Reina Ngawhare.' (This is another [word]. Take your younger brother, Paramena, over there. It's up to you what you do with him. It is good if you can find some clarity for him. The end. From your foolish father, Tamati Reina Ngawhare.)[52]

Tāmati Reina's views on land sales were diametrically opposite to those of Te Ito's Puketapu uncle, Te Tahana. As early as October 1851, he and other Ngāti Ruanui chiefs were seeking an alliance with Rāniera at Te Oropūriri and Wiremu Kīngi Te Rangitāke, the Te Ātiawa leader at Waitara, to resist what they saw as Pākehā claims to absolute sovereignty. In a letter written on behalf of Ngāti Ruanui, Reina invoked Hōne Heke's felling of the flagpole at Kororāreka, pointing out that a new flagpole recently raised at New Plymouth amounted to a claim of mana over the entire district. In other words, he suggested that the flagstaff could be seen as a pou whenua, a post like that put up by Kātātore, traditionally erected by chiefs to assert mana over the land.[53] Reina wrote:

Tenei te korero o nga tangata o tenei iwi o Ngatiruanui, kia purutia te oneone ko te waiu hoki tenei o te tangata ko te oneone. Kia rongo mai koutou e pouri ana o matou ngakau ki tenei kara, he kara tango whenua, otira me rapu he tikanga ki te Atua hei whakaha ia tatou kia kaha ki te Atua ki te whenua. He komiti nui ta matou kia kaha ki te Atua ki te oneone ... kua kite ano [ngā Pākehā] kua wakaturia he kara mo Niutireni e te Atua. Ko Taranaki, kei te kite mai nga kaipuke i Taranaki.

This is the talk of the people of this tribe, of Ngati Ruanui, to retain the land, for this is the milk of the people namely, the land. Listen, our hearts are dark because of this flag which will take our lands, but let us seek council of God to strengthen us that we may adhere to him and to our lands. This was a large meeting. Be strong to God and to the soil.... [The Pākehā] know that God has erected a flag for New Zealand – viz Mount Egmont [Taranaki]. Ships can see Mount Egmont.[54]

When a copy of this letter was brought from Te Oropūriri to Inspector Halse, he arranged for the Puketapu assessors Te Tahana, Rāwiri Waiaua, Tāmati Waka and Rāniera to write a letter in reply.[55] They advised Ngāti Ruanui to hold back from confrontation:

Tenei ano te kupu o nga kaumatua, e kore e pai kia tukua atu te tamaiti kia taka i te pari kia tere i te wai, otira me pupuru mai, me pupuru mai e tatou. Heoi ano, ka mutu i konei te korero mo koutou. Na matou tenei, nga rangatira Maori e whirinaki ana ki runga ki a tatou Pakeha.

This is what the elders said, that it is not right to allow a child to fall off a cliff, or to drift in the water, it must be held back, we all must hold it back. Well, what we have to say to you ends here. This is from us, from the Maori chiefs who put their trust in our Pakeha.[56]

But by October 1852, anxiety over the potential loss of land and political independence had intensified significantly among Tāmati Reina's people. That month, their missionary, Revd Woon, whom most of the people (presumably including Reina) had now abandoned, wrote to the *Taranaki Herald* to inform its readers that his former congregation had introduced a new legal system within which offenders were being fined, and that many had abandoned the Christian moral imperative of no sex before marriage. He was dumbfounded:

The Natives of my district are altering fast, and are certainly taking leave of their senses. They try me in the utmost in my endeavours to lead them in the right way. They are continually holding meetings to prevent the land being sold to Europeans ... Death having carried off so many there is a great disproportion of the sexes.[57]

The following year, 1853, Tāmati Reina embarked on a journey down the entire Taranaki coast promoting a pan-tribal, land-holding movement of political independence. It would become closely linked to Te Ito's work of tapu removal and later be closely identified with his Kaingārara movement.[58]

Te Ito, the Tohunga

In the press or official reports, Te Ito was invariably identified as belonging to Te Ātiawa or, more particularly, to Puketapu. While it is true that he and his family made their homes within the boundaries of Te Ātiawa throughout the 1850s and that they had strong kinship ties to the Puketapu hapū, its land and leaders, Te Ito's mission to free the land from tapu forces and unite Taranaki in opposition to land sales was more directly influenced by his Ngāti Ruanui relatives than his mother's Puketapu kin. Tāmati Reina probably had a particularly strong influence on the young Te Ito – perhaps even guiding him through the early stages of a personal psychological journey that led to his becoming a tohunga.

In pre-Christian Taranaki there had been a class of tohunga that specialised in expelling ngārara that caused sickness. Te Kāhui, a very knowledgeable tohunga from Taranaki, told Percy Smith that ngārara-atua-māori – ordinary atua that assumed the form of lizards, as opposed to those associated with mākutu (sorcery) – were dealt with by tohunga-taitai-ngārara (lizard-expelling priests) whose practices included the cooking and eating of ngārara.[59] We know nothing of the means through which Te Ito gained his mastery of these practices, but it is likely that at least some of his knowledge was passed down to him by his Ngāti Ruanui elders, including his adoptive father, Tāmati Reina. Reina and other Ngāti Ruanui leaders who set out on a path of political and religious independence in the 1840s must have seen in Te Ito the spiritual qualities and abilities needed to further their cause.

And indeed, within four years Te Ito would take their project to a new cosmological level, revealing a new divine purpose in the removal of tapu and opposition to land sales. In so doing, he would have greater success than Reina in forging strong links between Ngāti Ruanui leaders in the south and Te Ātiawa leaders in the north, especially with Wiremu Kīngi Te Rangitāke who, after his return in 1848, strongly resisted government interference in his exercise of mana and control over his land. As we will see in Chapter Four, Te Ito left Paraiti to live with Te Rangitāke at Waitara in the late 1850s, supporting him with his prophetic guidance.

Those who returned to Taranaki in the 1840s saw themselves as inhabiting a spiritually dangerous landscape – not only was it now being slashed by survey lines that brought social division, but it was also a place where many had been killed during the warfare of the 1830s. The blood of the slain stained the soil and their bones remained in the earth. When Waikato chiefs learned in 1841 that the land that they had conquered was being offered for sale, many were outraged. Whiteley reported the views of one Ngāti Maniapoto leader, Haupōkia, as follows:

> That land is tapued with our blood – with the blood of our fathers, with the blood of our sons, with the blood of our brothers – there lie their ashes, there are their bones deposited. Those [Taranaki] men are our slaves; we drove them to Kapiti or left those who remained as keepers of our land. And now they are going to sell our fathers and friends who have fallen in the battlefields to be eaten by the white man (this is the construction they put upon the act of growing food upon any tapued spot. The man who eats that food eats their friends whose blood was shed there, who died there and who was buried there).[60]

Many Taranaki returnees would have shared the view that the presence of death in the landscape rendered many sites tapu. When, for example, Charles Creed's Wesleyan congregation built their first chapel at Ngāmotu, New Plymouth, in 1841, these returned captives deliberately sited it on one of the 'old encampments of Waikato', 'strewn over with human bones'. In doing so they probably sought to defeat or contain the tapu of the site with the greater power of the Christian God.[61]

By the early 1850s, as epidemics raged through the Taranaki Māori population, many people attributed the unprecedented number of deaths to the dangerous nature of their landscape, contaminated as it was with many sites of uncontrolled tapu. In the next chapter we will follow Te Ito as he travels out from Paraiti to cleanse the tapu sites and objects believed to be the causes of widespread sickness and conflict and, through these practices, to assist people to live safely with their land.

CHAPTER TWO

The Mounted Tohunga and His Horsemen

Between the mid-1840s and mid-1850s, in addition to experiencing significant pressure to sell their land and deep anxiety surrounding their future independence, Te Ito and his relatives living at Paraiti in the north and in Ngāti Ruanui settlements to the south were in constant fear of sickness and death from epidemics, the shock troops of colonialism. Pākehā newcomers brought with them diseases to which Māori had no immunity. Influenza struck in 1844, whooping cough in 1847 and mumps in 1851, followed by a devasting outbreak of measles in August 1854. And there was undoubtedly much sickness that went unrecorded.[1] In 1849, Revd Richard Taylor wrote that Ngāti Ruanui people were 'dying in all directions'; one family he visited had one child living out of eight.[2] It has been estimated that Ngāti Ruanui settlements lost a third of their population between 1845 and 1852.[3] The modern notion that disease is spread through viruses was not generally known at this time; instead, the very high Māori death rate was widely attributed by Pākehā to damp and cramped living conditions. Epidemics were believed to originate in miasmas – foul odours or 'bad air' that emanated from rotting matter – which, in Europe, were most often invisibly present in slums.

Te Ito and many other Māori leaders had different explanations for the very high death rate in their communities. Some attributed it to their Christian baptism, which had caused the now rejected ancestral atua (ancestral spirits and demons) to seek revenge. Richard Taylor dismissed this explanation as mere foolishness, even when it came from a grief-stricken parent who had lost ten children:

> This morning as soon as it was light I held service with the natives and baptised five children. The heathen relatives of one were at first unwilling to have it baptised as its parent had already had ten children who were all dead and they attributed this great mortality to their having been baptised. This foolish idea is not uncommon.[4]

The idea was, of course, no more 'foolish' than Taylor's concept of miasmas.

Wāhi Tapu Ceremonies, 1850–53

In Taranaki, people attributed sickness not just to the actions of atua in general, but to their harmful presence in certain sacred places termed 'wāhi tapu', tapu being the condition that resulted from their presence. As the great Taranaki scholar Peter Buck (Te Rangi Hīroa) put it, 'it was the atua who punished, not a vague poisonous tapu'.[5] The term 'wāhi tapu' included burial grounds, pā and places where tohunga had performed their ceremonies to control states of tapu. According to Taylor, writing in the 1850s, the latter wāhi tapu, or 'sacred groves', were of particular concern. They had been 'only entered by the priest and merely contained the tombs of chiefs, offerings to gods and sacrifices, together with food baskets and fragments unconsumed by sacred persons [chiefs], rags and old garments of chiefs, their hair when it had been cut and such things'.[6] The atua that guarded such wāhi tapu usually took the form of ngārara (reptiles and insects), some of which were believed to have been deliberately placed there by tohunga.

Tāmati Te Ito probably began performing ceremonies to expel atua from wāhi tapu in 1850 or 1851, around the time that conflicts within

Te Ito's Puketapu hapū were intensifying and his Ngāti Ruanui relatives were formulating the concept of a pan-tribal alliance to hold their land. He would have been only in his early twenties at the time. This date for the beginning of Te Ito's work is derived from a comment by the Methodist historian the Reverend T.G. Hammond, who wrote that at the time George Stannard began his missionary labours at Waitōtara in southern Taranaki, 'anxiety about the disposal of land was becoming somewhat acute, and concern about the land precipitated other matters of a more or less troublesome character'.

> A man named Tamati Teito started a proposal to whakanoa (make common) all the sacred places of the Taranaki tribes. He contended that afflictions such as influenza came by disregard of the tapu at one time so much feared, and that the only way to be relieved from these constantly recurring maladies was to remove the causes.[7]

Stannard arrived at his new mission station, Waitōtara, in late 1848, and he began his mission work there the following year, developing friendly relations with Revd Richard Taylor at Whanganui. In June 1851, Taylor recorded that a group of people had come down the Whanganui River and had cooked and eaten food in one of their wāhi tapu, and he added that his congregation had told him that this practice had 'commenced in New Plymouth'.[8] The members of Taylor's Whanganui congregation would have been referring to the general New Plymouth area that included Oropūriri and Paraiti. It is reasonable to conclude that Te Ito, the person who 'started the proposal' to whakanoa all of the wāhi tapu, was the same person who had recently 'commenced' this work in New Plymouth. As we will see, subsequent events, such as his appointment to lead a troop of horsemen to extend the whakanoa work, support this assumption. Although Te Ito probably orchestrated the earliest of the wāhi tapu ceremonies, it is clear that they were subsequently performed by other Christian leaders throughout Taranaki and, as we have seen, also in Whanganui.[9] Some of these leaders may have been working under Te Ito's direction, but others may simply have been following his example.

In September 1851 Taylor visited Stannard's Ngāti Ruanui congregation in southern Taranaki, and learned that some time before, a mission 'teacher' named Pirimona had been conducting ceremonies to cleanse a local wāhi tapu. One of the participants told him that eating food within the sacred grove was intended to drive away ngārara, and Taylor was also told that these creatures were the embodiments of atua:

> I am thankful from this journey to find that the natives are gradually abandoning their strange infatuation about wahi tapus and are returning to the right way. Some time ago at Taw[h]itinui where this new custom most prevailed a teacher named Pirimona assembled the inhabitants in the wahi tapu or sacred grove in the midst of which the 'tuahu' or praying stone still stands, and having lit several fires in the middle of the grove whilst the entire population sat round in a circle he read a chapter from the Testament and cooked some potatoes which he hukihukied or strung on short sticks and then laid on the fires which being done he presented some of them to each person in the circle, but this eating is now being given up. On my speaking to a person who had done so he said, 'was it not right to drive away the ngararas, or reptiles, from them' (so they called their ancient gods). I told him by such practices they were more likely to get them back again into their hearts. This eating of food in their ancient sacred place was done to destroy its sanctity and drive away their old gods from their former abode.[10]

As noted in Chapter One, these lizard rites had strong traditional precedents. Te Kāhui, the Taranaki sage whose writings on mākutu (sorcery) and the practices of tohunga were translated and published by Percy Smith, explained:

> The ngarara-atua-maori is made tapu to give it strength; afterwards it is deprived of tapu by burning in the fire and is eaten in order to lessen the pain in the body [reduce the sickness]. But the ngarara still retains its power to affect man. In the same manner, men have had the power to annul the power of the same ngarara, even from the ancient time of Te-Tatau-o-te-po [the original house of teachings] right down

the generations to the present time. The names of the atua-ngarara (lizard gods) are: Moko-hiku-aro, Tu-tangata-kino, Rapa-whenua and Huru-kokoia.[11]

By conducting ceremonies to expel ngārara from wāhi tapu, Te Ito and others were thus improvising upon a well-established tradition in Taranaki. As noted earlier, there was also a distinct class of healers in Taranaki: lizard-expelling priests termed 'tohunga-taitai-ngārara'. The healing services of these tohunga were still being called upon in the 1840s, as the following journal entry written by Richard Taylor in 1846 reveals:

[At Hikurangi Pā, on the Whanganui River] I had a long conversation with two native prophets, they profess to cure the sick by their prayers to the evil one, as they look into the bodies of their patients and at once see what is the matter with them, and draw out the lizard which is feeding on their vitals.[12]

Of course, the 'prophets' had not prayed to the 'evil one'. They would have been more likely to have understood their healing as re-enacting a mythical struggle between two distant ancestors, Tāne and his older brother Whiro. As told by Moihi Te Mātorohanga, the tohunga whose teachings are included in Percy Smith's *The Lore of the Whare Wananga*, Tāne and Whiro's bitter dispute began when Tāne proposed that he and the other children of Rangi and Papa should separate their parents. Whiro was opposed to this plan, wanting to remain within the warm, dark embrace of his parents. Whiro's animosity towards his brother increased when Tāne was subsequently chosen over him to ascend to the highest heaven and obtain the three baskets of knowledge, afterwards becoming known Tāne-nui-a-rangi (Great Tāne of the heavens).[13] Whiro's anger eventually propelled him into an outright war with Tāne, resulting in his humiliating defeat and banishment to the dark underworld. From here, Whiro continued to attack Tāne's descendants, assuming the form of a lizard – a ngārara-atua-Māori – to inflict sickness and death. As ethnographer Elsdon

Best put it, while sickness persists, 'the old contest between him and Tane is still continued'.[14] He added that the most relentless and effective emissaries of Whiro were the dreaded Maiki brothers, Maiki-nui, Maiki-roa, Maiki-kunāwhea (a different set of atua from those named by Te Kāhui), all of whom continue to 'wage ceaseless warfare against the descendants of Tāne in the world of life'.[15]

Te Ito and the others who performed the whakanoa whenua rites at wāhi tapu in the 1850s were Christian, and so must have reconciled their understandings of atua and ngārara with the Bible and missionary teachings. Te Ito later understood atua and the Christian God to be related as parts of a divine hierarchy, and such a view was perhaps more widely shared by those performing the wāhi tapu rites. Some people were also debating the possibility that the ngārara had been sent from the underworld to this world by Satan, a Christian substitute for Whiro. But when members of his Taranaki flock suggested this to Taylor, he would have none of it. He agreed that Satan was indeed assailing them, but he was doing so with false ideas rather than with lizards:

> The custom of eating in wahi tapus was next considered, some said it was quite right to destroy the power of Satan for visiting them with sickness. I asked them if they seriously thought the eating of a few potatoes in a wahi tapu could have such an important effect and whether they thought if they were to meet a roaring lion that they could disarm his fury by eating a few potatoes before him? This seemed to make their custom ridiculous and further I asked them if they thought that evil spirits only dwelt in wahi tapus. I told them that they preferred dwelling in men's hearts as in the days of our Saviour. I said it was plain that Satan was striving to regain his dominion over them by putting all these vain ideas into their heads.[16]

Irrespective of whether the enemy was viewed as Satan or Whiro, in southern Taranaki at least, most people saw their wāhi tapu work as complementing that of the missionaries and were at a loss to understand why there was such strong missionary opposition to their ceremonies. Te Ito certainly viewed his work as complementary to that of the missions.

In the early 1850s, then, Te Ito's wāhi tapu ceremonies were being performed throughout Taranaki – certainly in the north, around New Plymouth where they were said to have begun, and in the southern villages visited by Richard Taylor, but no doubt also within Taranaki Iwi and Ngā Ruahine communities in the heartland of Taranaki. These ceremonies were an attempt to address the extraordinarily high death rate from diseases within Māori communities, but they were also to prepare safe habitation in a dangerous landscape to which many had recently returned.

At the exact time that this tapu-cleansing work was being undertaken, Ngāti Ruanui leaders were experimenting with new laws and communicating to Te Ātiawa leaders their concerns about threats to their freedom and independence, symbolised by the erection of the new flagpole in New Plymouth. In the north, divisions were widening within Te Ātiawa communities between land sellers and other leaders, such as Waitere Kātātore and Wiremu Kīngi Te Rangitāke, who wanted to hold the land and chart out a more independent future than that envisaged by the colonial government. Tāmati Te Ito's work as a young tohunga was probably supported by all or most of these land-holding leaders, north and south, including Te Rangitāke and Te Ito's mentor, Tāmati Reina.

Te Ito's Ope Whakanoa

By the beginning of 1852, the twenty-three-year-old Te Ito had assumed a greater leadership role at Paraiti. In January that year, he was the main spokesperson for a group complaining to the police about a Pākehā visitor who had been showing them a distinct lack of respect. Henry Halse, Inspector of Police, reported as follows: 'Jan 18. Sunday parade. Police on duty in town during Divine Service. Tamati, a Paraiti native, and three others came to the Barracks this morning and complained of unprovoked abuse received from Mr. Merrett. I went into town but did not meet with that individual.'[17] Joseph Jenner Merrett was an Auckland-based portrait and landscape artist, who married Rangitetaea of Waikato in 1843 and worked under the patronage of Sir George Grey in the late 1840s. According to his own account in 1852, he had 'cursed the native chiefs of this [Te Hua] district for the insult they offered to his Excellency, Sir George Grey'.[18] The 'insult' was possibly the refusal of Rāniera and his supporters to negotiate the sale of land at the time of Grey's visit in 1847. It is not clear where his abuse had occurred but, because it was Sunday morning, it is possible that Te Ito and his Christian family had travelled into New Plymouth from Paraiti to attend a church service there before visiting the police barracks. Although Merrett later received a warning from the police, he continued with his acts of verbal aggression, and in February the resident magistrate evicted him from Taranaki.

At this time Te Ito was probably heavily engaged in performing wāhi tapu ceremonies and building his reputation as a tohunga and local leader. He would soon gain greater formal recognition as an inspired tohunga matakite (seer) through his appointment, the following year, to lead an ope whakanoa – a troop dedicated to the removal of tapu from sites throughout Taranaki. It appears that in association with their push for self-determination, southern leaders agreed to expand Te Ito's whakanoa project and assemble for him a pan-tribal entourage of horsemen that would systematically remove the tapu from the whole of Taranaki by performing tapu-removal ceremonies at the numerous pā (possibly numbering in excess of a hundred) located throughout the district.[19] While it is unclear when it was decided to form this troop, it is recorded that Te Ito left Paraiti and travelled to the Australian goldfields soon after the Merrett incident, and that a pan-tribal ope whakanoa was organised for him when he returned in 1853.[20] It is possible that Te Ito went to Australia intending to earn money to support his tapu-removal work; perhaps he was accompanied by future members of his ope whakanoa who, like him, intended to purchase horses with money earned from gold mining.[21]

Gold had been discovered at Ballarat in the Australian state of Victoria in 1851, initiating the Victorian goldrush. By January of the following year, tens of thousands of migrants, including hundreds of

Māori, flooded into the state. Indeed, it has been estimated that at the peak of the goldrush around 1 per cent of the total Māori population was living in the central Victorian fields, mostly near Bendigo, where Māori miners 'abounded'.[22] A study by John Tully of Māori working claims at Eaglehawk (near Bendigo), Dunolly and Maryborough estimated their number to be between 400 and 500.[23] Te Ito and others who travelled with him from Taranaki had probably lived in one of the exclusively male tent camps, where they would have interacted on a daily basis with a wide range of nationalities. John Singleton, a surgeon on the goldfields, wrote that 'men of almost every European and Asiatic nation and language' were there, including 'Greeks and Germans, Danes and Swedes, French, Spanish, Portuguese and Italians, Hindoos, Negroes, Malays, Chinese, with Maoris and other Pacific Islanders'.[24] This Australian experience must have had a significant impact on Te Ito's understanding of cultural difference and colonial relations in New Zealand.

We cannot know how much money, if any, Te Ito made in Australia, but some Māori were said to have returned with significant sums.[25] Among the Māori miners in Melbourne was Winitana Tupotahi, cousin of the Ngāti Maniapoto chief Rewi Maniapoto, and a man who, by reputation at least, would have been known to Te Ito. He is said to have returned to New Zealand 'with a little hoard of gold, although he had suffered losses by robbery on the goldfields'. In Australia, this war leader 'had learned a good deal about shaft-sinking, tunnelling, and boarding up, knowledge that he transferred to military engineering when the Waikato war began'.[26] Te Ito had also gained mining skills, although he would put these to a very different use when he returned to Taranaki.

Robert Parris, the Taranaki Land Purchase Commissioner who would come to know Te Ito very well over the next decade, wrote that upon Te Ito's return to Paraiti in 1853, '[a] party of young men, varying from twenty to thirty, was made up for him from the different tribes, and *maintained for a very long time* doing nothing but digging over their tapued grounds, gathering stones and old trophies such as he chose to pronounce sacred [emphasis added]'.[27] It is likely that one of the leaders who 'made up' the ope whakanoa for Te Ito was Tāmati Reina. The ope began its work at the same time that Reina set out on his journey down the west coast laying the foundations for a land-holding movement with political independence.

Remarkably, there is an eyewitness account of Te Ito and his newly formed ope at work, written by none other than Percy Smith. Smith was born in 1840, and so would have been a boy of only thirteen or fourteen when he observed the events he remembered. Nonetheless, they must have made a significant impact on him. Here is his account in full, written around sixty-seven years after the scene he witnessed:

> We do not know what was the immediate cause of the movement that took place to remove the tapu of the old pas; but one man named by white people Tamati Tito, but whose proper name was Te Ito, suddenly came to the fore as a tohunga, or priest, with the assertion that he had the power to remove the tapu from the sacred stones. And this he proceeded to do by visiting all the old pas in the neighbourhood of New Plymouth and surrounding district. We have no record of his visiting *all* the old pas, but he probably did – I can at least vouch for his visit to Ngaturi, the old pa on which was afterwards built – during the Maori war – the Omata stockade.
>
> Either in 1853 or 1854, I was passing this place and there saw a large body of Maori horsemen, some fifty or sixty in number, some looking after the horses, others on top of the pa, which is not a large one – perhaps half an acre in extent – the ancient maioro, or ramparts, of which are still (1920) distinguishable. Being curious to learn what was going on, I went up to the pa, but was not allowed to go further than the entrance. I saw at the far side a group of men going through some performance which, after knowledge enables one to say, was the recitation of karakias [chants] by one of the men. This was Te Ito, and as I learned, he was whakanoa, or removing the tapu from the place. Though I saw nothing of any stone in this case, I heard at the time from others that Te Ito always searched for some sacred stone in the many pas he visited, and in most cases these stones were removed to other places and buried in spots known only to a select few of the old Maoris.[28]

Smith went on to say that in 1915, some of the stones buried by Te Ito in an old cultivation on Henwood Road, near Paraiti, were dug up by some local Te Ātiawa people. According to the farmer on whose land the cultivation was now situated, the first three stones that were found were very large, needing three men to lift them. On a nearby farm, a stone with a pounamu adze on top was found buried three feet deep. The stone 'was about eighteen inches in diameter, with a belt incised around it and a figure like a "6" carved on top'.[29] This stone was a mauri, a stone within which the mana of a place and its people had been bound. The land on which it was found had been one of the gardens adjacent to Te Ito's settlement of Paraiti.

Smith wrote that the presence of mauri stones such as those which had been buried in pā acted to preserve the mana of the people living there and 'also formed a connecting link with the ancestors of the tribe and with their ancestral homes in far Hawaiki'. He added:

> The people of this district round New Plymouth were (with few exceptions) driven helter-skelter from their homes by several incursions of the Waikato tribes in the early years of the nineteenth century. Their fortified pas were abandoned; and when the people returned to their homes in the early forties they did not re-occupy these old pas, but built new ones of a different type, or lived in open villages, though the former was the rule. Hence these sacred stones were left in the old pas, and it was this abandonment of them, and neglect of attention to the tapu of them, that gave rise to the belief in the early fifties that this neglect of the tapu was what caused so many deaths among the people.[30]

Land Sales and Puketapu Conflict

When he returned from Australia, Te Ito would have quickly discovered that political tensions within the northern Te Ātiawa had significantly increased while he was away and, most concerning, disputes over land sales within his own Puketapu hapū were escalating dangerously. It is difficult to determine Te Ito's position on land sales at this time. As we have seen, while his Ngāti Ruanui relatives were strongly opposed to selling, his Puketapu uncle, Te Tahana, was a strong advocate for Pākehā settlement. Puketapu people were unable to lease their land to settlers because the government had determined, without consultation, that any such leases would be null and void. Yet leaders such as Te Tahana could see a 'new economic future opening to them if they could acquire the stock and implements they needed to set up farms'.[31] Aside from gold mining with its limited, uncertain return, the sale of some of their land seemed the only realistic way to fund future development.

But the politics of Te Ātiawa land was a shifting kaleidoscope of divisions and alliances between sellers and non-sellers, which meant that Te Ātiawa and the government were struggling to conclude any general agreement. By mid-1853, things had reached a stalemate. Then, in August 1853, Donald McLean attempted to force the issue by making a payment of £400 to 'absentee' Te Ātiawa living in Wellington for what would become the Waiwhakaiho block of some 16,500 acres.[32] Although a deed for this block was subsequently signed in New Plymouth on 24 August 1853, the Waitangi Tribunal concluded that records of the transaction were entirely unsatisfactory:

> The deed itself escaped official recording and it could be that it was not originally seen as a complete transaction. Only a copy of the deed, found among McLean's papers, now survives. The reserves were purportedly delineated on an associated map, but the map cannot be located and there is no record of who sold. The copy deed does not recite the 'vendors' names but advises only that the deed was signed by [315] people.[33]

Tāmati Te Ito was probably one of the unnamed vendors for this block. In order to get agreement to the sale and boundaries of the block, the Land Purchase Officer, George Cooper, had been forced to negotiate separately with the heads of each family and agree to allocate them reserves of different sizes. It seems that Te Ito had not been promised any reserve land, and so on 8 February 1854 he wrote a very polite letter to McLean from Paraiti requesting such an allocation:

Paraiti

8 Pepuere 1854

E hoa, e Makarini,

Tena koe. E hoa, he kupu taku ki a koe, moku tetahi wahi whenua i ou wahi i Waiwakaiho ranei Mangati ranei i Te Keinga [?] ranei. Mau e homai kia pai koe ki taku kupu. Kei a koe te Whakaaro ki te homai ae ranei, kao ranei, ae me homai, me homai.

Heoi ano.
Na Tamati Te Ito

Paraiti

8 February 1854

Friend McLean

Greetings, friend. I have a request for you. Let me have a piece of land from within the Waiw[h]akaiho or Mangati or Te Keinga [?] lands. You could give this to me if you agree with my request. The decision is yours whether or not to give me this, but yes, do give it to me. That is all.

From Tamati Te Ito[34]

There is no evidence that Te Ito's request was granted.

The following month, Te Ito was a signatory to the sale of the adjacent Hua block, a block of 14,000 acres. His uncle Te Tahana had taken a leading role in the negotiations for this block and his name appears third on a list of 123 signatures after Te Ito's cousins, Rāniera and Matiu. Te Ito was one of the last of the Puketapu vendors to sign – his signature is number 101 on the deed; perhaps he was expressing his disquiet over the sale. The land was sold for £3,000 on the condition that the occupied pā, surrounding cultivations and burial places be excluded from the sale as reserves. Paraiti (50 acres) and Hua (100 acres, including Te Oropūriri) were designated as two of four such reserves.[35] It would be confirmed in June 1887 that Te Ito's grandmother, Hine Tieri, had been designated as one of three original owners for Paraiti Reserve.[36] Of the £3,000 paid to the sellers, £1,000 was held back to be used by them to repurchase sections at 10 shillings an acre, as they were entitled to a total of 2,000 acres in addition to the reserves.[37] There is no record of how this money was distributed among the sellers, and it is possible that Te Ito received none.

Two months after the sale, a meeting was held at 'The Hua', probably at Te Oropūriri, where it was decided that, 'if possible, a suitable place of worship should be erected in the town', chiefly for the use of Te Ātiawa living to the south at Ngāmotu and for the residents of the Hua block. Subscriptions were invited. Already, the Te Hua leaders – Te Tahana, Rāwiri Waiaua, Rāniera and Matiu – had each donated £1 and Miriama (Te Ito's mother) had given 5 shillings. Te Ito (recorded as 'Tamati Teito') later donated 15 shillings.[38] This donation is evidence of the tohunga's continued commitment to the Wesleyan Church, despite his whakanoa work. But the Wesleyan chapel would never be built. The sale of the Hua block and allocation of sections to sellers within it would soon become a source of such intense conflict that it would consume the lives of the Puketapu residents. Te Ito could not avoid becoming entangled in the conflict, to the extent that in one significant confrontation he was fortunate to escape serious injury or death.

In August, 1854, Rāwiri Waiaua was killed by his nemesis, Waitere Kātātore. Kātātore had been left out of the negotiations for the Hua block by Waiaua and Te Tahana, and partly as a result of this, he subsequently offered the government some land that had been excluded from the Hua purchase. Waiaua had planted wheat crops on a small part of this land and when these were burned by one of Kātātore's relatives, Waiaua made a counter-offer of a much larger block, named Tarurutangi, which included the land offered by Kātātore. George Cooper, the Taranaki Province Land Purchase Officer, told Waiaua that his counter-offer would be accepted if the chief was able to demonstrate his claim to the land by cutting the eastern boundary. Waiaua agreed to do so. At 8 a.m. on the morning of 3 August 1854, he and twenty-five men arrived on the disputed land with billhooks to begin clearing the boundary line; among them, according to his own testimony, was Te Ito.[39] They were met by Kātātore's party of twenty-nine armed men. Kātātore fired one barrel of his gun into the air and another into the ground as a warning. Then fighting broke out. Sixteen members of Rāwiri Waiaua's party were shot and six of them died, including Rāwiri himself.[40] Kātātore is reported to have told his men to 'spare Raniera's people', perhaps including Te Ito, and 'when the principal men were down' Kātātore reportedly 'called off his people'.[41]

The killing of Waiaua and his companions triggered a three-year period of intense conflict within Puketapu that has come to be known as the 'Puketapu Feud'. At Oropūriri, Rāniera strengthened the fortifications, adding a new outer double palisade, a rifle trench and a single inner palisade. The inhabitants of other pā, including those living at Paraiti, would have made similar defensive modifications.[42] The fighting, which consisted of small groups of armed men firing into pā and laying ambushes, made the whole of the Hua a dangerous place to live and work in the latter half of 1854, so it is likely that if Te Ito and his ope whakanoa were working at this time they were doing so south of New Plymouth. As the conflict continued into 1855, Te Ito appears to have left Taranaki altogether, moving again to Australia for a brief period.[43]

Mauri: Unearthing Stones, Burying Scriptures

While Puketapu were selling and feuding over their land north of New Plymouth, to the south, Ngāti Ruanui and Taranaki Iwi were becoming more determined to hold onto their source of life. In September 1852, a month before Revd Woon sent his letter to the local newspaper claiming that people were 'taking leave of their senses', George Cooper reported that on his recent journey through Ngāti Ruanui territory he had been told by their leaders that 'Ngati Ruanui were bound by an oath never to sell any land and they never would till the end of the chapter'.[44] Six months later, in February 1853, perhaps partly in response to the proclamation of the New Zealand Constitution Act through which most Māori became disenfranchised citizens, Mātene

Te Whiwhi and Tāmihana Te Rauparaha from the Ōtaki tribes Ngāti Toa and Ngāti Raukawa began canvassing support for a Māori King, visiting Taupō, Rotorua, Maketū and Waikato.[45] As we have seen, Tāmati Reina was also seeking to build an independence movement at this time. In May 1853, his Ngāti Ruanui people began constructing at Manawapou (south of present-day Hāwera in southern Taranaki) what would be at the time New Zealand's largest meeting house. Named Taiporohēnui by Mātene Te Whiwhi, it was to be a pan-tribal parliament house.[46] Taiporohēnui was also a ritual name for the west coast of the North Island, and in its new application it is said to have referenced a blocking of the tide of European settlement.[47]

In August 1853, while Taiporohēnui was under construction, the people of Taranaki Iwi buried a New Testament in their land. The purpose of the ceremony, according to the Reverend Johann Riemenschneider, the German Lutheran missionary who lived south of New Plymouth at Wārea, was 'to place for all of Taranaki and forever a sacred oath and divine *tapu* (ban) against all complete and partial sale to and settlement by Europeans'.[48] Although there is no evidence that Te Ito organised or attended this event, it is surely more than a coincidence that it was staged at the same time that he and his ope whakanoa were beginning their work. Both the placing of the New Testament in the earth and the removal of mauri stones from Taranaki pā by Te Ito and his ope whakanoa were undoubtedly informed by the same understanding. The Testament, containing God's divine word and spirit, represented a new form of mauri; the burial of this Christian 'mauri' complemented the removal of pre-Christian mauri by Te Ito.

Riemenschneider's appalled report of this dramatic event has been translated by his biographer, Peter Oettli, as follows:

> If the old heathen tapu is no longer effective or permissible the Nga Mahanga (Taranaki [people] between Warea and New Plymouth) had last winter thought of a certain new kind of tapu (ban) in conjunction with an uncertain Christian concept. They used it as a substitute for the earlier tapu to protect their land against the intrusion of Europeans. They held a great meeting in August in the episcopal [Anglican] village of

Puketaua (about nine miles to the north of Warea) concerning their land, at which they considered all kinds of plans how to secure it. Landmarks and agreements were already in existence, however both seemed to be too feeble to achieve their purpose. So, they had the unfortunate idea of burying a New Testament in the ground in order to place for all of Taranaki and forever a sacred oath and divine tapu (ban) against all complete or partial sale to and settlement by Europeans!

The native teachers and congregations of the Nga Mahanga on the episcopal side declared their support for the matter and a baptised episcopal native from the village of Kaihihi (14 English miles from Warea) undertook the burying of the Holy Scripture!

A few days later I was in the vicinity of Kaihihi. Here I was stopped by some episcopal natives who saw me on the road. They informed me in detail about the episode I have just described and they asked me about my opinion of it.[49]

Riemenschneider condemned the ceremony, of course, telling them: 'You have misused and violated His Holy word … by trying to turn it into a damnable magic device to make your plans and your land untouchable.'[50] News of the event and Riemenschneider's hostile reaction to it spread so rapidly that 'within a few days all Taranaki knew what [he] said'.[51]

In late April and early May 1854, a month after Te Ito had added his signature to the sale of the Hua block, a grand, pan-tribal hui was held at the large Taiporohēnui meeting house at Manawapou, attended by the Ōtaki leaders Mātene Te Whiwhi and Tāmihana Te Rauparaha and around five hundred Ngāti Ruanui. At a huge feast, which included 140 pigs, 1,000 baskets of potatoes, 900 baskets of kūmara, 700 baskets of taro and bread baked from 2 tons of flour produced by a local mill, southern Taranaki opposition to land sales was reaffirmed.[52] George Cooper, who had been invited to the hui, but who did not attend, drafted a report around the same time in which he also associated a land-holding compact with the burying of the Scriptures. The ceremony to which he referred was probably the one described by Riemenschneider. Cooper explained:

This compact has been joined in by the Ngatiruanui, Taranaki, and a considerable portion of the Ngatiawa, tribes: and the league has been ratified and confirmed at several aggregate meetings, with various formulas and solemnities, a copy of the Holy Scriptures having on one occasion been buried in the earth and a cairn of stones erected on the spot in attestation of the inviolability of the oath to oppose the sale of land by every means in their power which was then taken by the confederated chiefs.[53]

It is also probably the Ngā Mahanga ceremony to which Donald McLean was referring when he wrote on 20 February 1854 that a 'land league' had been formed in Taranaki and that 'by way of rendering it as binding as possible on the parties, a copy of the Scriptures was buried in the earth with many ceremonies thereby, as it were, calling the Deity to witness the inviolability of their compact'.[54] Although this letter was written more than two months prior to the Manawapou hui, within a few years, government officers and local settlers came to believe that a 'land league' was formed at this hui and that a copy of the Holy Scriptures were buried at this time. Peter Oettli's discovery in the Riemenschneider papers that the Testament-burying ceremony was performed by Taranaki Iwi in August 1853, not at Manawapou in May 1854, supports an opposing argument, first made by Keith Sinclair, that the Manawapou hui did not result in the formation of a 'land league' at which Taranaki leaders, including Wiremu Kīngi Te Rangitāke, swore a sacred oath not to sell any more land.[55] Instead, as Cooper wrote, the Manawapou hui was one of the 'several aggregate meetings' held to affirm a long-standing determination among southern tribes to hold onto their land. Judging from Cooper's account, the Testament-burying ceremony performed by Taranaki Iwi was also probably associated with one of the earlier 'aggregate meetings'. It may have been inspired by the work of Te Ito's ope whakanoa.[56]

While there is no evidence that Te Ito was present at the Ngā Mahanga Testament-burying ceremony in August 1853, or at any of the other 'aggregate meetings', including the Manawapou hui, there can be no doubt that his ope whakanoa work would have been supported by the leaders who attended them, many of whom would later become his Kaingārara followers. A comment by Revd Hammond, who probably got his information from the Waitōtara missionary George Stannard, reinforces the view that there was a close connection between Te Ito's work and the political intentions of the Manawapou leaders. Hammond wrote that Te Ito's project was probably in 'anticipation of circumstances in relation to the retention of land by the people'.[57] If Robert Parris was right, and the ope was 'maintained for a very long time', it is likely that the Manawapou leaders and their communities provided it with material support. An ope of some thirty horsemen must at least have been provided with hospitality in settlements located near to the pā and other sites that they were clearing. Perhaps, also, their visits occasioned hui at which issues related to the holding of land were discussed.

While Te Ito's work with the ope whakanoa was a continuation, although on a larger and more systematic scale, of his earlier practices that aimed to expel ngārara from wāhi tapu, it was also a departure, in that the ritual work was now a *pan-tribal* project. This work was led by a tohunga who had been chosen because he was able to 'see' where tapu stones and their guardian atua were hidden, whether they were near the summits of abandoned pā or 'under buildings, alongside rivers and in various other places'.[58] Not all of the organisers of the earlier wāhi tapu ceremonies, at least one of whom was a Christian 'teacher', had Te Ito's inspired ability to 'see' atua. Te Ito's success in finding stones and other objects that were considered to be tapu, and his ability to bring this tapu under his control, were evidence of his increasing mana. As leader of the ope whakanoa, he was becoming a tohunga whose influence extended across tribal boundaries, and as he rode across the tops of abandoned pā throughout Taranaki, he and his troop began to enact and embody a future unity that was earnestly desired by many. But he was not yet recognised as a poropiti (prophet).

CHAPTER THREE

From Tohunga to Prophet

When S. Percy Smith and W.H. Skinner visited Tāmati Te Ito at Paraiti in 1906, the old man shared very little of his life or knowledge with them. He did, however, offer his guests one or two gold nuggets of information. As we have seen, he confirmed that he had led the Kaingārara movement, and that its aim had been to unify Taranaki and restore the health of the people. But Te Ito also told his visitors that he had been with his Puketapu relative Rāwiri Waiaua when he was killed by Waitere Kātātore in August 1854, and 'being anxious to earn enough money to buy Rawiri's white horse, he went to Sydney in 1858, but on his return the horse was sold to his great disappointment'.[1] Percy Smith's date of 1858, four years after Rāwiri's death, is almost certainly wrong because, as we will see shortly, Te Ito was very present in Taranaki throughout the whole of that year. Waiaua was killed in August 1854, so it is most likely that Te Ito made his second trip to Australia, perhaps this time to goldfields near Sydney, in the second half of 1854 or the first half of 1855; that is, during the Puketapu Feud.[2]

In his *History of Taranaki*, Bernard Wells described Rāwiri Waiaua as a 'well-proportioned man, mild of disposition, profusely tattooed' who had been 'in the habit of paying visits to the town on a gray horse, wearing a white hat and green spectacles'.[3] White or grey, the horse must have been an impressive mount, one that Tāmati Te Ito would have wanted as a visible sign of his increasing stature. Indeed, impressive horses would later be closely associated with the mana of other prophetic leaders – Riwha Tītokowaru rode a white horse named Niu Tirene (New Zealand) 'which both Maori and Pakeha held in some awe', and the prophets Te Kooti and Rua Kēnana are both said to have ridden a white horse named Te Ia, which also had supernatural abilities.[4] Hipa Te Maihāroa, the South Island prophet, also rode a white horse.[5] We do not know the colour of the horse that Te Ito eventually acquired, but we do know that soon after his return from Sydney, this twenty-six-year-old tohunga, by now also a recognised seer (a tohunga matakite or pōrewarewa), rode it out of the shadows, in which he had been quietly working as the leader of Taranaki's ope whakanoa, to become the inspired prophet and leader of Taranaki's Kaingārara movement.

The Beginnings of Kaingārara

In the latter half of 1855 or early 1856, after his return from Sydney, Te Ito and his ope whakanoa shattered the taumata atua (resting place) of the powerful Taranaki atua Maru. It was probably with this dramatic act and subsequent ritual performances in southern Taranaki that Te Ito announced his transformation from tohunga to prophet. In a personal note to Percy Smith, the Pātea missionary T.G. Hammond wrote:

> The stone image of the god, Maru, which the Patea people formerly possessed, was burnt by Tamati Te Ito and his ope whakanoa ...
> The stone broke in pieces when burnt. The distinguishing name of the people who had it in charge was Wai-o-Tuere. Tapo of the 'Aotea' canoe was Maru's particular priest, and it remained in charge of his descendants from that time till burnt.[6]

Unfortunately, Hammond provided no further details about the nature of the event – we have no idea of numbers in attendance, the size of the fire, or the associated ceremonies. However, the deliberate destruction of Maru's image in a fire, upon which food may subsequently have been cooked, would have been viewed by Ngāti Ruanui as an exceptionally bold and dangerous thing to do – some may have even expected Te Ito to die as a result. When he did not die, but instead went on to perform what were seen as miracles, his mana would have significantly increased.[7]

Maru was a very powerful Taranaki atua indeed. Rangipito Te Ito, a distant relative of Tāmati Te Ito, and one of Percy Smith's main sources, wrote of Maru: 'Offerings (whakahere) were made to him of kumara, taro, aruhe, birds and fish; and after the offerings the god would communicate with his priest through the medium if the proper karakia had been recited.' Rangipito added:

> [Maru] was the principal god of Taranaki, indeed of all descendants of those who came in the 'Aotea' canoe, as also of Ati-Awa. This god was brought over by Turi in the 'Aotea' as a spirit, not an image, and the priests on board were those of Maru. He was an evil god who was very particular as to the behaviour of his worshippers, who were never to quarrel amongst themselves and always be on their good behaviour. He was their god of war to whom karakias were addressed and offerings made. When Titoko-waru abandoned Christianity (about 1868) he called up Maru to be his god, and hence his success in the war against the Europeans (1868–70). The old karakias that were still remembered were made use of again.[8]

However, according to another source, Kereoma Tuwhawhakia, Maru was both a good and dangerous atua. He could kill people, but he might also save them from death when they transgressed tapu, if appropriate offerings were made to the stone or wooden images into which the spirit of the atua had been called. Such offerings included the heads of dogs and the heads of fish caught in both sea and rivers.[9] The wooden images of Maru, termed 'whakapakoko rākau', were approximately 25 centimetres long, with a carved head at one end and a smooth, tapered shaft, wrapped tightly with flax cord, at the other. These were placed with the pointed end on the ground at tūāhu (shrines) and manipulated by tohunga who held the image between two cords. Hammond wrote that the whakapakoko of Maru used by a tohunga at Pātea was also burned, although possibly not by Te Ito in 1855 or 1856; it is said to have been burned 'when they embraced Christianity', which suggests it may have been destroyed at an earlier date.[10]

Kaingārara Doctrine

Revd Riemenschneider learned of Te Ito's personal and political transformation early in 1857, while his new church at Wārea was under construction.[11] Āperahama and Paora, two leaders of Ngā Mahanga, a hapū of Taranaki Iwi, had invited experts from Ngā Ruahine, the tribe immediately to the south of Taranaki Iwi, to build their church. Ngā Ruahine had a reputation as skilful builders and had constructed the Taiporohēnui meeting house at Manawapou in 1853. In the spring of 1856, therefore, extra crops had been planted at Wārea and the surrounding settlements, and during February and March 1857, some 120 Ngā Ruahine builders and their families were lavishly fed and entertained as they worked on the church project. Riemenschneider picked up 'dark hints' at the time that something more than construction work and friendly entertainment was afoot, and indeed, his congregation and the builders, led by Tāmati Hōne Ōraukawa, were discussing behind his back some of the new doctrines and practices that were being promulgated by Tāmati Te Ito.[12] Riemenschneider wrote that Te Ito had in 1856 gone to Ngāti Ruanui:

> [A]mong that people, he had developed his doctrines and his miracles to the highest degree, thus enchanting them. Secretly, they had also introduced the new cause to our people while building the church, but had, at the same time, out of fear kept their silence towards me until they returned.[13]

It seems that Ngā Ruahine had learned of these doctrines and practices from Ngāti Ruanui, and that the new ideas were now, alarmingly for Riemenschneider, being introduced to Taranaki Iwi. He would have been no doubt relieved, therefore, when having completed the shell of the church and decorated its interior with fine tukutuku panels, the builders departed in March 1857, leaving him and Āperahama to complete the project.[14]

Although the images of Maru had been burned, it seems that he and other atua or 'whakapakoko' (whakapakoko rākau) were accorded a place within the early version of Tāmati Te Ito's divine hierarchy. In what appears to be a well-informed report, published in the Māori newspaper *Te Karere o Poneke*, Karehana Te Whena wrote that according to Kaingārara doctrine, atua existed on three levels. The first was the CMS God of Paihia; the second was the Catholic God; and below these were the atua whakapakoko, probably including Maru:

> Tenei taku korero mo nga ritenga maori o tenei kainga o Patea. No Ngati Ruanui tenei kainga. Ka kite au i to ratou whakapono ki nga atua maori … E toru nga atua o taua iwi: ko te tino atua tetehi, otiia, e rua nga tino atua, ko te Paihia, ko te Katorika. Ko to ratou atua whakapakoko tetahi. Ka tahi tonu te karakiatanga o enei atua e toru. Erangi ano, ko to Paihia ki mua, muri mai ko te Katorika, kei muri i enei ko te atua maori. Ko te mahi atua tangata kei te hura i nga whatu a nga tupuna, he kai hoki i nga whatu a nga tupuna, he kai hoki i nga wahi tapu. He kai whakawa ano, ana, he katipo ano, he whare herehere ano to ratou. Tokomaha nga tangata nana te putake o tenei mahi hanga noa iho. Ko Tamati Te Ito te tino putake o taua mahi.

> *This is my account of the religious customs of this settlement, Pātea. This place belongs to Ngāti Ruanui. I have learned about their beliefs concerning the Māori gods … These people have three gods, but there are two main gods, Paihia and Catholic. The other one is the god of their ancestral god-image (atua whakapakoko). The prayers to these three gods are the same. However, the Paihia god is first, followed by the Catholic god, followed by the Māori ancestral atua. The work of the inspired person (atua tangata) is to remove the stones of the ancestors, they also eat in the wāhi tapu. They also have judges, police and jails. There are many people engaged in this work. The originator of the work is Tāmati Te Ito.*[15]

Te Ito, as an inspired prophet, was regarded as the embodiment of an atua who must have belonged to the divine hierarchy at the level of the whakapakoko. The name of this atua was Karutahi. A knowledgeable correspondent, possibly Riemenschneider (because he elsewhere refers to Te Ito as a Puketapu man), reported in the *Wellington Independent*:

> This Puketapu man, whose name is Tamati, asserts that Karutahi, an old Waikato deity, has entrusted him with a divine commission to abolish the ancient and sacred rite of tapu. Tamati has become the medium whereby the god Karutahi reveals to the Maori race the cause of their rapid diminution. It runs thus: The all potent institution of tapu has of late years been disregarded; the 'wahi tapu' or 'sacred place' has been desecrated; from the consecrated grove, flax and toetoe have been gathered ... vengeance [of the atua], assuming the form of a ngarara (lizard), enters the body of man, consumes his vitals, and thereby causes death.[16]

Karutahi is described in the above report as a 'Waikato deity' and indeed, it is believed that he is still present in the form of an eel, inhabiting a swamp near Meremere. When Transit New Zealand was carrying out an improvement to State Highway 1 in 2002, the Ngāti Naho hapū, for whom Karutahi now acts as a guardian, objected that the new route would pass through Karutahi's abode, and after negotiations, the original route was altered in 2002.[17] If Te Ito was a medium of this taniwha, then he was embodying the atua of a powerful neighbour who had twenty-five years earlier driven many Taranaki people from their homes. Now he was driving away from the same region demons that had been causing sickness and death. And he was doing so in concert with the Christian God.

Preparing For a New Divine Order

According to Riemenschneider, the prophet presented himself to his followers as 'a humble friend and faithful supporter of their Lord'.[18] Although he embodied 'an omniscient and wrathful god', he was also working on behalf of their Christian God.[19] This understanding was also voiced by Riemenschneider's congregation. Following a church service, in which Te Ito's supporters were excluded from Holy Communion, one of the local leaders turned to the missionary, whom he knew as 'Rimene', and said: 'Listen o Rimene, you and we all know what circumstances we are in and what our present raruraru [trouble] is, an all-consuming indispensable task. But, be that as it may, you see, we hold ourselves more before God and his house.'[20] The supporter added that Riemenschneider and other Pākehā could not possibly understand the work that they were engaged in with Te Ito, and that he should leave such matters to them.[21]

While Riemenschneider was sharply critical of Te Ito and only saw the work of Satan in his movement, Revd Whiteley was more sympathetic. In his report of 1857, for example, Whiteley wrote that tapu needed to be removed, 'in order that people may no longer be doubtful or [have] divided minds between the fear & bondage of Maori superstition and faith in the Christian Religion'.

> For it is a fact that though Christianity has been embraced very extensively, yet many are under the bondage of fear with regard to maori gods and maori witchcraft and maori tapu ... I believe the nation have changed their gods, they have sincerely abandoned their false gods and received the truth that the Lord Jehova is the one Lord – but in superstitious ignorance they have fancied that their old abandoned gods or demons or devils have still some sort of existence and some extent of power to inflict injuries and revenge upon them if opportunity should offer. They acknowledge that these false or imaginary gods have been abandoned but they have an idea that they have not been destroyed.[22]

The task that Te Ito and his followers had set themselves was of a much grander scale than that of the ope whakanoa which had earlier worked to remove tapu from wāhi tapu. Indeed, it was now one of millennial proportions – no less than the freeing of Taranaki from the influence of demons and their tapu, once and for all – thus ushering in a new era in which God could be fully present with his Taranaki people.

As Riemenschneider put it in his report to Germany, Te Ito and his followers believed that by clearing the district of the tapu associated with malevolent atua they were removing the main obstacle preventing 'the fulfilment of the divine order to come'.[23]

> The obstacles that still lie there between [God and Māori] are to be cleared away in God's name in order to make the path to perfection free and easy for them ... Fulfilment will and must take place when the work is completed ... No one should be allowed to criticise him or doubt his work or even talk about it.[24]

And it appears that Te Ito's prophetic vision was widely known. Explicit references to it would be made in April the following year, when, during a conflict between a land-selling chief, Īhāia, and Kaingārara forces led by Te Ito and Wiremu Kīngi Te Rangitāke, the latter called on the Taranaki people to fulfil the prophecy of Te Ito by defeating Īhāia, and thus repay him and Te Ātiawa for the 'great work of bringing their salvation from the powers of darkness'.[25] More about this climactic conflict will be revealed in the next chapter.

The Great Kai Ngārara Fires

Between January 1857 and February 1858, Tāmati Te Ito orchestrated a series of huge, ceremonial bonfires into which were thrown tapu stones, taonga, clothing, and material excavated from wāhi tapu. With these spectacular ceremonies, termed 'ahi kai ngārara' (kai ngārara fires), Te Ito and his Kaingārara followers were seeking to clear the tapu from the entire Taranaki district.[26] After one or more initial clearances in the south, Te Ito went north to stage a major ceremony at his home pā of Paraiti before moving back down the coast, organising fires at Poutoko Pā (near present day Ōakura), Wārea and Pātea.

Unfortunately, there are no detailed eyewitness accounts of the ceremonial practices that accompanied the fires; however, Revd Whiteley wrote in his report to the Wesleyan Missionary Society that there was much 'zeal and parade'. He added that in addition to 'superstitions and heathenish feelings and fears', the ceremonies included readings from the Bible and Christian prayers and worship, during which time 'great order and solemnity' were observed.[27] This period of worship would have been followed by one of feasting – perhaps the consumption of food cooked on the fires – signalling a collective shift from the dangers of tapu to the freedom of noa. While the kai ngārara ceremonies were similar to the earlier wāhi tapu ceremonies in that they were collective whakanoa events, at which food was cooked and eaten to remove tapu, the kai ngārara fires were on a much grander scale, involving much more pageantry. Tāmati Te Ito was 'attended with a large retinue' and heralded, as he rode into the place where the fire ceremonies were to be performed, by a 'blowing of trumpets'.[28]

In preparation for a kai ngārara fire, entire communities worked, usually for weeks, gathering tapu objects from the surrounding district and bringing them to one central place. Each evening, after they had been working all day, people gathered for a church service. During this collection phase, Te Ito 'roamed' across the landscape identifying places where the influence of tapu was strong – it might be in a stream, in an old wāhi tapu, in the thatch of a house or even in the clothing of a person. Stones were gathered from streams and the wāhi tapu were excavated to a certain depth, and the rocks and other material from them were transported by cart to a central spot where the fire would be built. If greenstone treasures and carvings had been stored in the thatch of a house, the thatch was burned. The taonga and any tapu clothing were presented to Te Ito to be burned in the fire.[29] It is likely that lizards were also captured during this preparation period and also presented to Te Ito for ceremonial burning. Certainly, as we will see, this would be the case when the kai ngārara ceremonies were taken up in Whanganui some years later.[30]

The scale of Te Ito's mission of tapu clearance and political unification can be most fully conveyed by describing his fire ceremonies in the order in which he orchestrated them. At the time that Te Ito staged his Paraiti event in June 1857, the local press noted that the 'Wizard of the South' had already performed his ceremony 'to the complete satisfaction of the Ngāti Ruanui tribe'.[31] However, the first fire ceremony for

From Tohunga to Prophet | 47

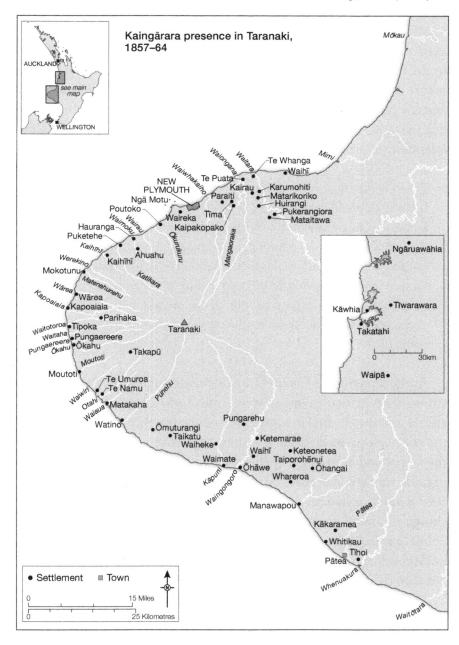

This map shows Kaingārara settlements and pā in Taranaki, 1857–64, circling the coast from north to south. Te Ito performed major fire ceremonies to remove tapu at some of these places, including Waiheke, Paraiti, Poutoko, Wārea and Pātea. His Kaingārara followers sent letters to him from most of the marked coastal settlements, including those in the Waikato (shown in the inset), when he was living at Paraiti, Te Whanga, Te Puata and Mataitawa during these years.
Source: Based on a map in Penelope Goode, 'The Kaingarara Letters: The Correspondence of Tamati Te Ito Ngamoke in the A.S. Atkinson Papers', MA thesis, University of Canterbury, Christchurch, 2001, p.19.

which we have documentary evidence was staged inland from Waimate at either Weriweri or Waiheke, both Ngā Ruahine settlements and home to the builders of Riemenschneider's church.[32] In January 1857, just before they travelled to Wārea to build the church, Tāmati Ōraukawa and his Ngā Ruahine people at Weriweri and Waiheke had carefully dug up tapu stones that marked the boundaries of gardens near their inland settlements. Richard Taylor wrote:

> They say that their old boundary stones have all been karakiaed [ritually chanted] over and no one can touch them without being killed, that many unwittingly doing so have lost their lives and that if any fragments of these formidable stones by any accident should be used in heating their ovens they would surely cause death. One of these matakites [possibly Te Ito] told the son of my host that he was bewitched and that he got a portion of one of these stones in his throat ... the poor youth told the man to remove it and as he could not the youth died.[33]

At the direction of Tāmati Ōraukawa, several tons of the excavated stones were carried to one spot and piled into a heap of considerable size. 'These they heated in a large fire and then cooked potatoes of which the entire pa partook. This was done to wakanoa or render common the stones and destroy the spell supposed to be laid upon them.'[34] It is possible that some of these boundary stones had, like the Maru image, been shaped, or had carvings on them. Earlier, at Pātea, Taylor had been shown a kūmara ground that had once been surrounded by '60 stones about four feet high, rudely sculptured into the form of a man'. Taylor's guide referred to these stones as 'tūāhu' and said that offerings had been made to the atua that they represented.[35]

Because Taylor only visited the Ngā Ruahine settlements every three months or so, he was unaware of the wider religious and political context in which this heightened concern about the excavated stones had developed. Indeed, Riemenschneider criticised Taylor for this lack of awareness and accused him of inadvertently sanctioning the Kaingārara movement at its outset by offering Holy Communion to

Te Ito's followers, something Riemenschneider had refused to do.[36] It seems that Taylor's congregation at Weriweri and Waiheke had, like the people of Wārea, deliberately kept their allegiance to Te Ito hidden from their missionary. While they had shown him the large pile of stones and explained that the tapu had been removed from them, the details of the ceremonial performance and the prophet's role in it appear to have been kept secret.

The burning of Maru and the Ngā Ruahine fire, while highly significant public events for the tribes of southern Taranaki, had not brought Te Ito to the attention of the settler press in New Plymouth. However, after Te Ito's next great fire, which he staged at Paraiti on 15 June 1857, the prophet and his movement became the subject of commentary and speculation in papers throughout the country.[37] Preparations for the event began at least ten days before.[38] They included transporting to Paraiti cartloads of stones that had been removed from wāhi tapu situated on Te Ātiawa land to the north of New Plymouth. The local paper reported that wāhi tapu had been excavated 'in various directions' – presumably, then, with some thoroughness.[39]

This unusual activity generated considerable interest among the settlers, and on 11 June, while it was still ongoing, Riemenschneider delivered a lecture about Te Ito to the Taranaki Institute. That day also happened to be Percy Smith's birthday. He wrote in his diary: 'My 17th birthday. Attended interesting lecture by Mr Riemenschneider on the movement going on amongst the native viz "Whakanoa" or making "common" their Tapu places, which is done by a "Prophet" named Tamati of Ngati Ruanui.'[40] Riemenschneider appears to have misinformed his audience, however, telling them that Tāmati Te Ito was engaged in the destruction of sacred places in order to expel an 'Evil Spirit' or 'kikokiko' which had been the cause of increasing mortality among his people. In fact, Te Ito was expelling many different atua kikokiko (malicious ancestral spirits).[41] The newspaper report of the lecture also included deeply insulting remarks about Te Ito, describing him as a 'Fanatic' and incorrectly claiming he was 'not of good antecedents'.[42] This disparaging view would be echoed in almost all future newspaper accounts of the prophet.

The fire was hugely significant for Te Ito, both personally and politically. Firstly, it was staged at Paraiti and hence was a very visible assertion of his new status among his Puketapu kin. Secondly, it was a wedding fire, held on the same day as his marriage to Mihi Watara. No details of the wedding ceremony have been recorded, but Revd Whiteley signed the marriage certificate and so it is likely that he also officiated at a Christian ceremony. Te Ito was then twenty-eight years old and his second wife, Mihi, was twenty-six.[43] Thirdly, the timing of Te Ito's fire ceremony, in mid-June, suggests it was also staged as a Puanga event, the local equivalent of Matariki. Puanga is a star (otherwise known as Rigel) in the Orion constellation and, because it is more visible than the Matariki cluster in Taranaki, its setting and rising two weeks later marks the beginning of the sacred Matariki period. In 1857, 15 June would have been near the beginning of this Puanga or Matariki period.[44]

The celebration of Matariki has a very long genealogy that stretches back into the pre-Polynesian past.[45] Throughout Polynesia, where it is variously known as matali'i (Hawaii), matari'i (French Polynesia), and matariki (Cook Islands and New Zealand), the appearance of the Pleiades cluster above the horizon signalled the renewal of life, including social and political life. Hostilities and hierarchies were suspended and feasting and festivities were engaged in by whole populations. It marked the onset of a time of *communitas* or, as the sociologist Émile Durkheim termed it, 'collective effervescence', when creativity and intimacy took over from order and hierarchy. Between 1815 and 1828, throughout Eastern Polynesia, the burning of god images and the destruction of marae were initiated by local priests during this period of renewal, in preparation for conversions to Christianity.[46] The cultures that participated in this 'Polynesian iconoclasm' included the Society Islands, the Austral Islands, Hawaii and the Cook Islands, but they did not include New Zealand Māori society. Now, however, a New Zealand iconoclasm – or more precisely, a Taranaki iconoclasm – was being conducted by Te Ito during this Matariki or Puanga period, with the objective of social and political revitalisation.

In its report on Riemenschneider's lecture and the Paraiti ceremony, the *Taranaki Herald* noted that at this time Te Ito's hands were 'quite full of similar engagements'.[47] However, if any such engagements were held in July or August 1857, they went unreported in the press and official correspondence. The next recorded kai ngārara ceremony was held on 9 September at Poutoko Pā, south of New Plymouth. This was a significant Taranaki Iwi settlement under the leadership of Tāmati Wiremu Te Ngāhuru (also known as Tawa-rahi). Te Ngāhuru, like Te Tahana, had been appointed as an assessor (to assist the local magistrate in New Plymouth), but unlike Te Tahana, he was also a Kaingārara supporter. In April 1854 he was sent to gather information about the proceedings and outcome of the Taiporohēnui hui at Manawapou, and it is thought that his report, now lost, misled officials into thinking the hui had failed to reach agreement about opposition to land sales.[48] Te Ngāhuru appears to have had a close personal relationship with Te Ito. In a letter written to the prophet in 1858, Te Ngāhuru referred to himself as Te Ito's 'matua', and in 1860, Te Ito's brother, Ropata Ngāromate, was living with Te Ngāhuru at Poutoko Pā.[49]

On Saturday, 5 September, police inspector Henry Halse wrote to the Native Secretary, Donald McLean, that a 'great meeting' would take place at Poutoko Pā the next day 'to witness the death of all kikokiko in and about that neighbourhood'.[50] As Christians, Te Ito and the Taranaki leaders had thought it acceptable, and perhaps most appropriate, to hold their ceremony on a Sunday; after all, it included Bible readings and Christian prayers. But possibly as a result of missionary intervention, the event was postponed until the following Wednesday. Halse, who attended the great hui, wrote:

> The only occurrence of the past week has been the meeting at Poutoko pa about the Kai ngarara ceremony. It took place on Wednesday and was attended as nearly as I could reckon by about six hundred and fifty-five natives. The particulars of which will appear in my diary. Tamati Te Ito is at Poutoko and was to leave this day for Warea and thence to Umuroa. Where he will proceed next, is not at present known, but it is supposed that he will be called upon to perform his ceremony all over the island. Painful as these proceedings must be to the long resident

missionaries, I believe much good will accrue out of them, as it is, the attendants at Native Chapels are on the increase, one object therefore of Te Ito's, namely, to induce the natives to hold fast to Christianity, is apparently being attained.[51]

Unfortunately (and ironically), Halse's diary and many of his official letters were lost in the Parliamentary Buildings fire of 1907, in which most of the old Native Department files were destroyed. Still, his brief note makes two very significant contributions to our understanding of Te Ito and his movement. Firstly, this is probably the earliest documentary reference to the name 'kai ngārara'. Here it refers to a fire ceremony rather than a movement; it is likely that Te Ito's followers came to refer to themselves as 'Kaingārara' due to their collective participation in the 'lizard-eating' ceremonies associated with the fires. Secondly, when Halse wrote in his note that 'it is supposed' that Te Ito would be 'called upon to perform his ceremony all over the island', he was probably reporting an expectation shared by the Kaingārara rather than offering his own prediction. It suggests that Te Ito's supporters expected that their prophet would become a nationally significant figure and that his movement would spread beyond Taranaki. This may have been a widely held view, even among his detractors. A Taranaki newspaper correspondent commented: 'Some knowing ones think that there is lurking behind an intention to combine all the race together, and become strong to have their own way with the white people. So, I am told, the natives themselves who have not entered into the thing say.'[52] However, Te Ito may not have shared this exaggerated expectation; in his interview with Percy Smith in 1906, he was quite clear that his focus had been only to unify Taranaki.

Te Ito arrived in Wārea, the next major settlement down the coast, a week or so after completing the Poutoko ceremony, and he immediately began work there, searching out tapu places and objects. He and the Wārea people were soon joined by a party of forty Ngā Ruahine, probably including Tāmati Ōraukawa and some of his church builders.[53] By hosting Ngā Ruahine, Taranaki Iwi were again strengthening the land-holding alliance they had entered into with their southern neighbours in 1854. The task of clearing the land around Wārea would occupy Taranaki Iwi and Ngā Ruahine for an entire month, their well-attended kai ngārara ceremony not taking place until 19 October.[54] In his report Riemenschneider described the clearance work in Biblical terms, writing that large numbers of people had been led into the 'desert' in their search for 'stones and bones'. Te Ito was this time dismissively labelled as a 'treasure-digger'.[55]

The missionary's report confirmed the observations of Halse and Revd Whiteley that church attendance had increased – people now 'crowded even more' into his chapel, he wrote.[56] However, he complained bitterly that they no longer dressed in their best garments for church; instead they came directly from their whakanoa labours wearing their work clothes and speaking what he described as 'the confused language of the Tower of Babel'.[57] For the followers of Te Ito, it made perfect sense to combine their whakanoa work with the protective ceremony of Christian worship – indeed, this was reflected in their earlier plan to hold the Poutoko kai ngārara ceremony on a Sunday – but for Riemenschneider the two activities were the absolute antitheses of each other. The Kaingārara were appropriating Christianity for their own ends and the Wārea missionary was finding himself increasingly marginalised by Te Ito, who, in a subsequent report, is further described as a clever 'seducer' disguised as Satan, the 'Angel of Light'.[58]

Although Riemenschneider excluded Te Ito's followers from Holy Communion, almost his entire congregation became Kaingārara converts, including the Ngā Mahanga chief Āperahama, with whom the missionary had established a close bond. Only Te Whiti-o-Rongomai, a local leader and the future prophet of Parihaka, withdrew from participation in Te Ito's whakanoa activities. As the missionary put it, using Te Whiti's baptismal name of Erueti:

Only Erueti stood like a rock on the rock of the brave confessions of Christ as the unifying saviour and when he could not do anything and could not give in to the demands made of him he withdrew completely to his remote fields in solitude for weeks. For he saw that Aperahama would not leave him alone and therefore, out of respect and in order to avoid an overt falling out he steered clear of him.[59]

From Wārea, Te Ito continued his journey south along the Taranaki coast, stopping next at Te Umuroa, a large Taranaki Iwi kāinga, inland from present-day Ōpunake. He may have staged a fire ceremony here, but if so, it appears to have gone unreported. The Umuroa leader Wiremu Kīngi Te Matakātea was a renowned warrior, whose troops had successfully repelled the Waikato invaders when they came with muskets in 1834 and 1836. A strong supporter of Kaingārara, he had established a successful school and had extensive cultivations of potatoes and wheat, the latter ground in his own mill.[60] During the prophet's visit, Te Matakātea and other leaders met with him to discuss the looming threat of land sales.

In November Te Ito continued south to Pātea, where he began preparations for what would be his last recorded whakanoa fire.[61] Revd Taylor, who visited Pātea in late November, again attempted to convince people of the folly of attempting to drive away the Devil 'by eating a few potatoes and repeating a karakia' but was told that he 'did not know the power and malignity of these evil spirits, hence many deaths among them'.[62] Interestingly, Taylor also reported on the activities of a prophet who he identified as 'Tiki' but who must have been Te Ito:

> Late in the evening a fishing party returned with a large quantity of fish and of the best kind being chiefly hapuku, this is the first of the season. I found that one of those natives who have distinguished themselves by expelling evil spirits and who is styled a prophet went with the party to sea and first had service with them, reading a chapter out of St Paul's Epistle to the Corinthians and then using our usual prayers so all the success was attributed to him and they viewed him with great admiration. When they returned they asked whether they should not again have prayers to thank God. Tiki, for such is his name, said no, the first was sufficient but he arranged for some to carry a portion of the finest fish, one to each of the neighbouring pas to show to those who trusted in him how successful he had been.[63]

ABOVE: A reconstruction of Te Oropūriri Pā as it might have appeared in the mid-1840s, based on excavations carried out in 2002 and 2004. This lightly defended kāinga with palisades enclosing seven whare puni, each on their own fenced sections, was probably similar to the neighbouring Paraiti Pā where Tāmati Te Ito and his whānau were living. *Illustration by Briar Sefton from Matthew Campbell, Simon Holdaway and Sarah Macready (eds), Finding Our Recent Past: Historical Archaeology in New Zealand, New Zealand Archaeological Association, Auckland, 2013, p.86, reproduced with the permission of the New Zealand Archaeological Association*

ABOVE: Land Claims Commissioner William Spain investigating New Zealand Company purchases in Taranaki in 1844. Spain is standing in front of an awning, beneath which two scribes are seated. Mt Taranaki is in the background. Spain's award of 60,000 acres to the New Zealand Company was later overturned by Governor FitzRoy, prompting Governor Grey's visit to New Plymouth in 1847. *'Mr Spain Investigating the Land Claims at New Plymouth (Mt Eliot June 1844)', pen and ink sketch, Puke Ariki, A75.441*

ABOVE: Te Awaiti whaling station, Marlborough Sounds, late nineteenth or early twentieth century. In the foreground two women stand beside a small graveyard. The station, established in 1827, became a temporary home for a number of Te Ātiawa people in the 1830s. In 1846, Te Ito's cousin Rāniera arranged for his Puketapu relatives to be shipped from here to New Plymouth. *Photograph by Robina Nicol, Alexander Turnbull Library, 1/2-233833-G*

OPPOSITE: Te Tahana Papawaka, a brother of Tāmati Te Ito's mother, Miriama. Te Tahana was a chief of Oropūriri Pā and was appointed one of the first native assessors in Taranaki in 1850. As a supporter of the government, he mediated between officials and his nephew, Te Ito, on a number of occasions. In this studio portrait, probably taken in the 1870s, Te Tahana is photographed holding a taiaha and wearing a tāniko-bordered cloak. *Alexander Turnbull Library, PA2-2822*

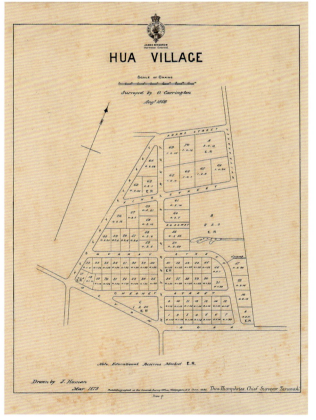

ABOVE: A flagpole standing on Mt Eliot (formerly named Puke Ariki) about 1849. Ngā Motu (the Sugar Loaf islands) and a boat are visible top right. This is probably the flagpole that Tāmati Reina Ngāwhare and other Ngāti Ruanui leaders objected to in 1851, viewing it and the flying of the British flag as a government assertion of absolute sovereignty. *'Mount Eliot Lately Purchased by His Excellency – Sir George Grey G.C.B.', tinted lithograph by unknown artist, Puke Ariki, A64.048*

LEFT: Bell Block, formely Te Hua, as surveyed by Octavius Carrington in 1856. This land, to the north-west of Paraiti, was offered for sale by Rāwiri Waiaua and others of Puketapu in 1848 and was subsequently purchased by the Native Minister, Francis Dillon Bell. One of the sellers, listed as 'Tamati (tamaiti)', was possibly Tāmati Te Ito. Te Ito was nineteen years old in 1848, and being under the age of majority, would have been legally described as a 'tamaiti' (boy). *Map by Julius Homan, 1880, Alexander Turnbull Library, sourced from LINZ, Crown Copyright reserved*

ABOVE: Wāhi tapu (sacred groves) included burial grounds and places where tohunga performed their ceremonies. This 1844 pencil and watercolour work by George French Angas is of a wāhi tapu situated inland from Kāwhia harbour. Decaying items that had belonged to a deceased Ngāti Maniapoto chief were enclosed within a double set of palings, the inner row painted red. Within the enclosure were the chief's garments fluttering in the wind, muskets, chests and a small sailing canoe to convey his wairua to Hawaiki. *Wahi Tapu or Sacred Place, or Property of a Deceased Chief Called Pehe, at Tepahe on the River Wihanakeke (11 October 1844)', Alexander Turnbull Library, A-020-024*

ABOVE: A tūāhu (tapu ritual site) consisting of four stones. In his description of a Taranaki wāhi tapu ceremony held in 1851, Revd Richard Taylor noted that 'the tuahu or "praying stone"' was still standing at the centre of the sacred grove. Very few stone tūāhu have been identified by archaeologists in New Zealand, and it is likely that most if not all in Taranaki were removed and destroyed by Te Ito's Kaingārara. *Photograph, courtesy of the Anthropology Photographic Archive, Department of Anthropology, University of Auckland*

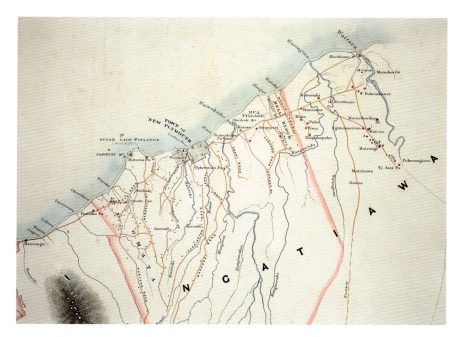

ABOVE: This map of Taranaki in 1862 shows land sold to the government (within the red lines), main settlements, and buildings destroyed by Te Ito's forces in 1860. The map was signed by the Provincial Surveyor, Octavius Carrington. *'Province of Taranaki from Waitara to Oeo', Puke Ariki, ARC2004-306*

ABOVE: The remains of Waiharoto Pā, Hāwera, photographed in 1961. Numerous storage pits are visible on the top of this impressive ring-ditch fortification. This, and other similar Ngāti Ruanui pā, were visited by Te Ito and his ope whakanoa in the years 1853 to 1855. *Photograph by Alastair Gordon Buist, Puke Ariki, PHO2004-352*

A watercolour painting of Rāwiri Waiaua in his last years by William Strutt. Waiaua was a Puketapu rangatira who, together with Te Ito's uncle, Te Tahana, became a leading supporter of land sales at Te Hua. In 1848, he offered land at Bell Block to the government. In 1852, he accused the people at Paraiti of killing his horse, and a subsequent dispute with Waitere Kātātore led to his own death in 1854.
Alexander Turnbull Library, E-452-f-010-2

pepuere 8 1854 paraiti

E Hoa e makarini tena koe e hoa
            ku
He pupu taku kia koe mo ku te
te ta hi wahi whenua i ou wahi
i waiwakaiho ra kei mangati
ranei i te kingi ranei ia mea
mau e ho maiki a poi koe ki taku
                          ka
kupu kei a koe te wharā ki te iho
                        ra
mai a e ra nei kao renei a meho
mai; meko ma heoiano

Na Tamati te ito

A letter written by Tāmati Te Ito to Chief Land Purchase Commissioner Donald McLean on 8 February 1854. This letter is a polite request for a section of the reserve land that had been set aside as a result of the sale of the Waiwhakaiho block. At the time of writing, Te Ito was leader of the ope whakanoa (tapu-removal troop) and living at Paraiti Pā. *Alexander Turnbull Library, MS-Papers-0032-0678A-06*

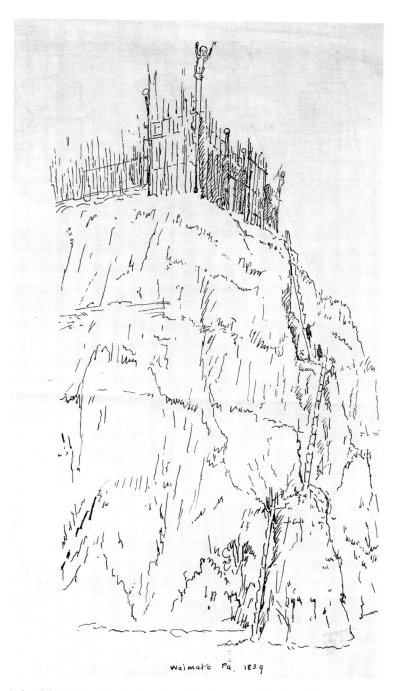

A sketch by Charles Heaphy showing palisades on top of the formidable Waimate Pā in south Taranaki in 1839. People are shown ascending or descending a ladder that provides access to and from the sea coast.
Pen and ink drawing, Alexander Turnbull Library, A-164-008

ABOVE: Riemenschneider's Lutheran mission station at Wārea, 1850. Riemenschneider was strongly opposed to Te Ito and his Kaingārara movement in the 1850s. His detailed reports, sent to his superiors in Germany from this station, provide valuable insights into Te Ito's activities and his rise to prominence as a prophet. *Puke Ariki, ARC2011-107*

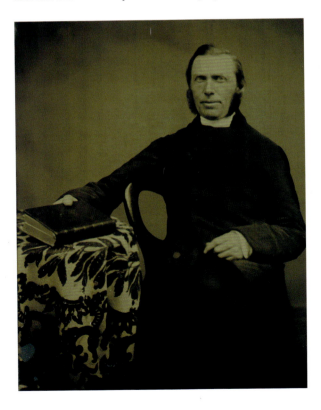

LEFT: The Lutheran missionary Reverend Johann Riemenschneider in 1859, shown here in an ambrotype portrait (produced on glass). Born in Bremen, Germany, Riemenschneider was accepted into the North German Missionary Society in 1837. He arrived in New Zealand in 1843, and after short stays in Nelson and Taupō, he established his mission station at Wārea in 1846. *Photograph by Hartley Webster, Puke Ariki, A82.030*

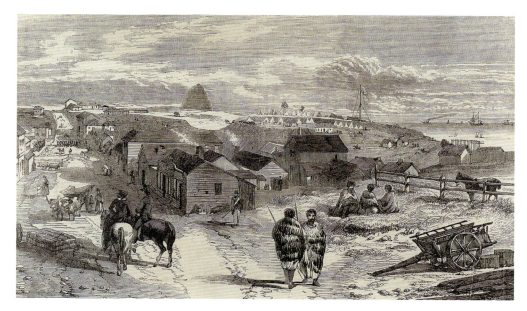

ABOVE: Devon Street, New Plymouth in 1856, with a military encampment on Mt Eliot (Puke Ariki) in the background. This engraving was produced around the time that Te Ito began his tapu-cleansing bonfires to the south. *'New Zealand, Encampment on Mount Eliot, New Plymouth', reproduced in* Illustrated London News, *23 August 1856, Puke Ariki, A95.782*

ABOVE: The marriage certificate of Tāmati Te Ito and Mihi Watara, showing their ages (twenty-eight and twenty-six) and place of residence ('Paraeiti') in 1857. John Whiteley, a Wesleyan missionary who knew Te Ito well, performed this marriage at the time of Te Ito's tapu-cleansing fire at Te Hua. *Department of Internal Affairs, Crown Copyright reserved*

A photograph of Taranaki military leader Wiremu Kīngi Te Matakātea, c.1880s. Originally known as Moki, Te Matakātea gained his new name (meaning 'clear-eyed') in recognition of his prowess as a marksman and military leader during the battles against Waikato invaders. A strong supporter of Te Ito, he owned a store, planted extensive wheat and potato crops and established a Kaingārara school at Umuroa. *Alexander Turnbull Library, PAColl-5800-31*

Taylor seems to have confused Te Ito with the atua that he had been inspired by or had invoked. A later report in *Te Karere o Poneke* identifies Tiki-kaha as an atua whakapakoko who, like Maru, belonged in the Kaingārara pantheon below the Paihia and Catholic Gods.[64] This same report describes Te Ito's Pātea fire as having been delayed until 26 February 1858, and notes that the services were led by a Catholic priest named Te Wano. As will become clear in the next chapter, the reasons for the delay were the same as those that brought an end to Te Ito's Taranaki fires: escalating conflict within Te Ātiawa over the sale of land to the government and subsequent military invasion.

Te Ito's great fires of land cleansing and political unification, staged in 1857 and early 1858, appear to have found a place within Taranaki oral tradition. Alan Taylor (1933–2016), an artist and scholar who was knowledgeable about Taranaki art and material culture and who must have learned of Te Ito's fires from local historians, wrote:

> The death rate in south Taranaki was so alarming that tribal elders threw onto a bonfire all they could find of their old culture – carvings, ornaments and figures of ancient gods – in the hope that this might lessen the calamity that had come upon them. The fire burnt for three days, but to no purpose: the death toll continued to rise.[65]

A clearly related oral tradition, recorded by the Ngāti Ruanui historian John Houston in his *Maori Life in Old Taranaki*, tells of 'carvings of wood and stone' being destroyed in a fire at Taki Ruahine Pā, situated between Hāwera and Pātea, 'subsequent to the introduction of Christianity'. Houston wrote that 'the fire burned for days, until in the end one special stone image burst asunder with a loud report, to the consternation of tribesmen'.[66] Perhaps the stone image was Maru.

Other Kai Ngārara Fires

But Taranaki was not the only district to be cleansed of tapu through atua-destroying fires. At the time of the Poutoko fire in 1857, police inspector Henry Halse wrote of Te Ito that it was 'supposed that he will be called upon to perform his ceremony all over the island'. While this may have been no more than wishful thinking on the part of his followers, in February 1862, four years after the last Taranaki fire, atua ngārara were being expelled from much of inland Whanganui with whakanoa fires.

We saw in Chapter Two that a movement to drive ngārara from wāhi tapu reached Whanganui from northern Taranaki in 1851. Now, just over ten years later, fire ceremonies, closely related to those conducted by Te Ito in Taranaki, were being performed across Whanganui to bring a 'full end' to the atua ngārara that had been causing sickness and deaths. In one report published in the *Wanganui Chronicle*, they were being led by an unnamed 'prophet'; in a second, they were led by an unnamed 'priest' – perhaps they were the same person. It is certainly possible that Te Ito was present in Whanganui at this time – there is no record of him being in Taranaki – but even if he wasn't and the ceremonies were being performed by another local tohunga, it is worth including a discussion of these reports here for the light that they shine on Te Ito's Taranaki fires.

The first is from the Reverend B.K. Taylor, the son of Richard Taylor, who had begun a journey from Whanganui to Waitara up the Whanganui River, intending to then head north across the ranges. His diary entry for 6 February 1862 reads:

> All the way up the river the most picturesque spots are quite disfigured by patches cleared of trees and shrubs and burnt where they have been searching for lizards. There is a kind of clairvoyant amongst them, who is called a prophet, and professes to know where the reptile is and having pointed out its abode, the search is immediately commenced, the trees are chopped down and a large circular hole is dug and it is generally contrived that a lizard is found there which is then burnt with much ceremony and its ashes carefully collected and sprinkled over potatoes that have been cooked in a native oven for the occasion. All partake of them and having eaten the ashes they suppose they have destroyed the power of the evil spirit and thus warded off diseases from them and their children.[67]

The second report is by a member of a geological survey team that travelled down the Whanganui River in mid-February 1862. Communities were, he wrote, being ravaged by sickness, and people blamed the atua they had abandoned when they converted to Christianity:

> These gods must be destroyed as well as cast off. They are found in the shape of lizards, spiders etc. In this neighbourhood they began to collect these objects about a month ago and on Saturday the 1st inst there was a large gathering of natives at Kaitoke to witness their destruction. About the middle of the day a large number of lizards were brought in in bottles which were hung on a fence surrounding a small piece of ground, about six feet square. A priest took the lizards out of the bottles and examined them carefully. Some he threw away as being lizards and nothing more. Above 20 of them he returned to the bottles with the exclamation 'this is for us', intimating that each of these was an atua. A fire was then kindled in front of the fenced square and a large iron pot hung over it. A number of articles of apparel and other things such as wooden meris [mere] etc. were, at the desire of the priest, brought forward and burned. These articles were supposed to have been tapu'd along with some ground in the neighbourhood from which, by this ceremony, the tapu was now removed. The lizards retained in the bottles were then emptied into the pot and burned to ashes, the remains were then emptied into the fire, into which potatoes were put to be roasted. When the process of cooking was accomplished the priest invited all who were sick, or who had sick relatives, to come forward and receive a potato which would be an infallible cure ... The proceedings of the day were brought to a close by the reading of the Church of England evening service with due emphasis and solemnity ... The same ceremonies have been going on in other parts of the district and were only brought to a close in the middle of last week when it was supposed that a full end had been made to those evil spirits that had been causing so much trouble.[68]

The first report by Taylor is lacking in detail. This suggests that he did not witness the ceremony, but that it was instead described to him after he came across the clearings.

However, the unnamed writer of the second report seems to have closely observed the kai ngārara ceremony at Kaitoke, south of Whanganui, and to have had a good understanding of what was taking place. As with Te Ito's fires, there was a period of preparation during which tapu items were gathered. In this case, they included the collecting of ngārara, a practice that must also have been followed in preparation for Te Ito's Taranaki fires, but which is not described in any published accounts. The processes of cooking the collected ngārara in an iron pot and of cooking potatoes in the fire into which the ngārara ashes had been thrown were also not described for the Taranaki fires, but they, too, may well have been part of the Taranaki ceremonies. In general, this Kaitoke fire ceremony bears all the hallmarks of one of Te Ito's fires, and it must have been orchestrated by a person who was knowledgeable about these earlier fires, if not by Te Ito himself.

Perhaps the leader had been a Kaingārara emissary. In the mid-1860s Piripi Te Kohe, a tohunga and member of the Kaingārara movement, visited the lower South Island to 'patu taipo' (destroy malicious demons), removing tapu from sacred places that had become dangerous due to their presence.[69] Te Kohe visited Murihiku (south of Dunedin), Ōtākou (Dunedin), and Arowhenua (South Canterbury), performing tapu-eating ceremonies at each place. The event at Arowhenua in 1866 was described as follows:

> He called the entire Maori population of the place together, and after a careful inspection, declared that he could see demons [ngārara kikokiko] inside Tamaiharoa [Te Maihāroa] and several others. With the unanimous consent of all present, he began the process of expelling these said spirits, and removing the tapu from the neighbourhood. First, he visited all the tapu places, taking a stick from one, and a tuft of grass from another ... With these materials he cooked food, which all the Maoris partook of, without distinction of age or sex. Being obliged to leave suddenly, Piripi deputed Tamaiharoa to complete the emancipation of his tribe from the power of familiar spirits.[70]

Hipa Te Maihāroa went on to become a prophet and founder of a significant South Island movement of independence. Following the departure of Piripi from Arowhenua, Te Maihāroa continued his mission of removing tapu from the land and its people.

In light of this southern spread of Te Ito's Kaingārara practices, the expectation reported by Halse that Te Ito would be called upon to perform his ceremony all over the motu was not as unrealistic as it might have at first appeared. But we have now moved too far from the pressing concerns facing Te Ito in 1858. In the next chapter we return to Taranaki and to the troubles brewing amidst his Te Ātiawa people.

CHAPTER FOUR

Mana Trouble

Among those who may have assisted Tāmati Reina with his preaching in southern Taranaki in the mid-1840s was Te Ua Haumēne, the future prophet of the Pai Mārire movement.[1] Te Ua was also a friend of Reina's 'son', Tāmati Te Ito, and a supporter of the Kaingārara movement during 1857, the year of the fires.[2] In a letter written to Te Ito in 1858, Te Ua addressed Te Ito as his 'friend' (hoa), and used the familiar 'Mati' rather than 'Tāmati'. He also included lines from a beautiful lament for Te Ito, who was now living distant from him at Waitara.[3] However, after Te Ua himself became 'inspired' in 1862, their relationship changed significantly.[4] He now referred to himself as 'te poropiti tuatahi' (the first prophet) and considered Te Ito to have been only a 'pōrewarewa' (seer). In Te Ua's theology, pōrewarewa were ranked third, below tūku (dukes) and pou (pillars).[5]

In what appears to have been a thinly veiled criticism of Te Ito and his fires, the Pai Mārire prophet announced, in September 1865, that the people of Taranaki had been quite correct to destroy their tapu things. Unfortunately, however, in their ignorance they had neglected to offer their fires as sacrifices to God, and so God had reduced their mana. If there had been a stronger, truly inspired seer the work would have been completed and the land retained, he said. This announcement was recorded by the Pai Mārire scribe Karaitiana in the Te Ua service book as follows:

Kupu Tuatoru: kei te patu mea tapu te tika. Ko te kūaretanga o Taranaki – kīhai i rapu ki te whakahere ahi. No reira ka tango te Atua i tētahi māna i te tāngata.
Kupu Tuawha: mehemea tēnā anō he pōrewarewa tino kaha he rapu pēnā, kua oti, arā, kua whakahokia atu ngā kēti ki ngā patiki.

Third Word: It is right to destroy tapu things. The foolishness of Taranaki was that they did not seek to offer the fires [to God]. Therefore, God took away some of the people's power.
Fourth Word: If there had been an inspired seer [pōrewarewa] strong enough to strive in that way it would have been accomplished. That is, the gates to the paddocks would have been restored [the land would have been secured].[6]

This chapter considers the intense political and military struggles that Te Ito was drawn into in the aftermath of his fires and suggests that, in light of these events, no prophet – neither he nor Te Ua – could possibly have been strong enough to complete God's work of unification at the time. Te Ito's vision was one of pan-tribal unity; he wanted to bring together all the people of Taranaki 'from Mokau to Patea'. If this was the work that Te Ua thought remained to be completed, then, as Te Ua himself would soon discover, the odds of success were very slim indeed. The fires of 1857 had succeeded to some degree in bringing Taranaki people together, but if in his more optimistic moments Te Ito believed that a greater degree of unity might soon be realised, the events of the next two years would dash any such hopes.

The First Challenge: Kātātore

Te Ito was presented with his first significant political challenge while preparations were under way for his Poutoko fire, hosted by Te Ngāhuru, in September 1857. Te Waitere Kātātore, the Puketapu leader who, as we have seen, signalled his strong opposition to Waiaua's offer of land to the government by erecting a carved pou, and who was considered by many to be a supporter of the Kaingārara, unexpectedly offered Land Purchase Commissioner Robert Parris some 40,000 acres.

Te Ito and the Kaingārara chiefs of Taranaki Iwi, Ngā Ruahine and Ngāti Ruanui viewed Kātātore's act with great alarm. A month after the offer was made, these Kaingārara leaders wrote to Parris insisting that he was not to bring surveyors near their land, and warning him that it contained tapu places that were guarded by atua in the guises of reptiles, spiders and taniwha:

> [H]e wahi tapu enei, e Parete – he mania. Ko nga kaitiaki i enei whenua he tataramoa, he ongaonga, he kotete; ko nga kai tiaki o enei wahi tapu he ngarara, he weta, he pungawerewere, he taniwha, he mokonui ... Kia rongo mai koe. Kaore tenei whare i hanga mo te aha ranei; otira i hanga o matou nei whare mo te whenua.

> *These are sacred places, oh Parris – slippery places. The guardian atua of these lands are brambles [bush lawyer], stinging nettles, seven-fingers [plants with serrated leaves]; the guardian atua of the sacred groves are reptiles, wētā, spiders, taniwha and giant lizards ... Listen, these rūnanga houses were not built without purpose; our houses were built to hold the land.*[7]

This letter was sent from the Ngāti Ruanui settlement of Keteonetea, a village near Tāmati Reina's settlement of Ketemarae, five days after Te Ito had staged his Wārea fire ceremony. All or most of the twenty signatories must have just arrived home from Wārea, where they would have discussed Kātātore's scandalous offer with Te Ito.

Immediately after the Wārea ceremony Te Ito also travelled south down the coast, stopping at Te Umuroa. There he wrote his own letter to his close kinsman and elder, Te Waitere Kātātore, urging him (with implied threats) to change his mind and not take any payment from the government. Given its significance, and the fact that so few of Te Ito's letters have survived, the whole text is included here:

Umuroa, Oketopa 31, 1857

Haere atu tenei karere aroha kia Te Waitere, tangihia atu ratou. E Koro, tena koe; otira, koutou katoa. Ka nui toku aroha atu kia koutou katoa i roto i te raruraru. Ka nui to koutou pohehe i roto enei ra. I marama ano koutou i taku waihotanga atu; inaianei, kua he. Kia rongo mai koutou – kua kanga koutou ki aku korero; ahakoa kanga mai koutou ki aku korero, ma koutou te kanga, maku tea o marama. Ka mutu era kupu; kei pouri koutou ki enei kupu.

E hoa, e Te Waitere, whakamutunga tenei tikanga au. E kore ranei koe e pai kia whakamutua tenei tikanga, no te mea kua kino, kua pakaru te tati o te whenua, me te ritenga mo taua kua he. E hoa, whakamutua te korero. E koro, kia ki te ai ahau i a koe. E koro, i mea atu ai au, kua nui te pouri o te kainga, kia aroha koe ki taku kupu; ka horomia e koe enei kupu ka tika, hei koha koa ma taua ka pai. Ko nga mea tenei e whakamutua ko te mahinga a to ngakau ki te tuku whenua. E Koro, whakamutua. Tenei tetahi. Ki te mea tangohia nga utu, kaua koe e tango; ahakoa mea iti, kaua e tango. Heoi ano.

Na tau tamaiti aroha, Na Tamati Te Ito.

Umuroa, October 31st, 1857

Go my loving messenger to Te Waitere and weep for them. Friend, salutations to you, that is the whole of you. Great is my love for you all in the midst of perplexity. Your confusion has been great in these days. You were all enlightened [thinking clearly] when I left you but now you are in error. Do you all hearken. You have cursed my speech [words]; but although you have cursed what I said, the curse will be for you, and for me this word of light [clarity and brightness]. So ends those words. Do not suffer yourselves to be depressed by those words.

Friend, Te Waitere, let this proceeding of yours cease. Will you not consent to that this proceeding of yours shall cease? It has become bad; the chart [map] of the land is broken [destroyed] and the rule [correct way of acting] for you and I has become void [lost]. Friend, cease talking that I may see you. Friend, [My elder] I have thought that great depression [sadness/darkness] exists at your place. Do you be kind to my word; if you swallow these words, [it will be] well. If treasured by us it will be good. The thing to be relinquished is this – the working of your heart to dispose of land. Friend [My elder], let this cease. Here is another thing: If payment is taken [made] do not you take any; however small, do not touch it. That is all. From your loving son [child]. From Tamati Te Ito.[8]

The reason that we are able to read this highly confidential letter is because it was opened by police inspector Halse (in the presence of Parris) and copied; the copy was sent to Donald McLean and subsequently published. Curiously, the letter opened by Halse bore Te Ito's signature but was in the handwriting of Te Ngāhuru, the Poutoko chief and assessor, and it had been brought to Halse by Te Ngāhuru himself.[9] This letter may, therefore, have been a copy made by Te Ngāhuru with Te Ito's permission (hence his signature) and originally intended for the eyes of Kaingārara leaders rather than those of Halse and Parris. Halse suspected this was the case. Presumably, the original letter penned by Te Ito reached Kātātore.

The structure and tone of this letter are revealing of the character of Te Ito, in particular his directness. The first paragraph conveys both Te Ito's compassion for his kin and his anger that his words have been trampled upon, or as he puts it 'kanga' (cursed). The words in question must have been about the importance of retaining land, but they may have also included Te Ito's prophetic pronouncements. It was generally thought that tohunga, prophets, and men of mana in general had the ability to return curses with interest, and the threat of such an outcome is suggested by Te Ito in a very direct way. The second paragraph begins with a reference to a jointly agreed plan ('tāti' – chart) for the land which Kātātore had now torn up. Rather than talking to the government, Kātātore is being invited to talk with Te Ito and reconsider the grave error he was making. But perhaps the most significant fact about this letter is its very existence! That the prophetic leader of Kaingārara wrote to Kātātore, presuming to have influence over him, strongly suggests that the latter was a Kaingārara supporter who had betrayed the wider Kaingārara cause, which was to hold on to the land.

Thus, Te Ito's letter to Kātātore suggests that the southern land-holding alliance had expanded to include Te Ātiawa, as the members of that iwi became Kaingārara. Historians Keith Sinclair and James Belich both thought that this letter was significant in that it suggested some relationship between the so-called 'land league' and Kaingārara, but the nature of the association was unclear to them. Sinclair noted that Te Ito, who was a 'great mover' in ceremonies for holding the land, spoke not of a league but a 'tāti' (chart or map) or 'tikanga' (policy or plan), connected to which were ideas about 'kaitiaki' (guardians) and new understandings of tapu.[10] Belich wrote that the nature of both the land-holding and Kaingārara movements was 'shadowy and disputed' and their connection was 'unclear', but 'the time and place of their origin suggest[ed] some link'.[11] Both historians felt that this letter and the one sent to Parris earlier, warning of guardian atua, cast new light on the nature of the so-called 'land league'.

We can now say that the Kaingārara movement which Te Ito formed after the initial phase of his whakanoa work, and which included many of the leaders who attended the Manawapou hui, was a further expression of these southern leaders' determination to both hold the land and to render it safe for habitation. As such, it was also a continuation and expansion of the organisational and ceremonial work that Te Ito and others had been engaged in during the 1852–54 period. By the late 1850s, the southern land-holding alliance of the early 1850s had morphed into Kaingārara and, as it did so, it expanded. This significant transformation went unrecognised by Pākehā settlers and government officials, who thus failed to appreciate the religious and prophetic dimension of a land-holding movement that they continued to refer to as a 'land league'.

The initial fierce opposition of Te Ito and his southern followers to Kātātore's offer contrasts sharply with what appears to have been a high level of enthusiasm for the sale among Kātātore's people living inland from Te Oropūriri at Kaipakopako Pā, an enthusiasm that was also shared by the wider Puketapu hapū. At the time of the initial announcement of the offer in August 1857, Halse commented that the excitement amongst the Kaipakopako people contrasted 'strangely' with their staunch resistance to land sales at the time of Rāwiri Waiaua's murder in 1854.[12] A few days after the announcement, a large hui took place at which, according to Parris, who had been invited to the meeting, there was a general feeling in favour of Kātātore's offer.[13] The following month, Parris reported that a second large hui was held at which there had been 'unanimous consent' to the offer and, as a consequence, all of Te Ito's Puketapu people were coming into town on 5 October 'for the purpose of publicly consenting to the sale'.[14]

Clearly, then, Kātātore's offer had created a serious rift between some of the Kaingārara leaders, including Te Ito, and the majority of Te Ito's own Puketapu hapū, and possibly also, by extension, the majority of his tribe, Te Ātiawa. Moreover, by November, Ngāti Ruanui and a significant number of Taranaki Iwi had abandoned their opposition to the sale.[15] Even Wiremu Kīngi Te Rangitāke appears to have accepted Kātātore's right to dispose of the land as he saw fit. When Kātātore told him, at the end of August, that he was going to offer the land, Te Rangitāke simply replied: 'E pai ana, kei a koe te tikanga' (That's fine, it's up to you to decide).[16]

Parris was understandably elated at this turn of events. He wrote jubilantly that he had broken opposition to land sales in Taranaki and had thus brought about 'the entire disruption of the league established for that purpose in this Province'.[17] Henry Halse shared Parris's excitement, writing that it was 'very satisfactory to know that the League no longer exists in this district and so feel that it is likely to die out where it originated, and that land can now be purchased from the natives without fear of causing trouble amongst them'.[18]

But this was very far from the truth. As a prophetic movement, Kaingārara remained strong and its leaders were looking to build on the success of their fires by establishing tribal rūnanga (councils) and their own independent school. Te Ito may have been unable to convince Kātātore to change his mind, but his influence and mana within Te Ātiawa and beyond was by now considerable. He was not only healing the land and people through expelling atua kikokiko, but he had also assumed a more chiefly role in mediating social conflicts within his own tribe, and between them and Pākehā settlers. Around the time of Kātātore's offer, for example, Te Ito had intervened in a case of suspected cattle theft by a settler named White, a man of ill repute according to Halse. White had been seen driving cattle south from New Plymouth and soon after, Tīpene, one of Te Ito's followers, had found that one of his bullocks was missing. Halse wrote:

> As might have been expected from the character Mr. White has earned himself, suspicion attached to him, and Te Ito directed Tīpene to take Mr. White's horse. Not deeming it advisable to take this case to court, I wrote to Te Ngahuru [the Poutoko native assessor] and Te Ito requesting them to cause the horse to be brought to me, which was accordingly done.[19]

Halse also knew better than to arrest Te Ito at such a sensitive time.

The Second Challenge: Īhāia

Te Ito's failure to persuade Kātātore and his Te Ātiawa supporters to hold onto their land did not deter him from his larger mission. In fact, he now threw himself into his whakanoa work with even greater energy than before. Riemenschneider reported that after concluding his work at Te Umuroa at the beginning of November Te Ito returned to Pātea, the place where he had begun his fires: '[T]here, he laboured in a more extensive manner gathering widely scattered magic [tapu items] together'.[20] The prophet briefly suspended this work in December to visit Kātātore, whose young child had just died, and at this time he again sought to persuade his relative to change his mind, but without success.[21] By the beginning of January he was back at work in Pātea and preparing for what would be his last fire. But before the ceremony could be staged, an event occurred that sent shock waves throughout the entire Taranaki district: on 9 January 1858, Waitere Kātātore was murdered. Te Ito immediately abandoned his whakanoa work in the south and hastened to New Plymouth, there to become, in Riemenschneider's words, 'a war oracle and prophet of victory'.[22] Te Ito was now faced with a second, more significant political challenge – to help build an alliance against Īhāia Te Kirikūmara, the chief who had ordered Kātātore's murder.

Īhāia, the paramount chief of the Ōtaraua hapū and a very astute political operator, had become a leading advocate for the sale of land, including that at Waitara, thus challenging the mana of Wiremu Kīngi Te Rangitāke. A deep rivalry had developed between the two chiefs, and Īhāia's animosity extended to Te Rangitāke's Puketapu ally, Kātātore, who prior to 1857 had also opposed land sales. In mid-1857 Īhāia, who had built a new pā, Ikamoana, on Puketapu land north of Paraiti, offered this land to the government. Of course, Kātātore and Puketapu opposed the sale and the offer was rejected by Parris.[23] Then, suddenly and unexpectedly, Kātātore made his counter-offer, which Parris and McLean immediately accepted. This was too much for Īhāia:

> After years of effort he had seemed poised on the brink of success. He had been the only important chief willing to sell land. He had offered the two most attractive districts in New Plymouth. Surely, it seemed, the Government could not have held out much longer. Now, at once, [through his rivalry with Kātātore] he had become a liability.[24]

On Saturday 9 January, when Kātātore made one of his weekly visits to town, Īhāia met him there and pretending great friendliness, shouted him food and large quantities of drink. That evening, as Kātātore and his four companions were returning home to Kaipakopako Pā, they rode unarmed straight into an ambush planned by Īhāia. Kātātore dismounted and attempted to flee, but he was shot and his body was badly mutilated. The leader of the ambush was Īhāia's brother, Tāmati Tīraurau.[25]

In the conflict that followed, the Puketapu forces based at Kaipakopako Pā fought Īhāia's followers under the military leadership of Te Rangitāke and the prophetic guidance of Tāmati Te Ito. Ōtaraua forces gathered initially at Ikamoana Pā, under the leadership of Īhāia.

In early January, probably before he left Pātea, Te Ito had sought the military assistance of Ngāti Ruanui in avenging Kātātore's murder, but it appears that their leaders had not forgiven Kātātore for offering land to the government and putting their sovereignty at risk. They wrote to Te Ito in late January telling him that they had no intention of providing him with any military support.[26]

Te Ito had more success in gaining assistance from the leaders of Taranaki Iwi, among them the renowned Te Umuroa chief, Wiremu Kīngi Te Matakātea. Te Matakātea was one of the main Kaingārara leaders, but more significantly in this case, he was married to one of Kātātore's sisters and so must have come under strong pressure from his wife's kin to support them.[27] Riemenschneider, however, considered that Te Ito's influence was the crucial factor. He wrote that the Te Ātiawa conflict was of no more interest to Taranaki Iwi than previous ones but that this time 'their new master', Te Ito, had found devious ways and means to drag them into his war: '[I]f they wanted to bring about perfection they had to obey and follow him, and they could not complete the work without him'.[28] Riemenschneider further claimed that he had strongly opposed Te Ito and had been able to keep the greater part of the tribe from joining the prophet, instead returning them into his fold of 'God and truth'.[29] Te Ito's limited success in involving Taranaki Iwi and his failure to involve Ngāti Ruanui does not necessarily mean that his influence was beginning to wane south of New Plymouth. Rather, Riemenschneider was probably right, and the southern tribes would have wanted to limit the conflict to Te Ātiawa as much as possible.

But with Kātātore's offer now effectively off the table, the death or banishment of Īhāia would greatly improve Te Ito's chances of uniting Te Ātiawa against land sales, and hence of bringing about the wider pan-tribal unity that he and the Kaingārara had been hoping and striving for. Te Ātiawa forces under the leadership of Te Rangitāke and their prophet Te Ito, and Taranaki Iwi under the leadership of Te Matakātea, besieged Īhāia at Ikamoana Pā in mid-January 1858, preventing any food supplies or ammunition from reaching their enemy.[30] By the end of the month it had become obvious to Īhāia that his situation had become dire and so, on 6 February, he and his forces quietly left their stronghold and moved north to Karaka Pā, situated on the north bank of the Waitara River amidst a grove of karaka trees.[31]

The following day, which was a Sunday, Te Ito and his forces burned Īhāia's Ikamoana Pā in a manner that suggests symbolic associations with the prophet's tapu-destroying bonfires. The *Taranaki Herald* reported:

> They destroyed his pa, bullock carts, ploughs and other farming implements by fire, and tomahawked his unfortunate pigs and left them to the flames. They then started after Ihaia who, after temporarily occupying an intermediate pa on this side of the river, which they also burnt after he quitted it, is now strongly entrenched on the opposite bank of the river.[32]

Supporting this siege from the outset were Taranaki Iwi forces loyal to Te Ito. On 16 February, some eighty men from Taranaki arrived at Te Ito's settlement at Paraiti with a 'long train of bullock carts conveying their arms and baggage'. They had concealed their arms under food they said they were taking 'for Tamati Te Ito'. The *Herald* reported that the native assessor from Poutoko, Tāmati Te Ngāhuru, was with them and used the fact that he was apparently participating in tribal warfare to call for an end to the practice of paying assessors.[33] Te Ngāhuru was in a difficult position. As a strong supporter of Te Ito and the Kaingārara he had, as we have seen, hosted one of the fires, at Poutoko, and towards the end of 1857, he had been arranging for another fire to remove the tapu from Puke Ariki in New Plymouth[34]. However, he valued his position as a paid mediator between Māori and Pākehā, even if this meant that he would sometimes be accused of being a double agent. Te Ngāhuru was therefore 'much vexed' by the *Herald* accusation that he supported the fighting, writing in reply that he had indeed accompanied the Taranaki men to Paraiti, but had only discovered the seventy guns after their arrival, at which point he had urged the men to return home.[35]

Īhāia and his forces were besieged at Karaka for almost three months. The zeal with which Tāmati Te Ito and Wiremu Kīngi Te Rangitāke's forces pursued Īhāia alarmed the settler population, some fearing that their houses might also become smouldering ruins.[36] Revd Whiteley, who had never forgiven Kātātore for leaving his Methodist Church for the CMS, and who was regarded as 'hopelessly one-eyed' about the virtues of Īhāia, stoked these fires and warned Donald McLean in March that Īhāia's besiegers were 'proceeding to extermination and annihilation on principle[s] foreign to Maori law and Maori fairness'.[37] In his opinion, there were two main atypical principles that were informing the besiegers' actions:

> [F]irst the ambition of Wiremu Kingi who aspires to the Kingship of all the land and wants Ihaia killed because he will sell land; and second the fanaticism of Tamati Te Ito who has made himself so popular among the credulous natives by his pretensions about old tapus and who now seeks by engaging in this quarrel to make himself a still greater man among them.[38]

Granted, Whiteley's views could be 'hopelessly one-eyed'. Nonetheless, his claim that Te Rangitāke's political ambitions and Te Ito's prophetic mission had become more closely aligned since Kātātore's death has to be taken seriously. The military conflict within Te Ātiawa was taking place in the shadow of a nascent King movement, from which both Te Rangitāke and Te Ito had so far remained aloof. But this does not mean that Te Rangitāke had ambitions to be the 'King of Taranaki', supported by his 'Wizard', Te Ito, as Whiteley would later claim.[39] Rather, just as the general desire of Ngāti Ruanui and Taranaki Iwi to retain sovereignty and land was in accordance with Te Ito's mission to free the land from tapu, so too was Te Rangitāke's desire to retain Te Ātiawa sovereignty aligned with Te Ito's prophetic mission.

If there were strong suggestions of Te Ito's prophetic influence in the February conflagration at Ikamoana Pā, when Īhāia's houses, flag and belongings were put to the flames, by April this influence was undeniably manifest in the words and actions of Wiremu Te Rangitāke. Riemenschneider wrote that in a speech, Te Rangitāke called upon his Taranaki Iwi allies to be vigorous in putting his plan into action and so repay him and the Puketapu people for the great work of Te Ito, or as the Lutheran missionary put it, 'for the great work of their salvation from the force of dark magic and deadly powers which had already been partly achieved by Puketapu through its great miracle man, Te Ito'.[40] A translation of this whaikōrero was published in the *Taranaki Herald*. The anonymous 'correspondent' who supplied the translated speech to the newspaper may have been Revd Whiteley, since he was attempting to mediate in the siege at this time. His 'literal translation' is as follows:

> Men of Taranaki! Be strong! Be brave, and capture Ihaia, Nikorima, and Pukere as payment for the tapu of [the tapu that has been taken from] Taranaki and Umuroa. Then we will stretch out their arms and burn them with fire. To prolong their torture let them be suspended over a slow fire for a week, and let the fire consume them. Like the three men of old whom Nebuchadnezzar commanded to be cast into the fiery furnace, even as Shadrach, Meshach, and Abednego, shall it be with Ihaia.[41]

The paper added that because the burning of the tapu of Taranaki had yet to be completed, the men of Taranaki Iwi believed that they 'must distinguish themselves to fulfil the prophecy of Tamati Teito'.[42]

As noted in the previous chapter, Te Ito's prophecy, as understood by Riemenschneider, was that the completion of his whakanoa work would bring about or make possible the 'fulfilment of the divine order'. Now, it seems, Īhāia was being represented as an additional obstacle preventing the completion of Te Ito's mission. The reference to the 'three men of old' in Te Rangitāke's whaikōrero is a curious one, because although in the Old Testament Book of Daniel, Nebuchadnezzar did indeed order the men to be thrown into a blazing furnace (made seven times hotter than usual), they walked through the flames unharmed. Did Te Rangitāke anticipate that Īhāia would also survive his furnace? Perhaps so, because in early June 1858, Īhāia did just that, abandoning his pā to his besieger's flames – Whiteley had secured an assurance from Te Rangitāke that he would allow Īhāia and his people to escape.[43] Īhāia headed north to Urenui and the Taranaki Iwi forces headed home.[44]

The Third Challenge: Where Should the 'Children' Live?

It appears that immediately following Īhāia's defeat, a Kaingārara rūnanga met at Waitara to discuss future plans, including the establishment of a new religious community to be located in the vicinity of present-day Parihaka. While there is no direct documentary record of this meeting, we can infer its occurrence from letters written to Te Ito by Kaingārara leaders in late June 1858. On Sunday 20 June, Te Ito's 'father', Tāmati Reina, along with Ropata Totoinumia, Wiremu Kīngi Te Matakātea, Āperahama Wetai, Te Rēweti, Īhāia Te Karawa and Kōmene, wrote to Te Ito at Waitara expressing their sorrow at leaving him. They added that they had just arrived at Kapoiaia (downstream from present-day Parihaka) after an exhausting journey, to find that the men of the settlement had already left to attend a hui at Waitaha, some 5 kilometres further south, where the flag of victory was flying. Ropata and Īhāia Te Karawa attended the hui the following day and sent separate reports to Te Ito.[45]

According to Ropata, the first item for discussion was land for a settlement:

> Tenei taku kupu ki[a] rongo mai i to matou taenga mai ki Waitaha. Ka mutu te waewae, ka waiwaikorero, ka mutu, ka takoto nga taonga, ka mutu, ko moe ki reira, ka mutu. I te ata ka timata te korero mo te wenua hei mahinga ma nga tamariki. Ko Maraeaute te ingoa o te wenua. Ki taku wakaaro kaore i oti pai. Ko te kore tenei e oti. Ko te kupu a Wi Tata i penei: Kati, ka rongo mai te Kaingarara, me hoki atu ano ki a ia.

> *This is my word to inform you of our arrival at Waitaha. When the dances finished there was a formal discussion. After that the presents [taonga] were laid down and once that had finished we slept. Then, after that in the morning the talk began about the land to be worked by the children [Kaingārara]. The name of the land is Maraeaute. In my opinion it was not resolved satisfactorily. This will not be resolved. Witata's word was as follows: 'stop! The Kaingarara [Te Ito] will hear. We had better return to him [for advice]'.*[46]

Īhāia Te Karawa also wrote that the issue of where the Kaingārara 'children' should live had been unresolved and had been left to Te Ito to decide:

> E hoa, kua rongo au ki ritenga o nga tamariki. E mea ana ratou kia mahi tena tamaiti i tona kainga, i tona kainga. Ka puta taku w[ha]kaaro, 'E pai ana, hei te rang[a]tahi nga kainga hei nohoanga, hei mahinga hoki'. Heoi ano ta tatou nei mahi kei nga kainga i w[h]akaritea mo tatou, he tuturu moutanga mo tatou. E tama ma, ko Te Umuroa, ko Waitaha. Ki te marama mai a Waitaha i a ia ka noho tatou ki Waitaha. 'Waiho ra kei to tatou matua te w[h]akairo. Me mahi tatou ki nga kainga katoa, e pai ana. Mana e ki mai e rua kainga, e pai ana, ko Umuroa, ko Waitaha'.

> *Friend, I have heard of the policy for the children. They say that each child should work in his own village. I expressed my opinion, 'it is good that the villages be places to live and work for the young people'. Our entire work is in the villages organised as permanent bases for us. For goodness sake! Te Umuroa and Waitaha. If he makes it clear it is Waitaha, we will live at Waitaha. 'Leave the decision to our father. If we are to work in all the villages, all right. If he should say two villages, all right – Te Umuroa and Waitaha'.*[47]

Te Ito had failed to persuade Kātātore to withdraw his offer of land to the government and, although he had also failed to persuade Ngāti Ruanui to join his alliance against Īhāia Te Kirikūmara, he had, with the assistance of Taranaki Iwi, achieved a victory of sorts for the Kaingārara cause. Now, he was being presented with a third significant political challenge: where should his southern followers live and work as they prepared themselves for the 'fulfilment of the divine order'? This question would prove to be so difficult to answer that it would never be resolved – Ropata was right.

The question of where the main southern Kaingārara settlement should be located was closely linked to the question of where the southern rūnanga should be based, and under whose mana it should operate. Te Umuroa, under the leadership of Wiremu Kīngi Te Matakātea, was already a thriving settlement and so it seemed to some to be an obvious choice. The previous year, in November 1857, the missionary Richard Taylor was told that Te Matakātea had 'quite a college' at Te Umuroa:

> They positively stated that he had full four hundred [children]. I asked who fed them all, he said that Wiremu Kingi did as he had an abundance of wheat and potatoes ... I think there is a feeling of independence and a distrust manifested in the European schools, and the object for which they are established, which may have a political origin.[48]

Te Umuroa had clearly become a significant centre of political independence, and Matakātea was determined that the Kaingārara council should be based there.

However, other southern Taranaki leaders living north of Te Umuroa, in particular Kōmene and Te Rēweti, were equally determined that the council should not operate under Te Matakātea's mana.[49] As reported by Ropata in the above letter, a firm offer of a large block land at Waitaha named Maraeaute (possibly after a prominent hill or pā) was made to the Kaingārara in June 1858, and its boundaries were recorded.[50] Te Watarauihi, who signed himself as 'kaiwhakawa tuatahi' (chief judge) communicated this to Te Ito in July, concluding his letter with a list of those making the offer: 'Ka mutu nga wenua i homai e nga tangata o Waitaha i roto i te runanga. Ka mea te kupu a Witata, Te Manu, Erana, Iraia, Hemi, Te Waitere, a nga wahine, a nga tamariki, nga tangata katoa; whakaae katoa ratou ki te whenua kia homai mo te Kaingarara.' (That ends the lands given by the people of Waitaha in the council. So says the word of Witata, Te Munu, Erana, Iraia, Hemi, Te Waitere, the women and children, all the people, they entirely agree that the land should be given for the Kaingarara.)[51]

But Te Ito could not possibly accept this offer because to have done so would have been to insult and alienate Te Matakātea, a leader of great mana and one of his strongest supporters. In December 1859, in a last desperate effort to resolve the dispute, Te Ngāhuru, Te Ito's elder, convened a hui at Poutoko Pā, but again no agreement could be reached. Indeed, it seems that feelings were running higher than ever during a fierce exchange of views. Te Ngāhuru succinctly summed up the conclusion of the hui in a letter to Te Ito: 'Ka nui te kaha o Wiremu Kingi ki te runanga kia hoatu ki Te Umuroa. Ka nui te pakeke o Komene, o Te Reweti. Heoi tena.' (Wiremu Kingi [Te Matakātea] is very determined that the council should be given to Te Umuroa. Komene and Te Reweti are just as opposed. That's all.) When, in support of Te Rēweti, Wītata described Te Matakātea's rūnanga as a 'runanga wahine' (council of women), it was possibly intended as an insult.[52] As he had in his dealings with Kātātore and in the conflict with Īhāia, Te Ito had hit the stone wall of chiefly mana.

The Waitara Rūnanga under Threat

At Waitara, a separate Kaingārara rūnanga under the leadership of Te Ito and Te Rangitāke had been operating its own court system.[53] While there was no question of where this rūnanga should be based – it would remain at Waitara – its leaders were confronted with a much more serious issue than location in the latter half of 1858. Despite their victory over Īhāia Te Kirikūmara, and to some extent because of it, their freedom and control at Waitara remained under serious threat. By the end of 1858, one of Īhāia's allies, Te Teira, was said to be 'working hard' to organise a sale of Waitara land to the government in defiance of Te Rangitāke and the Kaingārara.[54] In response, Te Rangitāke wrote to Governor Thomas Gore Browne and Native Secretary Donald McLean on 11 February 1859, strongly reaffirming his and the rūnanga's opposition to any land sale:

[K]ia rongo korua ki ta matou Runanga mo te whenua ... Kei Mokau te rohe mai o te whenua mo matou ake, ko enei whenua ekore e hoatu e matou ki a korua ringaringa ko te Kawana, kei rite matou ki nga manu o te moana e noho ana i runga i te kowhatu, ka pari te tai ka ngaromia taua kowhatu e te moana, ka rere nga mana, no te mea kaore he nohoanga mo ratou ... No konei i tuhituhi atu ai e au ki a korua ko

Te Kawana kia rongo korua i te Runanga o tenei tau hou, kia purutia ano te whenua, no te mea ko etahi o nga tangata Maori e hiahia tonu ana ki te utu whenua, no konei ka tata mai te mate.

[D]o you hearken to our runanga respecting land ... The boundary of the land which is for ourselves is at Mokau [Taranaki's northern boundary]. These lands will not be given by us into the Governor's and your hands lest we resemble the sea-birds which perch upon a rock, when the tide flows the rock is covered by the sea, and the birds take flight for they have no resting place ... I have therefore written to the Governor and you to tell you of the Runanga of this new year, which is withholding the land because some Maories still desire to sell land which causes the approach of death.[55]

In working to organise a sale of Waitara land, Te Teira and Īhāia were not only challenging the leadership of Te Rangitāke, they were also seeking to bring about the demise of Kaingārara. The future of Taranaki was at stake for both Te Rangitāke and Kaingārara. In his letter, Te Rangitāke said that he was writing to the Governor and McLean, 'kia rongo korua i te Runanga o tenei tau hou', which was officially translated as, 'to tell you of the Runanga of this new year'. This seems an odd way of putting things; rūnanga were probably not reconstituted annually in January or February. But 'tau' can also be translated as 'age' or period', in which case Te Rangitāke was writing to the Governor and McLean to tell them about 'the rūnanga of this new age' and its determination to prevent any further sale of land north of New Plymouth. Given that Te Ito's Kaingārara rūnanga were intended to bring about a new age of pan-tribal cooperation – that is, to bring people together from Mōkau to Pātea – this alternative translation is at least plausible.

So, Te Ua was right: with divisions between his chiefly supporters widening in the south, and direct challenges to the Kaingārara leadership and vision in the north, Te Ito had not by the end of the decade been strong enough to unite Taranaki in a single settlement, as Tohu and Te Whiti would do some eight years later at Parihaka. But to be fair,

Te Ua would not be strong enough either. It is important to recognise that, unlike his successors, Te Ito was attempting to realise a hugely ambitious dream at a time when the tribes of Taranaki were largely in control of their land and when a political alliance between their leaders, anchored in their independent mana and ancestral relationships to the land, seemed a realistic possibility. Despite his prophetic calling, Te Ito could not have known that within months of Te Ngāhuru's failed mediation hui, his vision would become a pipe dream. The government's crushing of the Kaingārara through a military invasion of Waitara that included the burning of Te Ito's pā there in March 1860, and the decimation of southern Kaingārara settlements and their leaders in April the same year, will be described in Chapter Six.[56] But first, we need to consider the extraordinary way that the Kaingārara continued to engage with atua and their tapu in 1858 and 1859, despite the geographical distance between them and their leader. We need to explore Te Ito's prophetic leadership through correspondence.

CHAPTER FIVE

Living with Atua
The Kaingārara Letters

The letter sent by Ngāti Ruanui leaders to Taranaki Land Purchase Commissioner Robert Parris in response to Kātātore's offer of land is extraordinary. As we saw in the last chapter, these leaders, most of whom were Kaingārara supporters, warned Parris in their note that he should not even think about allowing his surveyors onto their land because it included tapu places guarded by 'reptiles, wetas, spiders, taniwha and giant lizards'.[1] But did they expect Parris to take this warning seriously? Did they really think that Parris and the government would abruptly halt their efforts to acquire land if they knew that it was guarded by ngārara? The answer to both questions is almost certainly no. What then, were they saying? These Kaingārara leaders were telling Parris that their land was not a piece of property that could be bought and sold; it was, instead, a place in which they dwelt, and this meant living with atua and the tapu with which they were associated.

The letter is extraordinary not simply because of the unusual warning that the leaders delivered, but also because it strongly evokes the in-between world that the Kaingārara were inhabiting. This was a world that was, in a sense, both pre-Christian and post-Christian; a world in which the Kaingārara had begun to reconfigure their relationships with atua, tapu and missionary teachings. In this chapter our focus is on the way in which Tāmati Te Ito guided his followers in their ongoing relationships with atua and tapu through written correspondence. But before examining the Kaingārara letters written to Te Ito, it is important that we think a little more deeply about the meaning of the terms 'atua' and 'tapu' and what they might have meant to the Kaingārara.

It is clear that for pre-Christian Māori, a state of tapu arose from active relationships with atua.[2] While the term 'atua' is often translated as 'god', this is a post-missionary gloss and it is, at best, quite misleading. Although Christian missionaries chose the capitalised word 'Atua' to refer to their 'God', Māori atua were certainly *not* 'gods' in the Christian or classical European sense. Pre-Christian atua participated directly in social life as the embodiments of ancestral spirits that were controllable by tohunga, and sometimes even embodied by tohunga. Ritual techniques for controlling or directing the power of these atua had been developed and used by tohunga to ensure that people could safely and productively inhabit their world. Atua could empower leaders, but if offended they might also kill them, assuming the form of lizards (ngārara) that devoured their internal organs. The earliest recorded instance of such a fate was the death of the Bay of Islands chief Ruatara, soon after he returned to New Zealand, bringing the first Christian missionaries, in 1814. When Ruatara lay sick and in a tapu state, isolated from the village community, he was visited by two of the missionary party. One of the visitors, John Nicholas, later wrote that he had been told that an atua had, as a consequence of their breaking Ruatara's isolation, 'fixed himself in the stomach of the chief'.[3]

Tapu was not a transcendent condition imposed by transcendent gods. States of tapu were produced, controlled and negotiated by tohunga, with relationships between chiefs such as Ruatara and their vengeful, unpredictable atua ongoing daily concerns. And yet, unsurprisingly perhaps, it was a governmental, legalistic understanding of tapu that came to predominate in colonial and early ethnographic explanations of the concept. The ethnographer Elsdon Best wrote, for example: 'To put the matter briefly, it may be said that tapu means prohibition, a multiplication of "thou shalt not". These may be termed the laws of the gods and they must not be infringed.'[4] Writing in the 1850s, Richard Taylor defined tapu as 'a religious observance established for political purposes'.[5] Judge F.D. Fenton later concurred, describing it as 'an institution that has had the force of law among the people ... by it a chief or *ariki* was able to exercise a very great influence over his people'.[6]

A moral, governmental view of tapu was also widely assumed in accounts of the rapid collapse of tapu as an institution after conversions to Christianity. Richard Taylor, this time in full poetic voice, wrote that the introduction of Christianity had caused the political system to completely collapse: '[L]ike the chaff of summer's threshing floor, the wind of God's word has swept it away'.[7] In a more prosaic tone, Prytz Johansen pointed out that the demise of tapu required new forms of colonial governance: 'When the tapu institution disappears, fields, forests, and fishing grounds lie open to arbitrariness and a new protection is to be built up by the law as understood by Europeans.'[8]

But as an enduring condition that arose from an active relationship between atua and people, tapu did not simply come crashing down with mass conversions to Christianity in the 1840s – nor did atua suddenly cease to exist. Rather, the relationships changed, becoming in some contexts increasingly hostile. Atua, once amenable to knowledgeable control by tohunga with karakia (spells or chants) and rites performed at tūāhu, now came to be regarded as uncontrolled, malevolent spirits, termed 'atua kikokiko' in Taranaki and Waikato, that were causing widespread sickness and death. Elsdon Best succinctly equated 'atua', 'ngārara' and 'kikokiko' as causes of sickness in the following comment: 'Sickness made a person *tapu* because of the *atua* or demon, *ngarara* or lizard, *kikokiko* or ancestral ghost, entering into the body of the afflicted.'[9]

A legalistic view of tapu assumes that atua were, like the Christian God, transcendent, eternal and bringers of a divine order from above. It misses the point that tapu was a condition that was continually emerging and changing through interaction with atua, both benign and malevolent, controlled and uncontrolled. The name 'Kaingārara' referenced the movement's determination to combat a malevolent, uncontrolled multitude of atua, termed 'atua kikokiko', and their contagious, dangerous tapu. Lamenting what he saw as the weakened state of Māori society in the mid-nineteenth century, Te Mātorohanga, the tohunga whose teachings are collected in *The Lore of the Whare Wananga*, put it this way: 'Because *tapu* is the first thing, if there is no *tapu* all the actions of *atua* have no *mana*, and if the *atua* are lost everything is useless – people[,] their actions and their thoughts are in a whirl, and the land itself becomes broken and confused.'[10]

Indeed, the neglect of relationships with atua, and the resulting transformation of the latter into malevolent atua kikokiko, constituted such a profound transformation in the nature of both personhood and landscape that an intimate connection between them was lost. Tāmati Te Ito would certainly have agreed with Te Mātorohanga that the land had become broken and confused, but he and the Kaingārara were more optimistic, believing that a renewed relationship between people, atua and land was possible. Let us now turn, then, to a remarkable set of letters written to Te Ito by Kaingārara leaders through which they sought to attend closely to this revitalised relationship.

The Kaingārara Letters

The Kaingārara letters are a subset of a larger collection of 252 letters written between Māori that were plundered from two settlements during the Taranaki wars: Mataitawa, inland of New Plymouth, after it was occupied by colonial forces in October 1864; and Paiaka Māhoe, on the Taranaki coast south of New Plymouth in 1864.[11] Stuffed into sacks by soldiers, they were later passed on as potential sources of military intelligence to Arthur Atkinson, editor of the *Taranaki Herald* and an enthusiastic militia volunteer.[12] Colloquially (but also very unfortunately) known as the 'Atkinson Māori Letters', they are now held in the Alexander Turnbull Library in Wellington, which has recently digitised them and made them openly available online.[13] It is a rare privilege to have free access to such letters and, especially in light of the violence through which they have become available, they are used here with aroha and the utmost respect.

The fifty-two letters written to Te Ito were first identified and translated by Penelope Goode in her ground-breaking MA thesis.[14] In addition to providing initial translations of the often very obscure texts, Goode organised them chronologically and contextualised them with useful historical footnotes. Given the limited contextual information available to Goode, her translations are appropriately cautious. For example, 'ritenga', the prophetic guidance sought and provided by Te Ito in the Kaingārara correspondence, is usually translated by Goode as 'ruling'. But ritenga can also be glossed as 'ritual' or 'customary practice' and in this context it is often better understood as 'inspired prescription', or 'inspired guidance'. In many cases, the inspired prescriptions were sought in order that people might dwell safely with each other and atua and protect themselves from the malevolent influence of atua kikokiko. As we have seen, Te Ito himself was reported to have been inspired by a Waikato atua named Karutahi.[15]

More than a third of the Kaingārara letters (twenty in total) are requests for ritenga from Te Ito in relation to two domains of prophetic expertise previously associated with local tohunga: mākutu (sorcery); and the seasonal practices of fishing and agriculture. Most of the remaining letters are about the establishment of a Kaingārara settlement (eight letters which have already been discussed in the previous chapter), records of Kaingārara court hearings (four letters, referenced in the next chapter) and requests for guidance in marital relations (five letters). In the discussion that follows, the ritenga letters that reference the domains of mākutu and seasonality are interpreted and contextualised, in an attempt to provide a deeper understanding of Kaingārara engagements with atua and their tapu under the inspired guidance of a prophet whose words now travelled across tribal boundaries.

It has to be emphasised that the Kaingārara letters are extremely difficult to translate. Goode attempted a translation of the entire set of letters, but this, she admits, came at a price:

> Many of the fifty-two letters are difficult to decipher because of the state of the manuscripts, and the lack of supporting context means that it is often difficult, even impossible, to understand what is going on.

Given – most of all – the sheer numbers and abstruse themes of many of the letters, the cost has been to the scope of the translations. Definitive translations have not been attempted. The aim has been to offer working drafts as a basis for future study.[16]

While Goode's initial translations have for the most part been reproduced here, some have been revised in light of a better subsequent knowledge of supporting context. However, as with Goode's work, the revised translations must also remain provisional.

The authors of the Kaingārara letters address the prophet by three different names: Tāmati Te Ito; Tāmati Te Ito Ngāmoke; and Tāmati Ngāmoke. Te Ito's marriage certificate of June 1857 omits the name 'Ngāmoke' (lonely) raising the possibility that it was adopted subsequently to reflect the loss of one or more of his close relatives, possibly even a child. It was normal to mark tragedies by such a name change. For example, a Puketapu man, Hōne Rōpiha Ngāmoke Te Kekeu, wrote to Donald McLean in November 1857 saying that four of his children had died the previous month, adding, 'I am left alone, I am called now Hone Ngamoke (John Lonely)'.[17] These changes of name are reminders for us of the desperate circumstances many Kaingārara were faced with when they put their faith in Te Ito to guide them in their dealings with atua kikokiko.

Mākutu (Sorcery)

The earliest surviving letter sent by a Kaingārara leader to Tāmati Te Ito is dated the day before the prophet's great Wārea fire. On 18 October 1857, Taituha, a Ngāti Ruanui chief from southern Taranaki, wrote to Te Ito at Te Whanga, his pā at Waitara. At the time of writing, Te Ito would have been away from home preparing for his Wārea fire:

Ki a Tamati Te Ito
Kei Te Whanga pa

Oketopa 18 1857

Haere ra taku reta aroha ki taku tamaiti, ki a Tamati Te Ito. Tena ra koe, he [illegible] ra rawa toku aroha atu ki a koe. Kia rongo mai koe, ko nga mea i tuhia mai ai e koe kua wera i te ahi. I tahuna e au ki te kari, ko te hate. Ko te paipa, i purua ai te tupeka, i waohia ki roto ki te peke e urungatia ai e korua. Ka rongo rawa ake au. Kua purua e au ki taua paipa, kua pakaru i [a] au. Tena ra koe. Ka mutu. Naku, na Taituha

To Tamati Ngamoke at Te Whanga pa[18]

October 18 1857

Go, my loving letter to my son, Tamati Te Ito. Greetings to you. Great is my love for you. Hear this. The things you wrote about have been burnt in the fire. I burnt the shirt in the garden. As for the pipe, it was filled up with tobacco, and I put it inside the bag for you two to open. I heard perfectly well. I have filled that pipe and broken it. Greetings. That is all. From me, Taituha[19]

Taituha was here informing Tāmati Te Ito – who he refers to in the original te reo as his 'tamaiti' (child/son) because the prophet is of a younger generation than he – that he had followed Te Ito's ritenga: he had burned his shirt (and perhaps other items) in the garden and broken his pipe, which he had placed in a bag and sent with the letter to the prophet. The prophet had probably advised the destruction of the items mentioned because they had become tapu through an association with atua kikokiko and were thus causing Taituha to suffer in some way. Taituha may have been unable to attend Te Ito's October fire and so had, therefore, built his own small fire to destroy them. The way in which atua kikokiko had become associated with the items is unstated, but mākutu was probably suspected. Interestingly, Taitua wrote that he sent his pipe in a bag 'for you two to open'. The second person in this case was probably Wiremu Kīngi Te Rangitāke, with whom Te Ito was living at the time and with whom, as we have seen, he had become closely allied: another letter is explicitly addressed to both men.[20] However, it is also possible that second person was Te Ito's new wife, Mihi Watara.

A related letter reported a debate about how to deal with a tapu item referred to as a 'mai', a general term for garment. There had been a disagreement over where the garment should be destroyed. One opinion was that it should be burned at a Te Ātiawa pā named Matarikoriko, but others said it would be wrong to burn it at the mouth of a stream there and that it should, instead, be returned south to its Ngāti Ruanui owners for them to destroy. Hapurona Pukerimu, a powerful military leader and Kaingārara judge, wrote:

Ko te taenga atu o Ruka i haere mai au, i tiki mai i te mai nei.
Ma Hapurona e tahu.
Ka ki mai ha Rapata, 'Me tahu ki wea?'
Ka ki atu ha Ruka, 'Ki Matarikoriko'.
Ka ki mai ratou, 'E kore e tika kia tahuna ki reira ki te waha o Heringahaupapa'.
Ka hoki mai ha Ruka. Ka korero ki [a] au, 'Kua he taku kupu ki a koe, e Ha.'
Ka mea ratou kia kawea ki Tihoi, ki te tangata nona. Ka nohopuku au, kaore taku waha i hamu[mu.]

Ka mutu
Na Hapurona Pukerimu

When Ruka arrived I came to fetch the garment [from him]. It is I, Hapurona, who will burn it.
Rapata said, 'Where must it be burnt?'
Ruka said, 'At Matarikoriko.'
They said, 'It is not right to burn it there at the mouth of Heringahaupapa.'
Ruka came back to me and said, 'What I told you was wrong, Ha[purona].'
They said it should be taken to Tihoi, to the people who own it. I sat quietly. My mouth did not speak.

The end.
From Hapurona Pukerimu.[21]

Here, it appears than Te Ito was being asked for inspired advice from a distance on a complex set of relationships, including between the tapu of the garment, which probably needed to be burnt because it had come under the influence of a malevolent atua, and the tapu of the pā and stream, guarded by other atua. Inter-tribal relations were also at stake. It appears that distinct tribal tapu from north and south needed to be kept separate.

A third letter in this domain refers to the use of 'wai wera' (cooking water) to expel tapu in a context in which there had been accusations of adultery. Tāmati Reina of Ngāti Ruanui wrote to his 'son' Te Ito:

I tuhituhi atu ai au enei kupu aku ki a koe, te he hou ranei, te he tawhito ranei. Ko te rama tiaho, tena, ko te ramarama. Ko te ra hei tohutohu i te awatea: ko te marama e tohutohu i te po. Whaihoki ko koe hei tohutohu i nga mea ngaro o te ngakau. Ko [w]ai au ka mohio iho ki roto ki toku ngakau, ki tetahi atu tangata ngakau? Kei [a] au ranei taua he puremu. Whakaaturia mai kei tetahi ranei, a matouria mai kia wawe au te mohio. Heoi henei kupu. He kupu ke tenei. Ko te wai werawera i ringihia ki toku tinana. Ko te mahi a taua tangata ki a au kua mutu. Kua kahore noa iho.

I have written these words of mine to you for you to instruct me concerning both new and old errors. When the torch shines there is light. The sun is to guide the day and the moon is to guide the night. You, then, are to guide the hidden things of the heart. Who am I to know what is in my heart, or that of another man; is that sin of adultery mine? Show me whether it is someone else's, teach me so I may shortly know. That's all of these words. This is another word. The warm water was poured over my body. That man's work on me has stopped. It's all over.[22]

Prior to their baptism into the Christian faith, many chiefs throughout the country expelled their atua by touching parts of their body with cooked food, throwing locks of their hair into cooking fires or pouring cooking water over their heads, thus rendering themselves noa or free from tapu.[23] In Taranaki, the whakanoa rites were first performed by Wiremu Nēra Ngātai, who, in the 1820s, had been taken as a slave to Northland where he subsequently converted to Christianity. Returning to Taranaki around 1837, Nēra preached widely and prepared people for baptism with ceremonies, termed 'kokiro'. William Williams's *Dictionary of the Maori Language* translates 'kokiro' as 'set free from tapu'; it was, in other words, a whakanoa rite.[24] William Williams's brother, the CMS missionary Henry Williams, learned of this rite on a visit to Whanganui in December 1839:

> Heard much of a baptism which had been introduced by this man, Neira, which I condemned in toto. His ceremony appears to be washing the head, which has always been considered sacred by the New Zealanders, in warm water out of an iron pot, the person, at the same time confessing sins, vainly imagining that thereby his sins will be pardoned, a washing away of sin and a release of tapu very much according to native custom.[25]

'This man Neira' was, however, far from vain or misguided. Baptised into the Wesleyan Church under the name William Naylor (Wiremu Nēra), he had been preaching to almost all the hapū of south Taranaki and for two years had taught classes preparing candidates for Christian baptism.[26] It is highly unlikely that Nēra regarded his kokiro rite as replacing a baptism into the Christian Church or that he was seeking to remove Christian sins. It is more likely that he saw it as integral to the preparation for baptism, a removing of connections with atua. Bronwyn Elsmore was right to conclude that Williams 'totally misinterpreted Nēra's ministrations'.[27]

In pouring water over himself, therefore, Te Ito's 'father' had followed Wiremu Nēra's ritenga, although it had probably also been prescribed by Te Ito, and he had similarly freed himself from the tapu influence of atua, now understood to be atua kikokiko. We do not know the identity of 'that man' who was performing 'his work' on Tāmati Reina, but this work, now 'stopped', would have been mākutu.

Also in the domain of sorcery is a letter written to Te Ito by Te Ua Haumēne, a Kaingārara adherent who would, as previously noted, become an inspired prophet himself, founding his own indigenous resistance movement, Pai Mārire, in 1862.[28] Te Ua informed Te Ito that he had been unable to discover the cause of a person's emaciated condition, and asked the prophet if he had completed his search for the appropriate ritenga. It is likely that this ritenga was a prescription to ward off sorcery, since the emaciation would have suggested the presence of atua kikokiko. The name of the ill person is not provided in this undated letter, but he may have been Honeri, the son of Te Warihi, one of the Kaingārara leaders. In October 1858, Te Warihi wrote to Te Ito asking for help in discerning the cause of this son's illness:

Ki a Tamati Te Ito
Kei Te Whanga
Tiw[a]rawara pa

15 o nga ra Oketopa 1858

Haere atu ra taku reta aroha ki toku matua, ki a Tamati Te Ito. E hoa, e Tamati, kei te mate tetahi o matou, a Honeri. Ka nui tona mate. He aha ranei te take o tona mate? Kei a koe te tikanga.

Heoi ano, ka mutu.
Na Te Warihi

To Tamati Te Ito at Te Whanga
Tiw[a]rawara pa

Fifteenth day of October 1858.

Go my loving letter to my elder, Tamati Te Ito. Friend, Tamati, one of us, Honeri is ill. He is really sick. What is the cause of the illness? You decide what to do.

Well, that's all.
From Te Warihi[29]

The following month Te Warihi wrote to Te Ito to say that his son had died and that he had been left completely bereft.[30]

Seasonality: Fishing and Agriculture

This domain of prophetic expertise includes eleven letters that sought advice about seasonal practices previously carried out by local tohunga. The earliest of these letters is a report by Ropata Totoinumia, a Kaingārara leader, about a large gathering held at Waitaha, south of New Plymouth, at the beginning of Puanga, the Māori New Year, in June 1858. The rising of Rigel, which marked the start of the year, also signalled the beginning of the lamprey fishing season. Totoinumia reported that lamprey had been wrongly caught and eaten by several people within a tapu area marked by recently established rūnanga boundaries:

I muri iho ka patai au ki te tikanga o te he. Ka timata i [sic] a Hemi Te Pua ko te rapunga i te wai i Waitaha ... na ratou i rapu nga piharau, tunua, kainga. I kite ano ha Hemi, kaore ia ki atu kia hakiria.

Muri iho ka rapua e Hemi Te Pua, Kotahi tana ika, tunua, kainga.

Muri iho ko Te Ranapia. Ka korero i tona mahinga i te rarauhe hei wakaparu, kaore i wakaparua.

Muri iho ka heke ia ki te wai ki Pungaereere. Mau mai i a ia e rua nga ika, tunu ana, kainga.

Next, I asked about the nature of the error. Hemi Te Pua began the search by the stream at Waitaha ... they sought out the lamprey, which were roasted and eaten. Hemi saw them; he did not say they should be thrown away.

After that Hemi Te Pua looked for them. He had one fish, which was roasted and eaten.

After that Te Ranapia spoke of his getting bracken for a lamprey weir, but it was not made into a weir.

After that he went down to the stream at Pungarereere. He caught two fish, which were roasted and eaten.[31]

The guilty people publicly confessed their sins, but complained that the boundaries of the tapu areas had not been explained to them clearly enough, an excuse that the chief rejected. He asked them if they were willing to cease their transgressive behaviour and they agreed to do so. A second report on this new year meeting describes in less detail the fishing transgressions but records more fully these confessions of guilt.³²

Ropata Totoinumia also reported to Te Ito that he had clarified the northern and southern boundaries for line fishing and had warned people not to bring fish caught outside their district into their villages:

> Ka mea atu au, 'ka hiakai ki te ika me haere ki Te Namu. Ka tae ki reira, ka kai te ika, ka ora Te Takapu. Ka hoki ki tona kainga, kaua e tango ika ki tona kainga. Kaua e puta ki te moana i roto i enei rohe, i Waiwiri, i Otaha. Kaua e makamaka, otira ka karangatia e au kia rongo nga tangata katoa ko te wai, ara ko nga wai katoa, ko te tuwenua. Ko nga tangata o reira he papapa he mokomoko he weta he ngarara; te tuakana o aua mea he makutu.'

> *I said, 'When someone wants to eat fish, he had better go to Te Namu. When he gets there, he eats fish and Te Takapu will be safe. When he returns to his home, he is not to bring fish to his village. Do not put to sea within these boundaries from Waiwiri from Otaha. Do not cast out a line, however, I will make an announcement so that all the people are aware of the stream, that is, all the inland streams. The people of that place are stink-roaches, skinks, wetas, lizards; the older brother of these things is sorcery.'*³³

The chief's warning that sorcery is the 'tuakana' (older brother) of stink-roaches, skinks, wētās and lizards echoes that given to the government the previous year when Kaingārara leaders opposed Kātātore's offer of land. Then, the government was told that atua guarded sacred places within the block; now people were being reminded that these atua also guarded their mainland streams. In such a dangerous context, respect for the boundaries established by the Kaingārara council was vital for safe habitation.

It had always been the responsibility of tohunga to define fishing boundaries and to mark these with rocks (on which designs, often spirals, were painted) or stakes to signal ownership of the ground and show that the area was under the protection of an atua.³⁴ Te Ito had now assumed oversight of this role. However, people appear to have been having difficulty reconciling his inspired ritenga with local tradition. One local chief wrote to Te Ito complaining about the prophet's numerous prescriptions (ritenga mahamaha), of which he and his community had had no previous knowledge. All they had known previously, he claimed, was that fishing canoes needed to stay within certain boundaries.³⁵ And the distance between Te Ito and his Kaingārara followers became a significant issue when advice on fishing was needed quickly. In another letter, one of Te Ito's judges asked Te Ito to clarify a ritenga that appears to have prohibited trawling for kahawai. Here, a rapid reply from Te Ito would have been hoped for:

Ki a Tamati Te Ito Ngamoke
Kei Te Wanga pa
Waitara
Huawai pa
Waitaha

Tihema 21 1858

Haere atu ra e tuku reta ki toku matua, ki a Tamati Te Ito Ngamoke,
E koro, tena koe.
He ritenga tenei kua tae mai ki a au. Na nga tangata o War[e]a i mea mai te kupu kia haere atu etahi tamariki hei hoehoe kahawai, he tirohanga atu no ratau ki te kahawai e tu ana i te moana. Ka kimi mai ratou ki a matou kia haere atu hei hoehoe. Ka rapu au i konei, kahore i marama i au no konei ka tuhia atu taku reta ki a koe. Mau e whakamarama mai taua ritenga.
Heoi ano, ka mutu.
Na Te Watarauihi, Kaiwhakawa

To Tamati Te Ito Ngamoke at Te Wanga [Whanga] pa Waitara
Te Hauwai pa Waitaha

December 21 1858

Go, my letter, to my elder, Tamati Te Ito Ngamoke. Old friend, greetings to you. This is [about] a ritenga which I have received. The people of War[e]a said some 'children' [i.e., the Kaingārara] should paddle about, trawling for kahawai, because they saw the kahawai at high tide. They looked to us to say if they should go out paddling. I am seeking advice on this because it is not clear to me, hence I have written my letter to you. Will you clarify that ritenga for me. Well, that's all.

From Te Watarauihi, Judge[36]

There are six letters in the collection requesting ritenga in relation to the construction and launching of fishing canoes. Again, this was an activity in which the tohunga had always played a significant role, directing the 'consecrated industry' of construction and determining the time and place of launching, placing the activities under the protection of atua.[37] The earliest of the six letters, written in November 1858, informed Te Ito that a new canoe for Ngāti Ruanui was planned, but that construction would only proceed if the project had his blessing.[38] This must have been forthcoming, because two weeks later the same writer told Te Ito that the construction work had been completed and he requested a ritenga for the launch.[39]

The following month, in December 1858, the prophet was informed that a canoe named *Maru* – after the Ngāti Ruanui atua brought to New Zealand on the ancestral *Aotea* canoe – had been launched. However, there had been significant disagreement about the correct place from which to do this:

Ki a Tamati Te Ito Ngamoke
Kei Te Wanga pa
Keteonetea pa

Ti[hem]a 19 o nga [rā] 1858

Haere atu ra taku reta ki a Tamati.

E hoa, no te Paraire au i tae mai ai. Ko taku taenga mai kua riro te waka ki Ohawe. No taku taenga mai ka korerotia e au te kianga mai ki a au kia toia ki Waihi te waka. Ka pouri a Panapa mo ta ratou toaanga [sic] ki Ohawe. Ka mea ratou kia toia mai ki Waihi. No te Mane i kawea ai ki Waihi a Maru k[e]. Ki te he koe, mau e tuhi mai, kia h[o]ro mai.

Naku, na Te Kepa

To Tamati Te Ito Ngamoke at Te Wanga pa
Keteonetea pa

December 19th of the [days] 1858

Go, my letter, to Tamati.

Friend, it was on Friday I arrived. By the time I arrived the canoe had been taken to Ohawe. When I arrived it was discussed with me and I was told that the canoe should be dragged to Waihi. Panapa was dark about their dragging of the canoe to Ohawe. They said it should be dragged to Waihi. Instead, Maru was brought to Waihi. If you disagree, please write to me at once.

From me, Te Kepa[40]

Soon after, *Maru* was smashed at sea, no doubt vindicating the opinions of some leaders who thought that it had been launched in the wrong place. In a letter written on 27 December 1858, Te Ito was told of the loss, but the writer urged him not to be 'pōuri' (depressed or dark-hearted) because they had already cut down a tree for a new canoe.[41] The local leaders had independently determined that the correct course of action would be to destroy the fish that had been caught from the broken canoe. The fish were probably considered tapu because they had come under the influence of the atua that had been responsible for the destruction of the canoe. The atua involved here may have been Maru or one associated with Maru, after whom the canoe was named; as we have seen, a few years earlier, and in the same general locality, Te Ito had destroyed a stone image of Maru by throwing it into the first of his fires. Two successful fishing trips had resulted in catches of tuna (eels) and eighty mangō (dogfish), all of which were burned in a fire.

In addition to letters seeking advice on fishing, correspondence relating to the seasonal domain includes a letter written in October, the month for planting potatoes, informing the prophet that the Kaingārara leaders had acted in accordance with his guidance and that their potato rite had been completed:

Ki a Tamati Te Ito Ngamoke
Kei Te Wanga pa
Waitara
Hauwai pa
Waitaha

Oketopa 25 1858

Haere atu ra e ta maua nei reta aroha ki to maua nei matua. E koro, tena koe koutou ko [o] tamariki.
Kua tae mai tau reta ki a matou kua kite matou e tika ana tau kupu.
Kia rongo mai koe, ehara i a matou, na te tangata whenua i patai tonu ki a matou i nga taima katoa. No reira ka whakaae matou ki ta ratou kupu mo aua kai. Muri iho ka patua ano e matou, a, ka mate te ritenga o nga taewa. Engari ko nga wahie kua pau i a matou.
Ko aua taewa kei te takoto noa. Ki to matou whakaaro kia pirau noa atu ki roto ki te rua haua taewa. Heoi ano tenei ...

Heoi ano, Ka mutu.
Na Ihaia Te Karawa

To Tamati Te Ito Ngamoke at Te Whanga pa Waitara
Te Hauwai pa Waitaha

October 25 1858.

Go our loving letter to our elder. Old friend, greetings to you and your children. We have received your letter and recognise that your word is right. Listen here, it was not us, it was the people who lived there who kept asking us all the time and therefore we agreed to what they said about that food. Later we pounded [those potatoes], and the potato ritenga was completed. However, we used up all the firewood. Those [uncooked] potatoes are just lying about. In our opinion, those potatoes should just be left in the pit to rot away. That's all of this ...

Well, that's all.
from Ihaia Te Karewa[42]

It is unclear what the purpose of this rite was or why it had involved the building of a large fire that used up all the firewood. However, it is possible that, as in the early 1850s, the community had gathered around a fire upon which potatoes had been cooked in order to clear the land of atua kikokiko. In this case, the ceremony may have been performed in preparation for planting. It seems that Īhāia and other leaders had initially not completed the ceremony, but following Te Ito's advice – his word was 'tika' (right) – they did so. The question that remained was what to do with their left-over potatoes – should they also be cooked or left to rot?

We have no way of knowing the full extent of Te Ito's correspondence with his followers. It is possible that the fifty-two letters preserved in the Alexander Turnbull Library are but a small portion of the total number that he received. Most of the surviving letters were written in 1858, during the period between his fires and the build-up to the invasion of Waitara, and this was probably the case for the Kaingārara correspondence more generally. But it is important to also recognise that while his followers were writing to Te Ito seeking advice from him, or informing him of activities and problems, Te Ito was also responding in person to their concerns and sickness. In November 1858, for example, an old man who was dying had been brought to Ōakura south of New Plymouth. The influence of atua kikokiko must have been suspected and Te Ito was called upon to expel them. Police inspector Halse wrote:

Rangi Kapuao has been taken back to Oakura by his friends and by last accounts the next move will be to his pare [mourning shelter]. Tamati

Te Ito passed through the Town yesterday with a few followers (all mounted) to visit the old man and if it were practicable, to save him.[43]

The Kaingārara letters were sent to Te Ito from sixteen settlements located throughout the Taranaki district by members of Te Ātiawa, Taranaki Iwi, Ngā Ruahine and Ngāti Ruanui. In discerning breaches of tapu and prescribing ritenga to deal with these, Te Ito was essentially performing the same service for multiple hapū and iwi across Taranaki that had previously been performed by particular pre-Christian tohunga for their own particular hapū.[44] But now this work was understood to be 'mahi kikokiko' (the work of expelling malevolent atua) and it had become focused on the two domains – sorcery and seasonal work – within which malevolent atua and their tapu were potentially most active. These domains encompassed daily activities in which the continuity of life was most at risk from a failure to respect the guardians of land, waterways and sea. In advising the Kaingārara about their daily concerns, albeit from a distance, Te Ito was restoring relationships between people, and between people and place. For the Kaingārara who were living with atua kikokiko, Te Ito's visions and ritenga had become vital resources for their safe habitation.

But safe habitation also meant dealing with, if not expelling, another form of demon – colonial forces and their military commanders. Struggle was necessary to retain a measure of political independence in the face of colonial efforts to assert absolute sovereignty, and this in turn required a new form of rangatiratanga, of which Kaingārara would be an expression. The efforts of Te Ito and his Kaingārara followers to hold their land and assert their rangatiratanga at Waitara are discussed in the next chapter.

CHAPTER SIX

Prophet and Rangatira

While Te Ua Haumēne would express a pointed criticism of Te Ito's fires in 1865, he had earlier been a friend and supporter of the Kaingārara prophet. Towards the end of 1858, Te Ua wrote to Te Ito, expressing his love for him and his family, and his sorrow that they were now apart: Te Ua was then living at Te Umuroa and the prophet was living at Te Whanga:

E hoa, e Tamati Te Ito, tena ra koe, korua ko to waereere ko to kotiro. Ka nui to matou aroha atu ko [o] matua ko [o] hoa i ta matou waihotanga atu, a mo [o] hoa [a]no. Anei he waiata:

> Me mihi kau atu,
> Me tangi atu,
> I te ao e rere mai
> Te Wanga.

Friend Tamati Te Ito, greetings to you and your wife and your daughter. We – our elders and companions – were very sorry to leave you and your elders and companions, and all your friends. Here is a song:

> *I must yearn*
> *I must grieve*
> *As the cloud streams from*
> *Te Wanga*[1]

'Te Wanga' or, as it is more usually written, Te Whanga, was the name of Te Ito's pā at Waitara. It was one of four pā at the large Te Ātiawa settlement, the others being Kuikui (Te Rangitāke's pā adjacent to Te Whanga), Hurirapa and Wherohia. After the defeat of Īhāia in mid-1858, Te Ito had moved from Paraiti to reside at Te Whanga so he could be closer to Te Rangitāke at a time when the settlement was experiencing extreme tensions.[2] He continued to live there until September 1859, at which time, as a result of these tensions, he moved to Te Puata, a settlement containing two pā, on the Waiongana River between Waitara and Paraiti. Te Rangitāke would join him there in December. This chapter focuses on the close relationship between Te Ito and Te Rangitāke in 1859 and early 1860, and the heightened pressures that they faced during this period.

In 1859, the Kaingārara movement came under sustained attack from three sides at once: from leaders of the Kīngitanga in Waikato and its supporters in Taranaki, who urged Te Ito and Te Rangitāke to abandon their efforts to form an independent Taranaki alliance; from Waitara leaders, who were strongly opposed to both the King movement and Te Ito's Kaingārara; and from the colonial government, which sought to unilaterally impose its sovereignty by crushing Te Rangitāke. A recognition that there was a determined assault on both Te Rangitāke *and* the Kaingārara during this period opens up possibilities for a deeper understanding of the beginnings of the Taranaki wars, one that takes more seriously than previous accounts the significant roles that Te Ito and the Kaingārara played in the Waitara struggle.

Pressure from the Kīngitanga

By the end of 1859, Te Ito and his Kaingārara rangatira had been unable to resolve their differences over where they should establish their main settlement and rūnanga, and Te Ito had become so enmeshed in struggles within Te Ātiawa over the possible sale of land at Waitara that he was spending little time amongst the southern tribes. However, the Kaingārara remained an active movement for indigenous independence, with a working system of tribal courts and a successful school at Te Umuroa where pupils were taught in Māori. Kaingārara leaders had established their own judicial system by mid-1858, with Te Ito appointing local judges (kaiwhakawā) for Te Ātiawa, Taranaki Iwi, Ngā Ruahine and Ngāti Ruanui. Among the cases described in letters written to Te Ito are two of adultery and one of wife desertion. Other cases were about a theft of potatoes, slander (the use of an 'evil word'), the ownership of a horse, distribution of land, and domestic arrangements for a widow.[3] Transgressions of tapu also featured. When Te Ito was living at Te Puata, there was a very unusual inquiry into the circumstances surrounding the discovery in the pā of some reddish-coloured preserved heads (uru) – extremely tapu items – apparently concealed from the prophet. The fine that was handed down by Te Ito, and agreed to by the guilty party without protest, was £4 – £2 to the injured party and £2 to the court.[4]

With their system of tribal- or rūnanga-specific local courts and a large pan-tribal school at Te Umuroa, the Kaingārara were laying the foundations for a Taranaki independence movement that stood in the way of the larger ambitions of the King movement, centred at Ngāruawāhia in the Waikato. And just as the Taranaki movement was divided on where to locate its main settlement, there was also significant division among its members over whether or not to place their lands under the mana of the Waikato King. During a hui hosted by Te Ngāhuru at Poutoko Pā in November 1859, Kaingārara representatives debated the merits of doing so, but no agreement was reached. Rather, many continued to see Kaingārara as an alternative to the Kīngitanga and called for Te Ito to return south to them 'at once' to continue his work of making their land safe for habitation. One of the speakers, Hēmi Parai, said that all he asked for was that Te Ito extinguish the tapu on his piece of land so that he could safely live there again.[5]

The following month, at Waitara, these differences of opinion over the relationship with the Waikato King were brought to a head when a Waikato emissary secretly left one of the King's flags with Erueti, a fiery pro-Kīngitanga chief and member of Te Rangitāke's hapū. When Te Rangitāke discovered this ruse he was deeply aggrieved, claiming that it was a personal betrayal. Angela Ballara noted that the

Kīngitanga itself was viewed as a 'spiritual force, carried from marae to marae', and that one of its physical manifestations was the King's flag.[6] Thus the acceptance of this flag by a section of his hapū was indeed a serious challenge to Te Rangitāke's mana at this time, and it marked a significant turning point in his political career. When Erueti's faction began the construction of a flagstaff, Te Rangitāke threatened to quit the Taranaki district altogether. However, he was persuaded instead to go and live with Te Ito at Te Puata, some two kilometres to the south.[7] As this settlement comprised two pā, it is likely that the two leaders lived separately in each of these. Letters addressed to Te Ito at Te Puata indicate that he lived with there with his wife Mihi; his children, including at least two sons and his seven-year-old daughter Neirai; his younger brother Paramena; and at least two older brothers.[8] While residing at Te Puata, the prophet continued to advise his followers by letter on their dealings with tapu, and to pass judgment on transgressions committed by his Te Ātiawa followers.

The independent political path being pursued by Te Ito's Kaingārara movement and the rejection of the King's flag by Te Rangitāke (and probably also by many of the Kaingārara) had become issues of significant concern for the Waikato supporters of the King, especially for the powerful Ngāti Maniapoto chief, Rewi Maniapoto. So, in December 1859, about the time that Te Rangitāke moved to Te Puata, and taking advantage of the weakened political position of both Te Ito and Te Rangitāke, Rewi and another Kīngitanga leader sent a strongly worded directive to all the Kaingārara leaders ordering them to cease their activities:

Ngaruawahia
Tihema 29/59

Ki a Tamati Te Ito
Ki a Wiremu Kingi
Ki a Taranaki
Ki a Ngati Ruanui

E hoa ma, whakamutua ta koutou mahi kikokiko. Kaua e tohe.

Whakamutu rawatea.
   Heoi ano

Na Toma Whakapo
Na Rewi Maniapoto

Ngaruawahia
29/59

To Tamati Te Ito
To Wiremu Kingi
To Taranaki
To Ngati Ruanui

Friends, cease your work of expelling malevolent atua. Don't continue with it. Cease completely.
   That is all.

From Toma Whakapo
From Rewi Maniapoto[9]

This brief letter is fascinating and highly significant for a number of reasons. It is clearly addressed to all of the Kaingārara leaders of the main tribes: Te Ātiawa, Taranaki Iwi and Ngāti Ruanui (Ngā Ruahine would have been included with the southern tribes). Te Ito and Te Rangitāke are the only leaders addressed personally; Te Ito, the Kaingārara leader, is named first and Te Rangitāke, the head of the Te Ātiawa rūnanga second. As we have seen, 'mahi kikokiko' was the general term for the work of expelling atua kikokiko (malicious ancestral spirits). However, it is unlikely that Rewi Maniapoto was concerned about this specific activity – after all, Te Ito was no longer conducting his fire ceremonies, and his ope whakanoa work was long over. Rather, 'mahi kikokiko' here refers to the work, more generally, of the 'lizard-eaters'. It refers to the activities of the political organisation that had been built on an ongoing engagement with tapu through its leader, Tāmati Te Ito. In essence, Rewi wanted the

Kaingārara leaders to abandon their independent political ambitions and join with the Kīngitanga.

Pressure from Īhāia

In addition to dealing with pressure from the Kīngitanga that was widening divisions within the Waitara community, Te Ito and Te Rangitāke had to engage, yet again, with their bitter adversary Īhāia Te Kirikūmara, who had returned to New Plymouth still determined that Waitara land should be sold from under their feet. He too sought to take advantage of the weakened political state of the Kaingārara. Īhāia had been living near Urenui since his defeat by forces of Te Rangitāke and Te Ito, but in mid-1859 he had become ill and was admitted to hospital in New Plymouth. As well as wanting to avenge his defeat at Te Karaka, Īhāia considered that he had not received sufficient compensation for an earlier act of adultery committed by his wife and that only the sale of Te Rangitāke's land would satisfy him.[10]

Upon his discharge from hospital in November, he went to live with Te Teira, a Waitara chief who had supported him against the Kaingārara in 1858. Taranaki Land Purchase Commissioner Robert Parris wrote of Īhāia at this time:

> The pleasure of the old fellow's life seems to be centred in the sale of land. Wm King's [Te Rangitāke's] people have been using every stratagem to draw him off from Teira, but he is now just beginning to speak out. He has left the hospital cured and stops with Teira ma [and others]. He has been with me this morning in excellent spirits which I shall endeavour to control for he is liable to allow his temperament sometimes to exceed his discretion.[11]

According to Parris, one of the stratagems that Te Ito and some of Te Rangitāke's people had been discussing was the murder of Īhāia. In a letter that suggests that Te Puata had become a place of intrigue and deception, Parris wrote that a man named 'Bob' had moved into Te Ito's village and had been acting as a spy for Īhāia.[12] The spy is said to have been overheard discussing Te Ito's secret plan to kill Īhāia and his brother. Parris wrote: 'Mr. Bob will have to clear out from the Waiongona for he has so far committed himself as to make his residence there rather insecure.'[13]

Te Teira, like Īhāia, wanted revenge, both for Īhāia and for his own reasons. Various accounts point to a conflict between Te Teira and Te Rangitāke over a marriage arrangement: a girl who had been betrothed to one of Te Teira's nephews ran away and was sheltered by Te Rangitāke. Te Teira viewed this as an insult to his family, and although Te Rangitāke paid him compensation – a valuable horse and twenty sovereigns – he was not satisfied.[14] But, as the authors of the Waitangi Tribunal's *Taranaki Report* note, 'domestic incidents may obscure deeper frustrations'.[15] In this case, it is clear that both Īhāia and Te Teira had aligned themselves with settlers and government officials wanting to break the so-called 'land league' believed to be led by Te Rangitāke, to bring about his demise.

The Waitara leaders who opposed Te Rangitāke and Te Ito would have known this so-called 'league' had become the Kaingārara, and it is likely that some officials knew this also, although the name 'Kaingārara' was never used by them to describe a land-holding alliance.[16] Chief Land Purchasing Commissioner Donald McLean, Native Minister C.W. Richmond, and Parris were among the most influential government officials to identify the so-called 'land league' as the greatest obstacle in the way of progress in Taranaki. All advised the Governor that the league needed to be broken. Richmond wrote:

> It is true that W. King has never adhered to the Waikato King movement, nor yielded to the pretensions of the followers of Potatau (or Te Wherowhero), the former mortal enemy of Ngatiawas. But he is as steadfastly opposed to the Queen's supremacy as the Waikato party. In Taranaki he has always been the centre of the Land League, the ultimate object of which has always been identical with that of the proper King party.[17]

Donald McLean agreed, writing of Te Rangitāke: 'The interference assumed by him has been obviously based upon opposition to land sales in the Taranaki Province generally, as a prominent member of an anti-land-selling league.'[18] And we have already seen that Parris subscribed to the idea of a land league, writing to McLean at the time of Kātātore's offer of some 40,000 acres in 1857 that he hoped it would bring about 'the entire disruption of the league'.[19] In correspondence and reports, none of these officials recognised, nor would they ever officially recognise, Tāmati Te Ito as the prophetic leader of the Kaingārara movement.

Te Teira seized his opportunity to undermine Te Rangitāke's mana when Governor Gore Browne made his first visit to Taranaki in March 1859. At a meeting held in a paddock next to Robert Parris's house and attended by Richmond, McLean and Revd Whiteley, Browne was welcomed by Te Tahana who spoke, as he usually did on such occasions, of the benefits of Christianity and British law. McLean, on behalf of the Governor, then announced the new land purchase policy, including the promise that 'he never would consent to buy land without an undisputed title'.[20] After McLean had spoken, Te Teira stood up and told the Governor that he was anxious to sell his land at Waitara. The *Taranaki Herald* wrote:

> He repeatedly asked if the Governor would buy his land. Mr McLean, on behalf of his Excellency, replied that he would. Te Teira then placed a parawai (bordered mat) at the Governor's feet which his Excellency accepted.[21] This ceremony, according to native custom, virtually places Teira's land at Waitara in the hands of the Governor.[22]

But it immediately became clear that the land that had been offered did not come with 'an undisputed title'; other conflicting offers of land were subsequently made. In the midst of the confusion, Te Rangitāke stood and clearly announced: 'Listen Governor. Notwithstanding Teira's offer, I will not permit the sale of Waitara to the Pakeha. Waitara is in my hands. I will not give it up; ekore, ekore, ekore (i.e., I will not, I will not, I will not). I have spoken!'[23] He and those whom the press termed 'his followers' then abruptly left the meeting. We are not told who these followers were, nor how many departed with Te Rangitāke, but it must have been a significant number since the meeting broke up soon after. Te Ito and other Kaingārara leaders were almost certainly among those accompanying Te Rangitāke.[24]

Te Teira later clarified, in a letter to Browne, that he and his relative Retimana had only offered a small piece of land, 'sufficient for three or four tents to stand upon.[25] However, this letter appears to have been quickly forgotten, and a 'distorted' view took hold that Te Teira and his supporters were the true owners of all of the Waitara land.[26] Three days after the meeting in the paddock, Browne was visited by a deputation of settlers who persuaded him to drop his promise not to buy disputed land and to instead follow through on Te Teira's offer by individualising Māori titles generally. This, they said, would bring about the destruction of the tribal system and break the evil land league to which Te Rangitāke was said to be strongly affiliated.[27]

Te Teira wrote to Browne, urging him to act quickly. Te Rangitāke and his supporters were, he said, on a path of destruction and death, unlike those who lived 'by the word of God' and who sought everlasting life. Those who opposed Te Teira and the Governor needed to 'consider the great sacrifice made by Christ, the Lamb who knew no sin'.[28] The Governor should, he added, ignore the voices of those who would 'prevent the marriage and reject the food prepared by God'.[29] After being informed of Te Teira's letters, Te Rangitāke wrote to Browne in April 1859, pointing out that Waitara was a 'bedroom' for all of his people, and again insisting that he would never agree to a sale. One wonders what the Governor made of these letters, or if he even read them, given that it would later be claimed by officials that he had not been told that there were any dwellings at Waitara when he instructed Parris to proceed with the purchase.[30]

Under instructions from the Governor, Robert Parris went to Waitara on 25 November 1859 to inform Te Rangitāke that he intended to go through with the purchase. Four days later, the Waitara leader travelled into town with a party of thirty others to oppose the sale. Unfortunately, Parris named none of the supporting party in his official report, but it probably included Te Ito. Apparently, the meeting began with Te Teira and Te Rangitāke airing their differences in an orderly and dignified fashion in front of a large Pākehā audience. In this exchange, according to Parris, Te Rangitāke restated his opposition to the sale, 'but without advancing any reason for doing so'. The Waitara chief presumably thought it unnecessary to make it explicit to Parris and his audience that he and his people had their houses and cultivations there, and that he was representing them. Parris then formally questioned Te Rangitāke about his reasons and, unusually, he roped in Revd Whiteley to sign a record of the interview as a witness.[31] The government newspaper *Te Manuhiri Tuarangi* reported the critical exchange as follows: 'Ka Patai atu a Pareti, "ehara koia i a Te Teira taua wahi"? Ka ki ake, "no Te Teira ano, no matou katoa hoki; otiia, nana i tuku ki te moana, naku i rere ki runga, maku e to ki uta".' (Mr Parris enquired, 'Does not that piece of land belong to Taylor' [Teira]? He replied, 'It belongs to Taylor and all of us, but as he is setting it adrift to sea, I shall seize upon it and drag it to shore again'.)[32] However, in his official report to McLean following the meeting, Parris appears to have deliberately misinformed his superior, writing that in reply to his question, 'Does the land belong to Teira and his party?' Te Rangitāke said only, 'Yes the land is theirs but I will not let them sell it'.[33] With this misleading report, signed by Whiteley as a witness, Parris had, he thought, provided enough justification for the payment of a deposit of £100 to his friend, Te Teira, for his then undefined interest in the yet to be surveyed block.[34]

The Waitangi Tribunal investigation into the Waitara sale concluded that throughout the sale process the Governor was 'misadvised and misinformed' by officials, including Parris and McLean.[35] Parris was undoubtedly a strong supporter of Te Teira, who lived with him for a period in 1859. In his correspondence with the Governor and McLean, Parris extolled his friend's virtues, writing, 'Teira, whatever others may think or insinuate with regard to him as a man of rank has a character unsullied.' In contrast, he described Te Rangitāke as 'full of dogged obstinacy', a leader who was illegitimately dictating his authority over other people's land on behalf of the 'land league'.[36]

With the sale of Waitara land now proceeding, Te Ito and Te Rangitāke needed to chart a course between two bitterly opposed camps: one pushing for the sale to be completed and another advocating for the King. Supporting either camp would have meant abandoning their vision of a united, independent Taranaki. Things were falling apart for both leaders. In the midst of this political crisis, personal tragedy struck Te Ito's family. On 10 January 1860, Te Ito's daughter Neirai died, leaving her father heartbroken. He expressed what must have been immense grief simply and in the third person:

Hanueri 10 1860

He ritenga mamae tenei no Tamati ki a Neirai, ki tana kotiro.
Ka mea tana tangi, 'Kei wea [a] Neirai, e ngaro i a au?'

Heoi ano
Na Tamati

January 10 1860

This is a record of Tamati's grief for Neirai, his daughter.
His lament says, 'where is Neirai whom I have lost?'

That is all
By Tamati[37]

More tragedy would befall Te Ito and his wider Kaingārara whānau in the coming months. Government surveyors moved onto the disputed Waitara land offered by Te Teira on 20 February, and when the survey was disrupted by around eighty unarmed supporters of Te Rangitāke and Te Ito, most of whom were women, martial law was declared.[38] No doubt fearing for the safety of their children, Te Ito, Te Rangitāke and most of the local Kaingārara immediately moved their families and belongings 10 kilometres inland to Mataitawa.[39] Among the belongings that Te Ito carried with him to Mataitawa were letters written to him by his Kaingārara followers.

The Invasion of Waitara

At 4 a.m. on the morning of Monday 5 March 1860, some four hundred troops under the command of Colonel Gold left New Plymouth for Waitara in a column. The convoy stretched half a mile. Crossing the Waiongana River, soldiers occupied Te Ito's two abandoned pā at Te Puata, which were said to have been 'commanding the line of march'.[40] Upon reaching Waitara, the troops found that 'blue jackets' and marines from the HMS *Niger*, which had steamed to Waitara the same morning, had already occupied the settlement and raised the Union Jack.

Exactly what happened was the subject of an inquiry two years later in 1863, after George Grey returned to New Zealand as Governor. One of the soldiers who took part in the invasion, Captain Bulkeley, recalled:

> The Natives from the pas at the mouth of the river [including those at Te Ito's former residence at Te Whanga] must have left in the greatest of haste for after the pas were burnt remains of furniture, cooking stoves (American) and even money melted into a lump were found by soldiers and others. It was the largest pa I ever saw. I feel certain over 200 Natives must have constantly lived there.[41]

Te Ito's pa Te Whanga was labelled as such on a map drawn by the Government Surveyor, Frederic Carrington. This was included with the papers that informed Governor Grey's inquiry, through which he became convinced that the Waitara invasion had been unjust.[42] Te Ito's pā, Te Rangitāke's large pā Te Kuikui, and the smaller Wherohia Pā nearby were all burned to the ground by Te Teira and others of Te Ātiawa, who were now 'in the Queen's pay', assisted by marines and sailors. Lieutenant Henry Bates reported these events to Governor Grey in April 1863:

> In Obedience to your Excellency's instructions I have made enquiry at the survey office as to whether, at the time that the Government took possession of the block of land [at Waitara] called Te Pekapeka which had been claimed by Te Teira and sold by him to the Government, there were any cultivations or any pas belonging to the chief, William

King [Te Rangitāke] standing on that block; and if so, if any such were destroyed by the troops, friendly natives or others on the occasion of the Government taking possession of that block.

I beg to report for your Excellency's information that I have ascertained from Mr. O. Carrington (who for 22 years has been surveyor in this Province) that two pas situated on the block and called Te Kuikui (which was William King's residence) and Wherohia, the former of which was occupied by about 200 and the latter by about 35 natives of William King's followers, were burnt by Natives in the Queen's pay assisted by marines and sailors at the time of the Government taking forcible possession of the block. The extensive cultivations around these pas were likewise destroyed by the troops, friendly natives and others, and an inland cultivation belonging to Tamati Teito and other natives, some of whom were friendly, and which cultivation was situated at a 'kainga' or settlement on the Waiongona River called Poata [Te Puata] was also destroyed with the native houses standing near it; immediately upon which William King's natives retaliated by burning an exactly corresponding number of settlers' houses, no settlers' houses having been burnt or destroyed by them [prior].

The Position of the pas Te Kuikui, Wherohia &c. will be seen by the accompanying plan of the block sold by Te Teira.

I have the honour to be, Sir,
Your Excellency's most obedient, humble servant,
HENRY STRATTON BATES
Lieut. 65th Regiment and Native interpreter to the forces

P.S. There was also a pa called Te Huiarapa [Hurirapa] which stood on the block between the two pas above mentioned viz., Te Kuikui and Wherohia, this contained 30 or 40 natives. This pa was not destroyed but was occupied during the war by the friendly natives and is still occupied by Te Teira and his adherents. H.S.B.

I Certify that the above statements are correct.

Octa. Carrington.[43]

It is curious that although Te Ito's former residence, Te Whanga Pā, is shown on Carrington's map, Bates makes no reference to it in his report. Perhaps it was not occupied at the time – Te Ito was certainly no longer living there. This conclusion is supported by the fact that population numbers are given for the other three pā. It further suggests that all of the former occupants, many of whom would have been members of Te Ito's whānau, had left when he and Te Rangitāke moved to Te Puata in December 1859. Some may have gone to live at Te Kuikui or Wherohia, while others, including the members of Te Ito's whānau, must have gone to live with the prophet at Te Puata. It is significant that only thirty to forty people were said to have been living at Te Teira's pā, Hurirapa, the pā that was not destroyed. If this is correct, the vast majority of the people living at Waitara – more than 230 – had been Te Rangitāke's supporters.

Bates's report was said to have sent shockwaves through the offices of the Governor, George Grey, and the new Native Minister, Francis Dillon Bell. Bell claimed that Governor Browne had no idea that Te Rangitāke and his supporters had pā and cultivations on the Pekapeka block at the time he approved the sale and invasion. He wrote to Grey, claiming that Bates's newly discovered 'facts' were 'so contrary to what the Native Minister had always believed and to what Governor Browne and his then Ministers had asserted that the Native Minister was amazed at their now being advanced in the report of Lieutenant Bates as facts and he felt his opinion as to the Waitara case must be abandoned'.[44]

When questioned about Bates's report by Bell, Parris insisted that most of Te Rangitāke's cultivations were across the river from Waitara (which was hardly relevant); that Te Rangitāke and his people had moved inland to Mataitawa before the invasion (in fact, they were forced to do so, fearing an invasion); and that Te Kuikui was burned more than a week after the invasion (a minor point, but probably correct). As we will see in the next chapter, Te Ito's houses at Te Puata were also burned later, at about the same time.[45] True, Governor Browne had probably been misled by Parris and others in 1859, but Bates's 'amazing' facts would not have been news to anyone in living in New Plymouth, least of all Parris, who knew full well that the invasion had driven Te Rangitāke and his supporters from their homes.[46]

Te Ito and Te Rangitāke, 1860

Just as amazingly, perhaps, despite the brutal display of military force and the rampant destruction at Waitara, Te Ito and Te Rangitāke had not lost their Christian faith. Less than a week after the event, they joined Revd John Whiteley in a church service. Whiteley's journal for Sunday 11 March includes the following entry:

> Service at Te Horopuriri [Oropūriri] and Moetahi and then rode to Mataitawa. W. Kingi and his oracle Tamati Te Ito were at the first encampment so after some conversation I proposed a service. They asked me to baptise one of their children, afterwards I read 29 of Ezekiel and tried to preach to them on the name of the Lord. One of them afterwards seemed inclined to notice the parallel between the King of Egypt and his River Nile and W. Kingi and his River Waitara.[47]

It is unclear whether the service took place at Te Tahana's and Rāniera's pā, Oropūriri, or the first Mataitawa encampment; the latter is most likely, given that Te Ito and Te Rangitāke would have needed to reside a safe distance from the troops and Whiteley would not have described Oropūriri as an 'encampment'. The Biblical passage referred to by Whiteley makes interesting reading in light of the invasion. It begins:

> This is what the Sovereign Lord says: 'I am against you, Pharaoh king of Egypt, you great monster lying among your streams'. You say, 'The Nile is mine: I made it for myself'. But I will put hooks in your jaws and make the fish of your streams stick to your scales. I will pull you out from among your streams, with all the fish sticking to your scales.[48]

Was Whiteley implying that Te Rangitāke, like the Pharaoh, had no ultimate claim to his river? Probably. But the Te Ātiawa leader would not have found the analogy at all convincing. He would never have compared himself to a pharaoh, arrogant and aloof from his people. Nor would he and his Kaingārara allies have considered their ancestral river, or their land more generally, to be a form of property.

The authors of the Waitangi Tribunal's *Taranaki Report* described Te Rangitāke as 'the epitome of a rangatira'.[49] However, they made no mention of Te Ito or the Kaingārara. This report, and indeed most histories of the Taranaki wars, leave their readers with the impression that Tāmati Te Ito never existed, or if he did, that he was insignificant. The combination of priest and chief has been pivotal in much of human history and it was certainly so at Waitara, yet no New Zealand historian has recognised the relationship between Te Ito and Te Rangitāke as even slightly relevant to an understanding of the Taranaki wars.[50] As noted in Chapter Two, Keith Sinclair and James Belich did notice a connection between the chiefly land-holding group which met at Manawapou and Te Ito's religious movement. Sinclair pointed out that the so-called league had been misnamed by observers and that Te Ito, who was a 'great mover', spoke instead of a map or chart (tāti), policy or plan (tikanga). We now know that he and his followers also spoke of Kaingārara when referring to their ceremonies, their movement and even to Te Ito himself.[51] Belich did not pursue the matter of the name, but suggested that there must have been 'some link' between Kaingārara and the anti-land selling movement. Apart from Belich and Sinclair, the only other significant historical discussion of Te Ito is by Bronwyn Elsmore in her book *Mana from Heaven*. However, Elsmore viewed Te Ito's Kaingārara movement as simply a healing response to the introduction of the Gospel in Taranaki during the 'decade of the healers', a time of very high Māori mortality. She did not connect this to colonial struggles or to the holding of land.[52] Penelope Goode succinctly concluded in her thesis: 'Whatever the full picture was, the Kaingārara movement clearly attracted widespread attention among local Maori. The attention it has gained from scholars, by contrast, has been as meagre as their information has been repetitive.'[53] Goode's unearthing and translation of the Kaingārara letters should encourage historians of the first Taranaki war to revise their understandings of its origins. These letters reveal an active alliance of tribal rūnanga whose members recognised the inspired leadership of Tāmati Te Ito, based on his ability to 'see' and expel atua kikokiko from the landscape, thus making it safe to live in. His followers were not a land league, they were Kaingārara.

A recognition of the pivotal relationship between Te Ito and Te Rangitāke allows for a deeper understanding of the origins of the Taranaki wars in a number of respects. Firstly, through his relationship with Te Ito, Te Rangitāke was also connected to the wider Kaingārara alliance, crucially including the leaders of tribes to the south: Taranaki Iwi, Ngā Ruahine and Ngāti Ruanui. This does not mean that these leaders, or Te Ito himself, exerted authority over Te Rangitāke, forcing him to block the sale of Waitara land. As we have seen, the Kaingārara movement was by no means a strongly unified or heavily coercive organisation in 1859; it was not the illegal 'combination' so despised by settlers and government officials.[54] However, it can be argued that connections with the Kaingārara through Te Ito would have strengthened Te Rangitāke's resolve to hold the land. Moreover, following the invasion of Waitara, Te Ito's links with the southern tribes would assume a heightened significance. Te Ito's influence was a significant factor in the formation of a military alliance against Īhāia that included Te Ātiawa and Taranaki Iwi and, as we will soon see, this alliance would be activated again in a military resistance to the colonial invasion.

Secondly, in recognising the strong relationship between Te Ito and Te Rangitāke, it becomes necessary to acknowledge that at least some of Te Rangitāke's decisions were influenced by the prophetic advice and insights provided by Te Ito. In April 1859, after Te Teira had made his offer, Te Ātiawa began discussing the implementation of a general peace and the healing of the rift between Īhāia and Te Rangitāke. By May, good progress had been made, but Te Rangitāke 'still resisted extending the peace to Ihaia'.[55] Henry Halse believed that the rangatira was acting on advice from the prophet. On 21 May, he wrote to McLean: 'The peace question is being persevered in, but for Teito, who seems to control W. Kingi, [it] would have been brought to a conclusion long ago.'[56]

Of course, Te Ito did not 'control' Te Rangitāke, but he had probably advised caution. If so, it was wise advice, given the extreme hostility Īhāia would later express towards his enemy. Īhāia felt aggrieved that he had not received enough support in his war with Te Rangitāke, who, he said, would have been destroyed had this assistance been forthcoming. He made this claim in a letter published by the *Taranaki Herald* in July 1860, adding '[h]e is a feeble man, this William King: This old enemy of mine ... I do not wish the preservation of W. King, but his destruction will be a satisfaction to me.'[57]

A third outcome of recognising the relationship between prophet and chief is that the religious dimension of the conflict becomes more apparent and takes on greater significance. For Te Ito, Te Rangitāke and their Christian supporters, the land had to become a place where they could prosper peacefully with God. Te Ito had been preparing for such a future, driving atua kikokiko from both land and people. Land was not, nor should it become, mere property. However, Te Teira, Īhāia and their Christian supporters envisaged a different future. Christianity offered the prospect of Māori and Pākehā living peacefully together as individual landowners and fellow Christians. This is why, when Te Teira wrote to the Governor urging him to complete the purchase of Waitara, he emphasised that they were engaged in God's work, which would bring benefit to all who sought everlasting life through the great sacrifice of Christ, the Lamb without sin. Was he, perhaps, also implying a distinction between the misguided followers of Te Ito and the followers of Christ? As we know, Revd Riemenschneider certainly saw things this way.

Robert Parris, Īhāia and Te Teira would have been satisfied with the outcome of the invasion of Waitara. Parris supported the challenge to the mana of Te Rangitāke by Te Teira and Īhāia Te Kirikūmara because he, along with most of the settlers, wanted to see the collapse of the Kaingārara alliance, which he misidentified as a 'land league'. It is why he misled the Governor. It is also why Te Ito would later come to view the military invasion of Waitara as the beginning of a war between himself and Parris. This war, which Te Ito would refer to as 'my war with Parris', is described in the next chapter.

CHAPTER SEVEN

Mataitawa Years
1860–1864

In the last chapter we left Te Ito and Te Rangitāke participating in a divine service at Mataitawa with Revd Whiteley, six days after the invasion of Waitara. As they prayed, preparations were being made by Commissioner Parris for a survey of the land upon which their dwellings still stood, although these would soon be burned to the ground. At the same time, Te Rangitāke's relatives and other Kaingārara supporters were planning to construct a strong defensive pā on the same land.[1] During the week that followed, they carted timber to the edge of their now occupied settlement, and on the night of 15–16 March they threw up Te Kōhia Pā. This was an L-shaped, double-palisaded, musket-proof fort, within which some seventy warriors began readying themselves for an expected military assault.[2]

Their leader was Hapurona Pukerimu, one of Te Ito's Kaingārara judges. Hapurona's mother belonged to Te Ātiawa and his father was a chief of Taranaki Iwi. Also known as Tianara Hapurona (General Hapurona), he was a noted orator with a fiery temperament.[3] He wore a striking moko, its lines forming a criss-cross pattern across his face. His close connection with Te Ito was evident from correspondence. In October 1858, he sent three letters to the prophet: one (discussed in Chapter Five) asking advice regarding a garment to be burned, another advising Te Ito to allow a group to travel through his territory, and a third suggesting that Te Ito should leave an undisclosed ritenga to Hapurona to consider since he was on the spot and so best able to assess the situation.[4] In one of these letters, Hapurona described himself as Te Ito's 'matua' (a close relative belonging to Te Ito's father's generation) and in another he referred to Te Ito as his 'tama' (son).[5]

Invasion and Resistance

We cannot know how many of Hapurona's warriors readying themselves within Te Kōhia Pā were Kaingārara followers, but it is likely that most were. If so, at this point the war was primarily a military struggle between British troops led by Colonel Charles Gold, supported by his Te Ātiawa allies in the 'Queen's service'; and the Kaingārara under Hapurona. We saw previously that Te Ito had inspired Te Rangitāke's forces in their defeat of Īhāia; perhaps he had also inspired his supporters prior to this battle. It began at midday on Saturday 16 March: Colonel Gold opened fire on Te Kōhia, and Hapurona's troops answered him with their muskets. Exchanges of fire continued throughout the day, with Gold's troops unable to breach the very strong defences of the pā. The following morning, after retiring for the night, the troops resumed their attack, but when they finally entered the pā several hours later they found it evacuated; Hapurona had left two men behind to keep up the firing, thus successfully deceiving Gold.[6]

Hapurona's Kaingārara troops retreated inland to Mataitawa where, three days later, on 20 March, Te Ito was again visited by Revd Whiteley. The missionary found 'W. Kingi, Tamati Te Ito and 70 or 80 men who were mostly in the stockade [Te Kōhia] on Saturday. Many of them had their faces now in eternity. How solemn this thought.'[7] Most, if not all, historical accounts of the Te Kōhia battle have emphasised the successful retreat of Hapurona's forces with few, if any, Māori casualties (James Cowan, for example, listed no Māori deaths resulting from this battle and wrote that casualties were 'slight'); but this comment suggests that Whiteley assumed that British and colonial forces would pursue and overcome these men eventually.[8]

The settlement of Mataitawa was situated on a long narrow ridge. From it, Te Ito and his people had a clear view of forested land stretching out before them towards the west coast. The settlement was not fortified; however, a military defence, Manutahi Pā, had been built to protect Mataitawa from an attack from the west. The first families to establish homes here in February 1860 were those who had been forced to leave Waitara and Te Puata – probably several hundred people. During the years 1860–64, the settlement prospered under the leadership of Te Ito and Tāmihana (Wiremu Tāmihana Poihaka), a close relative of Kātātore who had lived at Kaipakopako Pā in the 1850s.[9] Soon after the invasion of Waitara, Te Rangitāke moved north to Kihikihi (just south of Te Awamutu), where he lived briefly with Rewi Maniapoto before moving to Manutangihia, a Ngāti Maru settlement in the forested ranges of the upper Waitara River. There he would live 'in strict seclusion' for the next twelve years.[10] In Te Rangitāke's absence, a new pivotal relationship between prophet and rangatira – now Te Ito and Tāmihana Poihaka – was forged at Mataitawa. By 1864 hundreds of acres had been planted in crops, the well-organised settlement had greatly expanded, and there was possibly a Kaingārara court in operation.[11]

Te Ito's New Fires

Two weeks after his 20 March 1860 visit to Mataitawa, Whiteley made a further visit to the inland settlement, this time accompanied by Riemenschneider. The latter wrote that on their way there they had noted a large fire blazing between New Plymouth and Waitara, and when they met Te Ito at Mataitawa he immediately asked: 'is that fire over there not my village?'.[12] In his journal, Whiteley confirmed that the blaze they had seen was indeed the burning of a pā at Te Puata:

> We then [after leaving Mataitawa] went up to Waitara. Mr Rogan [Taranaki Land Purchase Commissioner] told us Tamati's pa at Puata was burnt by the natives of Te Teira's party without the knowledge of the Colonel ... On passing Puata we found that the pa was really burnt,

at least the houses and a part of the fencing. Thus, the great wizard himself is humbled, but I expect he will seek utu.[13]

Far from being humbled, however, Te Ito was understandably incensed and did indeed exact utu. As already noted, the military interpreter Bates said that the prophet burned exactly the same number of settlers' houses as were burned in his village.[14] Te Ito knew how to light fires. When Whiteley visited Te Ito again a day or so later, the two men had a long argument during which the prophet told the missionary that in future this would be the way that he would exact payment for 'every aggression that might be made upon his property'.[15]

But Te Ito had done more than exact revenge; he had struck fear into the hearts of the local settler population. A Taranaki correspondent for the *Nelson Examiner and New Zealand Chronicle* wrote:

> A new and horrible feature presented itself last night. At eight o'clock the town was immensely excited. Fires were seen at the Bell Block and two rockets went up from the stockade there. Messengers left town and returned with the intelligence that five homesteads had been burned by W. King's natives the estimated value of which was 12,000 pounds. Rundle's with all his grain ricks; Arden's with all their furniture; the two Willis's and Northcroft's. This, as I learn, was done in retaliation for an act committed by R. Brown, in command of the friendly natives at Waitara, and who, on Wednesday, burnt an old ruined pah, somewhere on the native land, sacred to one of their prophets. We do not expect any further similar mischief, provided no aggression of the same kind is committed by us, as W. King is desirous of keeping aloof from such proceedings.[16]

This report is revealing of settler attitudes towards Te Ātiawa settlements, including that of Te Ito: high value, calculated in monetary terms, is placed upon settler houses and land; whereas Te Ito's home, from which he had recently been force to flee, is described as merely an 'old ruined pah', which for some mysterious reason was 'sacred' to him, an unnamed 'prophet'. Te Rangitāke had decided to distance himself from such 'mischief'. In fact, the Te Ātiawa chief did also say that he had attempted to dissuade Te Ito from pursuing a new fire campaign, but his argument must have fallen on deaf ears. An unnamed correspondent from 'Camp Waitara' wrote: 'Te Rangitāke disavows any participation in the firing of settler houses at the Bell Block, but asserts he vainly endeavoured to prevent the incendiary, Tamati Teito, the prophet, destroying the property of settlers who possibly had no hand in the destruction of his pa.'[17] Given the extent of destruction that the prophet and his people had been subjected to since 5 March, Te Ito's response was not at all surprising, and Te Rangitāke's position on the burning of his and Te Ito's homes and crops appears, in contrast, to be a surprisingly forgiving one. It was true that the settlers whose houses had been set ablaze were Te Ito's neighbours, with whom he and his family had previously lived on relatively friendly terms, one neighbour writing of Paraiti, 'we settlers knew every Maori there'.[18] But Te Ito's actions brought into sharp relief deeper veins of colonial racism that underlay the military invasion. His response was both personal and fully proportionate.

When Governor Grey later demanded that compensation be paid by Te Ātiawa for the loss of the settler houses, the Ngāti Hauā leader, Wiremu Tāmihana, who was then negotiating terms for peace, firmly rejected the demand, pointing to the significant Māori losses, some of which could not be adequately measured in monetary terms:

Na te Kawana te take o ena. Ka whawhaitia a Wi Kingi ka oma atu i tona pa, ko te pa ka tahuna ki te ahi. Ko te whare karakia ka tahuna me te pouaka Kawenata. Pau katoa i te ahi nga taonga kakahu, paraikete, hate, tarau, kaone; pau katoa. Nga kau, kainga iho e nga hoia; nga hoiho 100, maketetia iho e nga hoia. Ko te tino mea tenei i manukanukatia e te ngakau o Wi Kingi, ko tona hahi i tahuna ki te ahi. Me i puta he kupu ma te Kawana kia kaua e tahuna tona hahi kia waiho marie ona taonga me ana kararehe, ka puta hoki tona whakaaro ki te tohu i nga taonga o nga Pakeha.

The Governor was the cause of that war. War was made on Wiremu Kingi, and he fled his Pa. The Pa was burnt with fire; the place of worship was burnt; and a box containing testaments: all was consumed in the fire; goods, clothes, blankets, shirts, trowsers, gowns, all were consumed. The cattle were eaten by soldiers and horses, one hundred in number were sold by auction by the soldiers. It was this that disquieted the heart of Wiremu Kingi – his church being burnt with fire. Had the Governor given word not to burn his church and to leave his goods and animals alone he would have thought also to spare the property of the Pakeha. This was the cause of the Pakeha's property being lost (destroyed).[19]

Viewed in light of the destruction detailed in Tāmihana's speech, Te Ito's burnings were a balanced response. The fact that Te Rangitāke's advice to Te Ito fell on deaf ears is also significant. It suggests a wider difference of opinion between the two leaders over their defensive strategies, and indicates that Te Ito was the more militant, less conciliatory of the two. Based now at Mataitawa, Te Ito and the Kaingārara were pursuing an independent fire strategy, one that would soon be taken up by Te Ito's southern followers.

In late March 1860, Te Rei Te Hanataua, a great Ngāti Ruanui leader and supporter of Te Ito, led a small war party to the southern outskirts of New Plymouth.[20] Here, his followers plundered abandoned farm houses, confirming the worst fears of the settlers that the southern tribes would come to the aid of Te Rangitāke. When on 27 March the bodies of five settlers, including two boys, were discovered near Ōmatā, a force of over three hundred British troops and volunteers was sent from New Plymouth to rescue the remaining settlers. In an engagement that has since been named 'the battle of Waireka', Taranaki Iwi, under the leadership of the Kaingārara chief and Te Umuroa leader Te Matakātea, and Ngāti Ruanui, led by Te Hanataua, pinned down the colonial force who, in the official version of events, were dramatically rescued by a naval brigade of sixty men from the HMS *Niger*.[21] The details of the battle and the number of casualties are disputed, but it is certain that Te Rei Te Hanataua was among a number of important chiefs who were killed. He was later buried at Poutoko, Te Ngāhuru's pā.[22]

Immediately after this battle, Taranaki Iwi settlements between Ōmatā and Wārea were shelled by the HMS *Niger*, causing very heavy damage and significant loss of life. Then, towards the end of April, troops under the command of Colonel Gold again marched south to Wārea, burning settlements, destroying crops and flour mills, and looting cattle and horses as they went. In retaliation, Taranaki Iwi burned down almost every settler house south of New Plymouth.[23] An expedition from New Plymouth in September found that over 120 houses had been burned. Churches were left untouched.[24]

We need to be clear about why the southern Taranaki tribes so readily supported Te Rangitāke's cause. Historians have been strangely silent on this question, assuming that these tribes joined Te Rangitāke simply because they saw his cause as a just one. James Cowan wrote that the invasion of Waitara was 'quickly followed by a decision of Taranaki, Ngati Ruanui and Nga Rauru to come to Wiremu Kingi's aid', and within ten days a force of five hundred warriors was 6 miles from New Plymouth. Yet he provides no account of the reasoning behind the quick decision or how it was reached.[25] Nor have any contemporary historians of the wars pursued this question further.[26] The authors of the Waitangi Tribunal's *Taranaki Report* argued, however, that Hapurona had thrown up Te Kōhia Pā on the edge of the disputed Waitara land with a view to its being readily abandoned, and that its real strategic purpose was to gain the support of southern tribes by showing that the Governor was clearly in the wrong. In support of their claim they cite, strangely perhaps, advice from Governor Thomas Gore Browne to Colonel Gold: 'The first blood shed is a matter to which the natives attach great weight, and other tribes would join William King in a demand for utu if he could satisfy them that he had not been the first aggressor.'[27]

But, as already explained, Tāmati Te Ito's pivotal relationship with Te Rangitāke was critical for the mobilisation of southern support. It is indeed likely that in building Te Kōhia Pā to invite attack from Gold, Hapurona was pressuring the southern Kaingārara to come to his aid by showing the government to be the first aggressor. But the effectiveness of his message crucially depended on the prior existence of Kaingārara

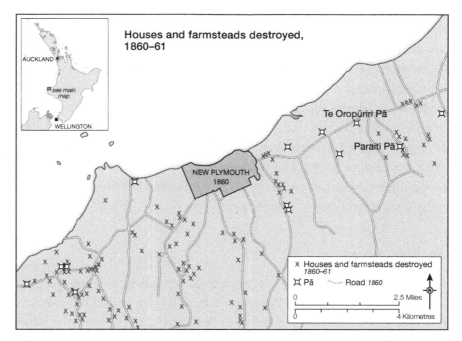

This map of the northern Taranaki area around New Plymouth shows the locations of settler houses and farmsteads destroyed in the first Taranaki war of 1860–61. Most were burned by Te Ito and his Kaingārara followers. *Source: Based on a map by Ian Smith,* Pākehā Settlements in a Māori World: New Zealand Archaeology 1769–1860, *Bridget Williams Books, Wellington, 2019, p.250; after a map by Octavius Carrington, 'Province of Taranaki from Waitara to Oeo', 1862, Puke Ariki, ARC2004-306. Carrington's map is reproduced in full colour in the first set of images.*

and Te Ito's leadership of it. Te Ito's influence over the Kaingārara may have been waning a little in the lead-up to the invasion, but the letters written to him show that he continued to provide inspired direction to his followers in 1860.[28]

By September 1860, almost all of the settler houses to the north and south of New Plymouth had been burned to the ground in what appears to have been a systematic campaign, inspired by Te Ito's actions. To the north, Te Ito and Tāmihana Poihaka maintained their incendiary campaign for months, directing it from Mataitawa. The *Taranaki Herald* reported in late August that several houses at Te Hēnui were in flames: 'The rebel party about Henui who are busily employed burning houses are Puketapu, Wi Kingi's tribe, Waikatos and some Southerns. They were on Paynter's, Hamblyn's and Barriball's farms this afternoon destroying pigs etc. Tamihana and Teito, the prophet, are their leaders.'[29] In all, a total of around 150 farmsteads were destroyed on the outskirts of New Plymouth.[30] Their owners crowded into the fortified town, which was now very much under siege.[31]

It is tempting to suggest an association between Te Ito's Kaingārara fires, intended to expel atua kikokiko from the land, and his fires of revenge, intended to expel settlers from the same land. Indeed, because the parallel is so strong and obvious, it must have also been made by the Kaingārara themselves. It would not, however, have been noticed by most settlers, who never understood the purpose of Te Ito's ceremonies.

'My War with Parris'

In June and July 1860, Te Ito's Mataitawa settlement expanded significantly when Waitara and Puketapu whānau were joined by warriors from the south and a large number of Waikato fighters. Soon, the latter would become a huge thorn in Te Ito's side. Waikato warriors, mainly Ngāti Maniapoto, had participated in a significant defeat of government forces under the generalship of Hapurona at Puketākauere Pā, near Waitara, on 27 June. Fired up with enthusiasm after this success, waves of mostly young Waikato fighters had arrived in Taranaki, where they were proving difficult for Te Ito and Tāmihana Poihaka to control.[32]

At the end of August, Te Ito visited Tāmati Wiremu Te Ngāhuru at Poutoko Pā. The old chief was now ill and Te Ito had left off his house-burnings, travelling south from Mataitawa (no doubt at considerable personal risk) to attempt a cure. Unfortunately, Te Ito was unable to help Te Ngāhuru and, after a lingering illness, the Poutoko chief died in December.[33] The *Taranaki Herald* wrote at this time that Te Ito was leading resistance:

> It is reported that Tamati Teito, the prophet, and leading man in the rebellion, and who has taken Kingi's place at the head of his party, has visited Tamati Wiremu, the friendly chief at Poutoko and is said to have expressed himself as follows to him: 'If my war had been with

Parris alone, the war would have ended long ago; but the great *he* (evil) has been Waikato' ... Teito, we hear, wished to fight in an honourable way (at least so he says now); to hoist a red flag when he was prepared to fight; and when it was not flying we might go where we pleased; and he was willing to allow us to recover our dead for burial [at Puketākauere] but that the Waikatos would not allow it.[34]

Although this report describes Te Ito as having assumed Te Rangitāke's place as 'the leading man in the rebellion', in fact he shared leadership with Tāmihana Poihaka and Hapurona. In his cited comments Te Ito personalised the fighting, describing it as 'my war with Parris'. In doing so, he was following a rhetorical convention in which leaders spoke as the embodiments of their hapū or iwi; Parris was the government. In Te Ito's view, the participation of Waikato forces had inflated his 'honourable' war with Parris into a much larger affair that was now being fought out in the shadow of the Māori King. The great mistake, 'the great *he*', was Waikato's involvement.

Te Ito's honourable war had indeed spiralled out of his control. By September, there were over 2,300 troops in Taranaki, including British regiments and reinforcements from Australia. Hapurona's fighters had been reinforced by some 600 men from Waikato and around 800 from southern Taranaki.[35] In November, Ngāti Maniapoto and Ngāti Hauā suffered a heavy defeat at Māhoetahi, between Waitara and New Plymouth, with at least thirty killed and many more wounded. The survivors fled up the Waitara River to Hapurona's pā. Early in 1861, government troops, now led by General Thomas Pratt (who had replaced Gold), advanced up the Waitara. They attacked the series of pā that had been erected south of the river by employing a technique termed 'sapping': a trench, deep enough to protect the soldiers, was slowly dug towards the fortifications, which could then be bombarded or mined. In March 1861, as Pratt's saps were slowly approaching the large Pukerangiora Pā held by Hapurona's forces, the Kīngitanga leader Wiremu Tāmihana Te Waharoa travelled south to discuss possibilities for peace. After arranging a truce with Pratt, he entered Pukerangiora and a lengthy debate ensued. According to a later account, this was concluded by Tāmihana Te Waharoa proclaiming: 'Waikato! Back to Waikato! Te Ati Awa! Away to Mataitawa! Ngati Ruanui! Return to your homes! Let the soldiers be taken back to the town of Taranaki; Waitara shall be left under the protection of the law.'[36] But after weeks of dogged sapping, Pratt felt he was close to achieving his objective and so was in no mood to negotiate. Instead, Governor Browne sent Native Secretary Donald McLean to investigate, and upon receiving reports that there was a genuine desire for peace, the Governor himself travelled to Taranaki to meet Te Ātiawa leaders.

Te Rangitāke indicated that he was prepared to meet the Governor at Mataitawa, but Browne insisted that they meet at New Plymouth. Apparently on the advice of Te Ito, Te Rangitāke decided not to do so. The *Taranaki Herald* reported: 'There is just the chance that Kingi will not meet the Governor. It is said he is kept back by the prophet imposter, Tamati Teito, who has unbounded influence over him.'[37] The newspaper was exaggerating, but the report does suggest that the relationship between Te Ito and Te Rangitāke was an enduring one. In the end, the Governor met with Hapurona and other Te Ātiawa chiefs, who agreed to his terms of peace on behalf of the Mataitawa people. The agreement included a clause in which the Governor claimed the right to divide the Waitara land and allocate it to its former owners as he saw fit, and to retain the blockhouse and redoubt that had been built there.[38] Not surprisingly, neither Te Rangitāke's nor Te Ito's names are among the sixty-five that are included in the agreement signed by Hapurona. Instead, Te Rangitāke simply sent a letter to the Governor on 8 April 1861 agreeing to peace.[39]

Mataitawa, 1862

Te Ito and Tāmihana Poihaka remained at Mataitawa throughout 1861 and 1862 as its main leaders. As such, they were closely watched by government spies. When Te Ito left Mataitawa on a visit to his Ngāti Ruanui whānau in May 1861, Wellington Carrington (brother of Frederic), then serving with the military, wrote to inform Donald McLean, adding, 'I expect some mischief although they say it is only a "toro" [visit]'.[40] In January the following year, under the heading 'Native Intelligence' the *Taranaki Herald* told its readers: 'Tamati Teito, who has been on a visit to Ngati Ruanui, will shortly return, and it is believed will pass on his way to Mataitawa by the bush road.'[41] The 'bush road' referred to in the *Herald* report was the Whakaahurangi track, an ancient route that passed behind (to the east) of Mt Taranaki, linking Ketemarae in the south and Mataitawa in the north. Te Ito had probably been on another visit to Tāmati Reina and his Ngāti Ruanui kin. But rather than returning directly to Mataitawa in early 1862, might Te Ito have first travelled further south to participate in the ceremonial cleansing of Whanganui, as described in Chapter Three? It is certainly tempting to think so.

Despite Te Ito's earlier irritation at the behaviour of Waikato forces, by 1862 he, Tāmihana Poihaka and their Te Ātiawa relatives at Mataitawa had become openly and strongly allied to the Kīngitanga. Revd Whiteley, who continued to visit and preach at Mataitawa, returned from one of his Sunday visits at the end of August 1862 with a message that he wanted publicised in the press: '[Europeans] must not be alarmed at any demonstration which will be made on Wednesday next, on the occasion of the anniversary of Potatau's accession. They wish it to be understood that their flag is not a *kara whawhai*, or fighting flag.'[42]

An apparently knowledgeable *Taranaki Herald* correspondent who attended the anniversary celebrations on the Wednesday wrote that he missed the flag-raising ceremony, but that when he arrived a karakia, termed 'taimaha', was in progress to ensure a plentiful harvest the following year. The ceremony concluded with a church service. It is possible that the karakia was spoken by Tāmati Te Ito, who may have also attended the church service. During the speeches that followed, Tāmati Reina stood and proclaimed: 'Heoi ano nga mea e taepatia ana e au, ko te Kingi, ko te oneone' (The only things that I am fencing off or seeking to preserve are the King and the land).[43]

The newspaper account of the hui went on to note that Mataitawa appeared to be a prosperous settlement where food was plentiful and many people wore new clothes. Then, chillingly, the writer questioned why the place had not been invaded and its crops not destroyed during the war:

> As regards the place itself in a military point of view, it is worth observing that Mataitawa, though looked upon during the war as Wiremu Kingi's great stronghold, has never yet been fortified in any way, and if such a thing had been possible as for armed Englishmen to travel through the bush, it might have been taken without more difficulty than ordinary fighting presents; and, as this was the very centre of their food plantations, it is a little surprising that so zealous an officer as General Pratt did not try to ascertain the state of it before peace was concluded.[44]

Presumably the writer (probably Arthur Atkinson) thought that a peace settlement concluded after the destruction of Mataitawa would have been preferable to one that was signed beforehand.[45] Two years later, Pratt's mistake would be corrected: as we shall see, in October 1864 'armed Englishmen', some of whom were led by Atkinson, did indeed travel through the bush and destroy the beautiful, thriving settlement.

Mataitawa had clearly prospered under the leadership of Tāmati Te Ito and Tāmihana Poihaka. It appears also that Te Ito was still regarded there and elsewhere as the inspired leader of the Kaingārara. This is suggested by a letter written to him in April 1863, agreeing with his judgment and accepting his punishment if required. The writer, Minita, began:

Te Poutoko

14th Aperira 1863

Ki a Tamati

E koro, tena ko koe.
    Kua tae mai tau reta ki [a] au, kia kite au i au korero. Ka nui te pai tika a tau reta me tau kupu mai ki [a] au noku te he. E tika ana noku ano te he tuatahi. Kaore ianei i huna e au ki a Henere aua he. Kua kitea mai ena e koe. Kei mai koe kei te huna atu au ki a koe. Mehemea ianei kei te ngaro i ahau henei. Ka tika tau ki mai kia whiua au. Otira kei a koe te whakaaro mo tena taha.

Te Poutoko

14 April 1863

To Tamati

Friend, Greetings to you.
I have received your letter and have seen what you have to say. Your letter is very fair, including your word to me that I am at fault. It is correct that the first offence was entirely mine. I certainly did not conceal those offences from Henere. You have seen them; don't say I am concealing them from you. If I were really hiding them your opinion that I should be punished would be right, however it's up to you what you think about that side of it.[46]

It is interesting that the writer of this letter knows that Te Ito has 'kitea' (seen) the offences. Perhaps the prophet had been shown some evidence, but it is also possible that the writer was acknowledging that the offences had been 'seen' in a visionary sense.

The Resumption of War

A month before this Kaingārara letter was written, on 4 March 1863, the new Governor George Grey arrived in Taranaki to inquire into the Waitara question. He was accompanied by General Duncan Cameron; the Premier, Alfred Domett; and the Minister of Native Affairs, F.D. Bell. Then in early April, soon after a military redoubt had been built, provocatively, at Tātaraimaka, south of New Plymouth, Tāmati Te Ito spoke with Bell, informing him that he intended to return to his land at Waitara.[47] In forwarding the documents relating to his inquiry into the invasion of Waitara to London on 24 April, Grey wrote of his concern about the repercussions of Te Ito carrying out his plan:

> The original occupants of the land are likely to return there and quietly occupy it. If they do, we must either turn them off by force, or leave them in possession, they having taken repossession of the land against the will of the Government. If the first of these events occurs,

a general war will probably take place. If the second of them occurs, the Government will be placed in a position which will weaken its authority and influence ... If we, on our part, attempt to put those Europeans on it ... my opinion is that the Natives will instantly try to turn them off and bring on a general war.[48]

Te Ito did all that he could to prevent the general war that Grey apparently was less anxious to avoid. Throughout April Te Ito carried on a correspondence with the Native Minister, Bell, urging him to remove the troops from Waitara so that he and his people could quietly return there. He well knew that Taranaki Iwi had resolved the year before that Tātaraimaka would not be given up because Waitara had not been returned, and that they viewed the construction of a redoubt at Tātaraimaka on 4 April as an act of war.[49] Tragically, Grey and Bell did not respect the urgency of Te Ito's call for action and delayed the official proclamation of the abandonment of government claims to Waitara until 11 May. On 4 May, Taranaki and Ngāti Ruanui fighters killed nine soldiers at Ōakura in an ambush that was probably intended for Grey, triggering a resumption of war.

Two days later, Te Ito wrote angrily to Bell:

O Friend, I told you to make haste, you waited for the evil, you heard the word that was said in answer to your enquiry, [Te Ito had said he wished to return] the man is dark (sorrowful) although the big weed is alive: had you hastened to take away your Europeans (soldiers) that great evil would not have happened, but you cling to the evil. O, Mr. Bell, through you arose that evil. Had you hastened to give up Waitara at the time you and I were writing all would have been well. You could not see it for your eyes were diseased. Write to your Europeans to go away.[50]

The Waitangi Tribunal was in full agreement with Te Ito:

We can thus reach some conclusions on the resumption of the war. The Government contends that the second war dated from the Oakura ambush of 4 May, a view that posits Maori as the aggressors and responsible for the second war. That position has long been regarded as untenable. The second war arose from the Government's breach of the peace, the failure to inquire promptly and honestly into Pekapeka [Waitara], the military reoccupation of Omata and Tataraimaka, and the military trespass on Maori land. These were hostile acts, in our view, which were undertaken during the truce and which could have implied only that the war had been unilaterally resumed. They were contrary to the honest conduct expected under the principles of the Treaty of Waitangi.[51]

This 'evil' that Te Ito had tried to prevent not only brought about the resumption of a devastating war in Taranaki, but Grey also claimed Waikato involvement and used this assertion to justify his invasion of Waikato on 11 July 1863.[52] For Te Ito, it dashed any hopes of rebuilding the Kaingārara movement.

Among the southern tribes, Te Ito's mana as a prophet was about to be at least partially eclipsed by that of Te Ua Haumēne, and the practices and beliefs of the new religion, Pai Mārire, would soon displace those of the Kaingārara. Te Ua, who had been a Kaingārara supporter and a leader of one of the rūnanga, had been inspired to assert his own prophetic leadership in September 1862.[53] He received his vision – a visit by the archangel Gabriel – soon after a mail steamer, *Lord Worsley*, was wrecked on the coast near his home at Te Umuroa. Te Umuroa was, as noted earlier, a Taranaki Iwi settlement where an independent school had been established by the Kaingārara rangatira, Wiremu Kīngi Te Matakātea. But by the time of the ship's grounding, Te Matakātea had renounced his allegiance to both the Kīngitanga and Te Ito's Kaingārara, and he escorted the passengers and crew of the steamship to safety in New Plymouth.[54] Te Ua, who must have also withdrawn his support for the Kaingārara by this time, wrote:

When the Lord Worsley had been five days on shore, in the days of September, I was one night seized with an illness (or affliction) and I felt as if someone were shaking me. I heard a voice saying 'who is this sleeping? Rise up! Rise up!' I then became porewarewa (under mesmeric influence).[55]

While southern Taranaki, possibly influenced by the teachings of Te Ua, subsequently agreed upon an aggressive response to government incursions into their territory, leading to the Ōakura ambush of May 1863, Te Ātiawa adopted a defensive stance. The Waitangi Tribunal concluded:

> There was little sign of Te Atiawa aggression after the resumption of war in May 1863 and yet their lands were also about to be invaded and confiscated. 'Kingi's Natives', as they were called in the local press, reinforced their old pa and were sometimes engaged in skirmishes with the settler militia, usually over cattle, but they did not go on the offensive. Kingi himself was not involved.[56]

In fact, neither Wiremu Kīngi Te Rangitāke nor Tāmati Te Ito Ngāmoke would participate in any future military aggression. By this time Te Rangitāke had moved to the headwaters of the Waitara River, and his former prophetic advisor, Te Ito, continued to lead a peaceful community at Mataitawa, where domestic conflict would briefly become a more immediate issue for him. The prophet was accused of paying 'excessive attention' to Tāmihana Poihaka's wife. This charge briefly plunged the entire Mataitawa settlement into confusion, but the issue appears to have been resolved rapidly and peacefully at a public event, during which both sides faced off with haka and entered into dialogue.[57] The vast chasm separating local settler understandings of Te Ito and the reality of his prophetic leadership among Taranaki Māori is clearly evident from the newspaper report of this incident. The local correspondent for the *Otago Daily Times* wrote:

> It appears that Tamita Teito's [sic] excessive attention to Tamhan's [Tāmihana's] wife led to a quarrel with the accompanying demonstration [a haka]. This Tamita Teito has always been an element of discord in the Province, much of the mischief of 1857 [probably referring to 1858] was caused by his instrumentality, and in 1860 he urged-on the Waitara Maoris in their opposition to the Government by his pretended prophecies and was the first to commence burning the settlers houses;

his residence prior to Colonel Gold's advance was at Ikamoa [actually, Te Puata], a short distance from the banks of the Waiongona River, about four miles from the Waitara – this fertile flat is now one vast nursery for thistles, the seeds from which are scattered in all directions by every blast. He is a man who bears a very immoral character.[58]

It is likely that Te Ito and his wife, Mihi Watara, separated about this time and that Te Ito married his third wife, Hinearapiti. This would accord with the evidence presented in the Native Land Court by Hinearapiti's daughter, Maiterangi, who was born around 1863.[59]

Just as Te Ito, the prophetic advisor to Te Rangitāke, was the less willing to compromise of the two, so it was for his relationship with Tāmihana Poikaha at this time. At least this is how a correspondent for *The Press* interpreted it. Describing the situation at Mataitawa he wrote: 'There are now two parties among them – one headed by Tamati Teito (the prophet) is for commencing hostilities at once; the other is afraid of losing their land ... he is very much afraid of confiscation.'[60] Tāmihana Poihaka was right to fear confiscation, but if he thought that by refusing to provide military support to the southern Taranaki tribes he would avoid this outcome, he would be sorely mistaken. Te Ito was both less conciliatory and more realistic in this regard.

The Invasion of Mataitawa

But the invasion of Te Ātiawa land that began in February 1864 was not provoked by Te Ito, Tāmihana Poihaka or any other Te Ātiawa leader. It began with the building of a redoubt at Sentry Hill, midway between Paraiti and Waitara, by troops under the command of Colonel H.J. Warre. In April, some two hundred Pai Mārire fighters responded to this provocation by attacking the redoubt. During their advance in broad daylight they are said to have performed ritual acts – raising their hands and shouting 'hau' – in an effort to protect themselves against the bullets that would kill around fifty of them.[61]

Te Ito and his people would never return to live at Waitara. Instead, they would be driven further inland, forced to abandon their new homes at Mataitawa. By October 1864, Te Ito and Tāmihana Poihaka had resolved their differences and neither now wanted any involvement in the new war. Tāmihana sent a message to New Plymouth, possibly via Rāniera's brother, Matiu, informing local authorities that he and his people wanted peace.[62] They were abandoning Mataitawa and going to live among Ngāti Maru in the upper reaches of the Waitara River.[63]

Colonel Warre had no intention of entering into peace negotiations, however. Instead, on 8 October, without any justification, he assembled a large force (a ridiculously large force, according to one account) that included 200 men of the 70th (East Surrey) Regiment, two field guns, and 100 Bushrangers under the command of Arthur Atkinson.[64] Manutahi, the lightly defended pā protecting Mataitawa, was quickly taken (no significant resistance was offered) and then the force marched up the hill to Mataitawa. Atkinson's *Taranaki Herald* reported:

> Leaving the Bushrangers to destroy Manutahi, Col. Warre went on with Major Saltmarshe's party of the 70th and the mounted men and friendly natives to Mataitawa, but no resistance was attempted here. Indeed, it would have been hopeless, unless they had been in large numbers, as there was not, nor ever had been, any fortifications, William King and his people having relied on Manutahi as sufficient defence. The place was destroyed, eleven horses, (some of them belonging to friendly natives) and fowls and ducks and other small deer [sic] brought away, and the force returned.[65]

In the hills behind Mataitawa, the force came upon about 100 acres under cultivation, including potatoes that were flourishing. Fishing nets, fish hooks, a taiaha, carts, ploughs and other items were taken as plunder. Also taken were the Kaingārara letters, stuffed into sacks and passed on to Atkinson.[66]

Te Ito, Tāmihana Poihaka and their families had joined Te Rangitāke at Manutangihia in the upper Waitara River. There they would remain in relative safety for the duration of a war that Te Ito had struggled to prevent and no longer wanted to be part of.[67]

ABOVE: A photograph of a sketch by William Francis Gordon of Īhāia Te Kirikūmara's pā, Ikamoana, after its destruction by forces led by Te Rangitāke, Te Ito and Te Matakātea in February 1858. Te Ito's forces were reported to have killed Īhāia's livestock and destroyed his carts, one of which is represented here. *'Ruins of Ihaia's Pa "Ikamoana" after Its Demolition by the Puketapu Tribes Taranaki 1858'*, Puke Ariki, PH02009-011

LEFT: In January 1858, following the murder of Kātātore, Īhāia Te Kirikūmara and his forces were besieged at Ikamoana Pā by Te Rangitāke, Te Ito, Te Matakātea and their supporters. The following month Īhāia retreated across the Waitara River to Karaka Pā. This drawing depicts the military situation immediately after this move. A note on the bottom of the map identifies the pā coloured pink as being in the 'occupation of Ihaia and his allies' and those coloured blue as being occupied by Te Rangitāke and his allies. *John White, 1859, Alexander Turnbull Library, MapColl-832.2bkcmf/ [1859?]/Acc.699*

This sketch of a tohunga engaged in a divination rite was reproduced in a book by the Reverend Richard Taylor. It is unlikely that Taylor ever witnessed such a performance, but he had been told that tohunga manipulated whakapakoko rākau (god-sticks) by pulling on a string wrapped around the pointed shaft as shown in this drawing. Some whakapakoko from Taranaki may have been burned in Te Ito's fires. *Reproduced in Richard Taylor, Te Ika a Maui: Or, New Zealand and Its Inhabitants, Wertheim & Macintosh, London, 1855, p.62*

Te Ua Haumēne, founder and prophet of the Hauhau or Pai Mārire religion. During the years 1862–65 many of Te Ito's Kaingārara followers shifted their allegiance to Te Ua, and some may have regarded him as a successor to Te Ito. But Te Ito, who was living at Mataitawa during the years 1860–64, was not a supporter of Te Ua and maintained a distance from him. *Photograph, Alexander Turnbull Library, PA2-2825*

ABOVE AND LEFT: Two photographs of an adzed fishing waka, 1934. A note on the back of the top image reads, 'Last canoe to be launched on Aotea harbour, north of Kawhia'. The Kaingārara letters reveal that Te Ito provided ritual advice for the construction and launching of a number of similar waka in 1858. *Alexander Turnbull Library, 1/4-015175-F, 1/4-015176-F*

OPPOSITE: The second page of a letter written by Tāmati Reina Ngāwhare at Ketemarae to his 'son' Tāmati Te Ito at Te Whanga, 16 September 1858. Reina is asking for advice about both old and new sins and he tells Te Ito that he has poured warm water over himself to remove tapu. Te Ito's younger brother, Paramena, was residing with Reina at the time of writing. Reina signed himself 'papa kuare' (foolish father) in the margin. *Alexander Turnbull Library, fMS-Papers-2327-02-13*

he katoa kei te noho pūku i roto i
te ngakau o te tangata i toku ngakau
i to tetehi atu tangata ngakau koia
tenei te aroha atu o taku reta kia koe
Ko te aroha i he ai a Hopa haunga nga
he o kite ana e te kanohi maoki ko
te mea nga ro ko te puremu ko te takahae ko tenei he ko te he nga ro ka mea
te tangata kia waiho hei taonga mo
na ki roto i tona ngakau i toku nga
kau i to tetehi atu tangata ngakau
i tuhituhi atu ai au e nei kupu aku
kia koe kia tohutohu ria mai e koe
te he hou ranei te he tawito ranei
ko te rama tiaho tena ko te ramara
ma ko te ra hei tohutohu i te awa
tea ko te marama kei tohutohu i te
po whai hoki ko koe hei tohutohu
i nga mea nga ro o te ngakau ko ai au
ka mohio i boo ki roto ki toku ngakau
ki to tetehi atu tangata ngakau kei au
ranei tana he puremu whakaatu
ria mai kei tetehi ranei a matou
ria mai kia ware au te mohio
hei he mi kupu he kupu ke tena
ko te mahi we rawera i ringihia ki
toku tinana ko te mahi a tana tangata
kia kua mutu kua kahore nooiho
tenei hoki tetehi ko tu taina ko
Puramena kia ri ro atu ia koe
ki kona kei a koe ano he tikanga
mona ka ki te koe i maha ma
mona e kaiana kanūtu na tou
Nā Tamati Reina e nga hiare

haphakuare

LEFT: Īhāia Te Kirikūmara, rangatira of Ōtaraua hapū. Te Kirikūmara fought in battles against Waikato tribes in the early 1830s, and in 1833, under the terms of a truce, he was taken to Waikato as a captive. On his return to Taranaki he became a strong advocate for land sales to the government, offering land at Waitara three times. His fierce opposition to the Kaingārara led to military conflict with Te Ito and Te Rangitāke in 1858. *Photograph, Alexander Turnbull Library, PA2-2120*

RIGHT: Robert Reid Parris, *c.* 1890s. Parris was appointed Land Purchase Commissioner for Taranaki in 1857 and later served as Assistant Native Secretary, Compensation Court Judge, Resident Magistrate and Civil Commissioner (1865–75). Parris facilitated the 1860 Waitara purchase, which led to the Taranaki wars. He met with Tāmati Te Ito a number of times to debate issues of land confiscation and rangatiratanga. *Photograph, Alexander Turnbull Library, PAColl-9508-1-07*

ABOVE: Bell Block blockhouse with two bastion towers, 1864. Built by local troops in early 1860, this was the main government military post on the road between New Plymouth and Waitara during the 1860–61 war. Te Ito's nearby settlement of Paraiti would have been clearly visible from the blockhouse. The post was abandoned in 1865. *Watercolour by Joseph Osbertus Hamley after drawing by E.A. Williams, Alexander Turnbull Library, E-047-q-026*

ABOVE: Māhoetahi stockade, October 1864. This stockade, near the Waiongana River, was erected by British troops after the defeat of Ngāti Maniapoto and Ngati Hauā forces in November 1860 during the first Taranaki war. The post was later occupied by Te Ātiawa loyal to the government, under the leadership of Mahau, who built a whare rūnanga here in about 1868. *'Mahohitahi Oct. 10th 1864', pencil and watercolour by Henry H. Warre, Alexander Turnbull Library, E-294-001*

LEFT: Hapurona Pukerimu, photographed in the late 1860s or early 1870s. Hapurona's mother was Te Ātiawa and his father was a chief of Taranaki Iwi. A great orator and strong supporter of Te Ito, Hapurona led the Kaingārara miltary response to the invasion of Waitara. In 1865, he referred to himself as Tianara Hapurona (General Hapurona). He died in 1874. *Alexander Turnbull Library, PA2-2566*

RIGHT: This photograph may be of Wiremu Kīngi Te Rangitāke about 1880. Te Rangitāke was the son of the great Te Ātiawa leader Te Reretāwhangawhanga, who led a migration of his people from Taranaki to Waikanae in the 1830s. Te Rangitāke led a return migration to Waitara in 1848. Te Ito became his prophetic advisor in 1858, during the conflict with Īhāia Te Kirikūmara and the response to the invasion of Waitara. *Alexander Turnbull Library, 1/2-022668-F*

OPPOSITE: Plan of sections at Mataitawa, 1871, by Octavius Carrington. After the flourishing settlement led by Te Ito and Tāmihana Poihaka was invaded and plundered by government troops in October 1864, Crown grants of land were made available for soldiers. The initial plan was abandoned, however, because the ridge on which the sections were to be located was too narrow. *Archives New Zealand Te Rua Mahara o te Kāwanatanga, R22824169*

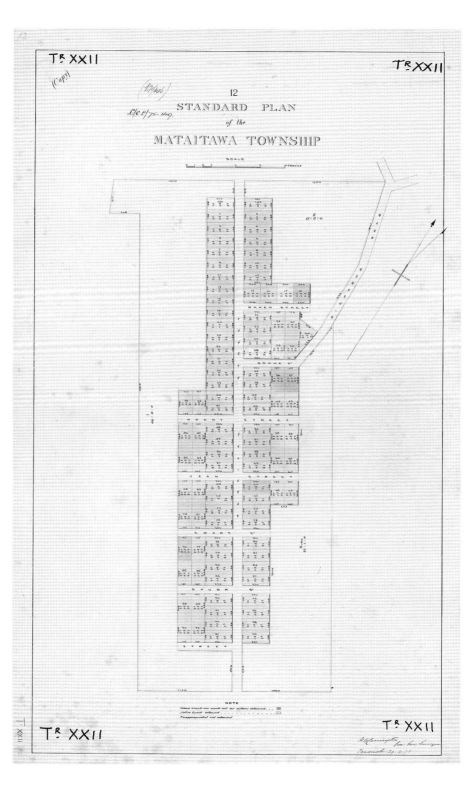

ABOVE: A watercolour of New Plymouth from Marsland Hill, 1860, by Edwin Harris, possibly copied from an original artwork by Charles Emilius Gold. St Mary's church is shown in the centre of the painting. A Māori chapel is at the top right, beyond the troops. The strong military presence suggests that the town was under siege at the time. *Alexander Turnbull Library, C-030-010*

ABOVE: Early in 1861, troops lead by General Thomas Pratt began employing a technique termed 'sapping' – digging covered trenches along which soldiers could approach a defended pā. This is a recent photograph of the end of Pratt's last sap approaching Pukerangiora Pā. It was abandoned when a truce was arranged in March 1861. *Photograph by Ron Lambert*

OPPOSITE: This photograph is labelled on the back 'Tamihana. Taranaki'. The subject is probably Tāmihana Poihaka, who shared the leadership at Mataitawa with Te Ito during the 1860–64 period. He was reported to have been one of the main leaders in the campaign to burn settler farmsteads. *Alexander Turnbull Library, PA2-2796*

FELL & ATKINSON,
SOLICITORS.

23

These flags are depicted on any drawing in the Gordon collection Dominion Museum. As Mr Atkinson's letter was written in pencil I have inked it over to preserve it — Room for the Maori flags. **Nelson, New Zealand** W.F. Gordon

28ᵗʰ March 1899

The raising of the King's flag at Mataitawa 1862

The top which was the new flag was red & white with KINGI, a (G very small) diagonally across the half of it outer, a rather large red cross & three hollow squares with red crosses inscribed [⊞ red on white]

The second flag was blue (triangular) with 3 little red crosses inscribed in squares (no inscription)

The lowest was like the top one (red & white) but with NIUTIRENI (no cross to the E) written downwards across the inner half of the flag

These flags were raised at Mataitawa with appropriate ceremonies (partly Maori Karakia, partly Church service) on the 10ᵗʰ Sep. 1862 — being the anniversary of Potatau's accession

It was the official recognition of the King by the Ngatiawa tribe

Mr Parris was invited & he kindly invited me & except Lᵗ Waller 65ᵗʰ Regᵗ we were the only white men present. We had been delayed on the road waiting for Tahana & the flags were up just before we got there but the Karakias were still going on —

These flags could not properly be called Hauhau flags as Te Ua was only just then developing the Pai marire or Hauhau scheme. I do not think he had then got as far as a flag — indeed I used to and do still believe that his first niu or worshipping post was the flag staff at Kaitake — I saw that flag taken, & have myself the truck of of the mast. but the soldiers got the flag — tho' the Bush rangers, coming down behind from Patuhai above got into the pa first but the flag was lower down. & I did not get even

a note of it. The Waireka flag (that I saw was plain red. The illustration is more or less copied from a diagrammatic sketch in my diary of the time 10ᵗʰ Sep. 1862. as to size I could only say they bore on what I remember as a "lofty" staff & did not look insig= =nificant (See back) March 29ᵗʰ 1860

Letter written by Arthur Atkinson to W.F. Gordon, 28 March 1899. Atkinson recalls attending celebrations at Mataitawa in 1862 to mark the accession of Pōtatau as Māori King. The letter begins with a description of three flags, sketched on the top left, which were flown at the hui. The top flag is described as red and white with the word, 'KINGI' written on it. The flag immediately below it is said to have been blue with small red crosses, and the bottom flag is described as red and white with the word 'NIUTIRENI' (New Zealand) written on it. Prior to the celebrations, the Mataitawa leaders reassured the Pākehā population with a press release, pointing out that these were not 'kara whawhai or fighting flags'. *Museum of New Zealand Te Papa Tongarewa, CA000162/001/0014/0003*

ABOVE: This photograph of a drawing shows Māori ploughmen with horses and oxen protesting the confiscation and settler occupation of land in the vicinity of Parihaka in 1879. The ploughman with the team of oxen is probably being arrested. The tense scene is being observed by groups of Māori and Pākehā in the foreground. *'Māori Ploughing Settler's Land at Tikorangi 1879', photograph of an ink drawing by Philip Walsh, Alexander Turnbull Library, 1/4-012533-F*

ABOVE: In this chilling image, men from Native Minister John Bryce's Armed Constabulary are gathered on a rise above Parihaka, awaiting orders to advance on the undefended settlement. On 5 November 1881, as these and other troops moved towards a gathering of 2,500 unarmed followers of Tohu and Te Whiti, they were welcomed by children dancing and skipping. *Photograph by William Andrews Collis, Alexander Turnbull Library, PA1-q-183-19*

Tohu Kākahi, a leader with Te Whiti-o-Rongomai of the Parihaka community. Tohu was of Te Ātiawa and Taranaki Iwi descent, and lived at Wārea in the 1840s and 1850s. He was probably not a follower of Te Ito, but he did join the Hauhau movement. Tohu supervised the Parihaka ploughing campaign of peaceful resistance in 1879 and 1880. The date of this portrait is 1883. *Wood engraving by John Patrick Ward, Alexander Turnbull Library, PUBL-0113-02*

An 1880 sketch of Te Whiti-o-Rongomai, who with Tohu Kākahi led the Parihaka community. Te Whiti lived at Wārea during the 1840s and 1850s, and was taught by Revd Johann Riemenschneider. When most of Riemenschneider's congregation joined Te Ito's movement in 1856, Te Whiti distanced himself from it. After expressing some initial rivalry towards Te Whiti, Te Ito joined his and Tohu's community at Parihaka in 1871.
Photograph of a sketch by William Francis Robert Gordon, Alexander Turnbull Library, PA1-0-423-10-4

The Parihaka settlement in 2003, with Mt Taranaki in the background. In June 2017, the Parihaka Treaty settlement was formally signed. Treaty Negotiations Minister, Chris Finlayson, apologised on behalf of the Crown for its shameful actions in the 1870s and 1880s, which included the imprisonment without trial of Parihaka residents, the denial of their basic human rights, the invasion and forced eviction of Parikaha people, the sacking of the settlement, rapes committed by troops, and the arrests of Tohu and Te Whiti. *Photograph by Trevor Read, Stuff Limited*

CHAPTER EIGHT

A Gun Broken
The Path to Parihaka

We know little of Te Ito's life during the period from October 1864, when he and Tāmihana abandoned Mataitawa, to the beginning of 1868. But Robert Parris, who by now was Civil Commissioner for Taranaki, reported that by early in 1868 the prophet had made his home at Te Kaparoa, a small settlement inland of Mataitawa, between present-day Lepperton and Inglewood. Te Ito must have had a number of garden clearings in this area – in the early 1870s, settlers at Norfolk, near Inglewood, built huts at a place they knew as 'Tamati's clearing'.[1] For some months, the prophet and the others of his community maintained generally friendly relations with their neighbours, the family of a military settler named Davis.[2] However in June, when the Ngā Ruahine leader and prophet Tītokowaru began his military campaign in southern Taranaki in response to the confiscation of his tribal lands, the Davis family, along with many other settlers living on relatively isolated farms throughout Taranaki, became increasingly fearful. Tītokowaru had deliberately ignited these fears as part of a strategy to halt further settler occupation of confiscated lands. On 9 June 1868, his forces killed three settlers who had ignored warnings to cease felling timber on his land, and on 12 June a soldier, Trooper Smith, was killed. Tītokowaru wrote, in a now famous letter, that the upper part of the trooper's body had been cooked and eaten. He continued: 'My throat is constantly open for the flesh of man. I shall not die! I shall not die! When death itself shall be dead I shall be alive.'[3] It was to prove a very successful fear tactic.

Soon after, on 21 June, Mrs Davis happened to be talking with Te Ito about these events in the south and asked him whether it was dangerous for her and her family to remain on their farm. Te Ito replied, enigmatically: 'If your fears carry you away, you had better go.'[4] In the climate of terror that Tītokowaru had created, these words became direct threats, and soon rumours of impending violence – in some accounts the Davis family had been killed – spread rapidly throughout Mataitawa. Mrs Davis told her husband what she thought she had heard; her husband told his friends in Mataitawa that 'armed Natives' had warned them off their land; and on the advice of other settlers, the Davis family began to pack up their belongings. On learning of this, Te Ito urged them to stay. He wrote to Parris, pointing out that the settlers' fears were completely unfounded and that in fact it was he who was fearful that forces would be sent inland to make his people's lives 'unpleasant'. Parris went to investigate and found that the whole affair was based on an 'imaginary feeling' and that there was 'not slightest ground' for concern.[5] H.R. Richmond, Taranaki Province's Superintendent, quickly issued a public notice: 'A report having been circulated in New Plymouth to the effect that certain natives in the neighbourhood of Mataitawa have assumed a hostile or menacing attitude, the Superintendent desires it to be generally known that this report is quite without foundation.'[6]

But the report may not have been entirely 'without foundation'. Te Ito shared Tītokowaru's anger over the massive confiscation of Taranaki land that had followed the escalation of a conflict he had sought to prevent. This confiscation, which had been promulgated under the New Zealand Settlements Act in September 1865, included Mataitawa. The Act stipulated that all 'rebels' who submitted to the Queen's authority within a reasonable time would receive 'sufficient' land in their district as a Crown Grant.[7] However, at Mataitawa and elsewhere, priority had been given to the allocation of sections to military settlers such as Te Ito's neighbour Davis, and local Te Ātiawa shared a widespread frustration over the decisions of the Compensation Court, which had begun sitting in June 1866.[8] Parris, who was now a judge of the court, had been struggling to allocate enough reserves for returning 'rebels', and he had been kept busy travelling from hui to hui throughout the province, attempting to reassure both settlers and Māori that their concerns would be addressed.[9]

In August or September 1868, in this climate of frustration and fear, Te Ito reportedly had a prophetic vision. He is said to have announced he had dreamt that a fire would come from heaven on a certain day and would destroy all the Pākehā within the town of New Plymouth. An unnamed correspondent added that the prophet and his followers withdrew deep into the bush, where they remained for more than a week in expectation of the cleansing fire from above.[10] We need to treat this hearsay account with caution, but the burning of New Plymouth would have been viewed as a realistic possibility at the time. On 6 September 1868 there was 'a great fire in Devon Street', New Plymouth, in which a large warehouse was burned down and the adjacent *Taranaki Herald* printing building was damaged, and then on 24 November, twelve houses were destroyed in 'another great fire in Devon Street'.[11] In his report on Te Ito's activities, however, Parris makes no mention of the prophecy, writing dismissively that the prophet had been going out at night 'performing incantations and invoking the spirits from whom he professed to receive inspiration'.[12] Did Te Ito and his followers still believe the prophet to be under the influence of an atua, such as Karutahi? Parris's brief note hints as much.

If heavenly fire did not cleanse the land of settlers, Te Ito's subsequent fiery rhetoric certainly unsettled them. On 30 September, soon after the reported announcement of the prophecy, Parris was invited by Te Ito to visit him at Te Kaporoa to discuss an unspecified concern.[13] After some confusion over the date initially proposed, and a fruitless journey inland by Parris on 1 October, the Commissioner travelled to Te Kaporoa six days later accompanied by Richmond; Major Charles Stapp, commander of the militia; Te Ito's uncle Te Tahana and Mahau (who, like Te Tahana, was a native assessor). It would be a small hui

– Te Ito had only seven people (most of whom would have been family members) living with him at the time.[14] As Parris might have expected, the issue of concern for Te Ito was the confiscation; he proposed to his guests that the settlers be told to abandon the confiscated lands allocated to them by the government. Parris expressed surprise at such a radical suggestion and said that during none of his earlier visits had it been raised; he dismissed the idea out of hand. Te Ito became extremely angry and, as Parris put it, 'indulged in very unbecoming language with reference to the Government... saying that he should not be guilty of violence himself but other tribes might'. Te Tahana and Mahau responded by expressing their strong support for Parris.[15]

From Te Ito's perspective this meeting had ended very unsatisfactorily, the discussion having been too quickly cut short. The following day, therefore, he wrote to Superintendent Richmond inviting him to discuss the matter further. Richmond suggested instead that Te Ito meet him at Māhoetahi, a Puketapu pā on the road between New Plymouth and Waitara. Mahau had occupied Māhoetahi after a significant defeat of Waikato forces there in November 1861, and he and his section of Puketapu had since remained in control of the pā.[16] It was here in 1867 that the Puketapu hapū had debated the allocation of returned land, and more recently in August 1868 that Mahau's people had built a large meeting house.[17]

It was raining heavily, and Parris only half-expected Te Ito to turn up.[18] But when he and Richmond arrived at Māhoetahi they found that Te Ito and his followers had already positioned themselves at one end of the smoke-filled meeting house, while his uncle Te Tahana and his Puketapu supporters were at the other end. The *Taranaki Herald* reported:

> The building, designated as 'the house of our forefathers' was built in the usual native style and neatly lined throughout with reeds. It is 27 feet wide by 85 feet long; the floor was strewn after the manner of our ancestors with a good substitute for rushes and new matting was laid down for the reception of the guests.[19]

Mahau, who for some reason hadn't received sufficient notice of the hui, had not yet arrived. Because Te Ito had called the meeting, he opened the speeches, saying that his heart was dark but that he hoped it would become light through discussion with his friends. Te Tahana replied, speaking in favour of peace and warning Te Ito that any violence would be answered with military force. He is quoted as saying, 'if we give a blow we expect it to be returned'. Rōpiha, one of Te Tahana's Puketapu party, followed, urging Te Ito to return to them: 'You are like birds in the bush', he said. He wanted Te Rangitāke to come and live at Waitara and Te Ito to return to his former home at Te Puata on the Waiongana River. 'Take your gun and hang it up', he said.[20]

But Te Ito's mood only darkened further, leading to a tense exchange between him and Parris. Te Ito stood up, holding his gun, and asked derisively, 'Who was the Governor? Who was the Superintendent? And who were those people who were afraid? And why was this fear?' A foreign tree had taken root at Waitara, he said, and it needed to be removed, 'root, trunk and branches'. Throwing down his gun, he added that if the tree was removed the weapon would be thrown away; if not it 'would be held'.[21] Parris replied that the tree was a pūriri, too firmly embedded in the ground, and that Te Ito should come back to his friends who were 'part of him'. Te Ito would have none of it and replied, 'with alacrity', that he had meant what he said, and that if the Pākehā were not removed he would kill them. Richmond intervened to say that he did not believe Te Ito, and Parris added that under normal circumstances he would have had the prophet arrested, but since Te Ito had called the meeting to openly express his thoughts he would ignore the threat. Te Ito then repeated it.

Parris knew that Te Ito's grievance was deeply and widely held across Taranaki and that arresting Te Ito risked retaliation, inflaming a tense political situation, so he offered to talk with him further in private. However, a group of settlers from Mataitawa attending the hui had become alarmed and gathered around Richmond, urging him to intervene. Richmond told them they should take their families into the blockhouses at Manutahi and Sentry Hill as a precaution. The settlers immediately departed to gather up their families and belongings. Parris had to return to town, but before doing so he spoke with Mahau and they agreed that he and Te Tahana should take matters in hand and attempt a resolution overnight.[22]

When news of Te Ito's speech reached New Plymouth that evening, exaggerated rumours spread throughout the town like wildfire: some appear to have thought the Taranaki war was about to resume in the north. In the morning, Parris took out warrants for the arrest of Te Ito and three others in case he needed them. However, just as he was about to leave for Māhoetahi, Te Tahana and another assessor, Kipa, arrived to say that they had been talking with Te Ito all night and had convinced him to withdraw his threat.[23] The prophet had since left Māhoetahi and gone to live at Te Puata with Mahau. A meeting of magistrates headed by Parris agreed to leave Te Ito for Mahau to deal with and the relieved settlers went back to their normal business. Perhaps Te Ito saw the rich irony in the outcome of his whaikōrero: he had been pressured to return to the very home from which Mahau, Teira and troops had forced him to flee nine years before.

Richmond immediately issued a public notice:

Superintendent's Office,
New Plymouth October 15, 1868

Some alarm having been caused to the settlers in the Mataitawa District by the conduct of certain natives living there, the Superintendent wishes it to be generally known that there is no longer any danger to be apprehended, as they have consented to withdraw entirely from all opposition on the subject of the confiscated lands.[24]

In retrospect, it seems extraordinary that one man's whaikōrero in a meeting house could have had such dramatic effects. Te Ito had, with his utterances, struck almost as much fear into the hearts of the settler population as Tītokowaru had with his violent actions to the south. But although Te Ito would have remained opposed to the confiscation (and Richmond's notice was surely misleading on this point), it appears that his dialogue with Te Tahana and Mahau had convinced him that threats of violence could not succeed as a long-term strategy. From this point on, therefore, he began to align himself more closely with the pacifist ideas being developed by Tohu Kākahi and Te Whiti-o-Rongomai at Parihaka.

Te Ito and Te Whiti

For Te Ātiawa, 1869 would be a year of reconciliation. The period was bookended by two very significant hui held at Parihaka: one at Christmas 1868, and the other beginning on 17 March 1870. While there is no record of Te Ito's participation in this process of political healing, he would certainly have maintained a keen interest in it, both as a Te Ātiawa leader and as a prophet. Rangatira from throughout Taranaki, presumably including Te Ito, were invited to attend the grand events at Parihaka, their success contributing significantly to Te Whiti-o-Rongomai's increasing public status as a leading advocate for peace in the district. Te Whiti and his relationship with Te Ito feature prominently in newspaper and official reports upon which the following discussion is largely based, yet it is evident that Tohu Kākahi played a less visible but equally central role in the founding of the Parihaka community.[25] Te Whiti's relationship with Te Ito became particularly significant in the context of a developing relationship between the prophet and his Te Ātiawa supporters more generally. Tohu drew more strongly on the support of southern iwi connected with the *Aotea* waka.[26]

According to Parris, who was personally invited to Tohu and Te Whiti's 1868 Christmas hui, this was the first formal meeting between a government representative and the people of Taranaki Iwi since the beginning of war in March 1860.[27] It was also the first time that Wiremu Kīngi Te Rangitāke had visited the Parihaka community, although he and the community's leaders had been in frequent communication since its beginnings in 1866.[28] Te Rangitāke was accompanied on his visit by members of his family, and although the old chief declined to meet with Parris, his brother, grandson and five others treated the Commissioner in a 'very friendly and sociable' manner. After speeches of welcome, a feast was brought out for the guests by a hundred men and women. Parris, who was deeply impressed by the welcome, noted: 'After they laid down the food they performed a "Ngeri", a very interesting sight, one I have not witnessed for many years – something like a war dance, but void of its distortions of countenance, and more joyful than defiant.'[29] Parris had been accompanied to the hui by Mahau and Te Tahana, the Puketapu assessors, and Poharama Te Whiti, the great Te Ātiawa chief from Moturoa in New Plymouth. Te Whiti-o-Rongomai began his address to his guests by asking Parete (Parris) and each of his companions in turn, 'e tangi ana koe ki a wai?' (who do you cry for?). In other words, as was appropriate for the beginning of a hui, he was bringing to mind those who had passed away. Parris wrote that he did not meet the 'chief tohunga', Tohu, but that during Te Whiti's speech Tohu had been engaged in 'some superstitious ceremony or other'; in fact he had probably been reciting karakia to give direction and support to Te Whiti.[30] The duality of leadership here between public voice and less visible spiritual guidance appears to have had parallels in Te Ito's relationships with Te Rangitāke and Tāmihana.

The old Moturoa chief, Poharama Te Whiti, who had accompanied Parris to the hui, was already an advocate for peace, and over the next few years he would become a strong supporter of Tohu and Te Whiti.[31] Te Ito had invited him to his October hui at Māhoetahi but Poharama had declined the invitation because he did not receive an assurance from the prophet that his intentions were not confrontational. Soon after his dramatic performance at Māhoetahi, Te Ito had sought to patch things up with Poharama by sending two women to him on a peace mission, and later travelling to Moturoa himself.[32] In contrast to Te Ito's small, tense hui in October, this Parihaka hui was a much grander and more conciliatory occasion, one that Poharama would have willingly attended. Soon afterwards, perhaps encouraged by the Parihaka leaders and Te Rangitāke, Poharama assumed a leading role in healing the divisions within Te Ātiawa that had been caused by the Waitara sale and subsequent war.

In January 1869, Poharama and Īhāia Te Kirikūmara, Te Rangitāke's former adversary, visited Te Rangitāke at his inland settlement. The meeting, which must have been one of strong emotions, concluded with an agreement that Te Rangitāke's section of Puketapu would begin returning to what remained of their land. At the end of January, therefore, some twenty Puketapu people, led by the Mataitawa chief, Tāmihana, and his wife, the daughter of the great Puketapu chief Toheroa, settled at Te Ito's former kāinga, Te Puata, now described by Parris as 'Mahau's place'.[33] In February the following year Te Rangitāke's son, Eruera Kīngi, brought twenty to thirty members of the Manukorihi hapū out to live at Waitara. Parris wrote:

> William King did not come himself, but his party is considered to represent him. They visited all the Native kaingas from Urenui to Warea (Pariaka) where they are expected to arrive this day, and will remain to attend a large meeting which is to be held there in March. They arrived at my office last Monday morning early, accompanied by Teira, Hemi Pataka, Tiraurau and others who came from Waitara with them; when I gave them some food, and after a very friendly conversation they went to Moturoa to the chief Poharama's place.[34]

When Parris returned to New Plymouth after a visit to Auckland on 16 March 1870, he was met by Wiremu Kīngi Te Matakātea, Ropata Ngāromate and a number of other leaders anxious that he should attend the second great hui called by Tohu and Te Whiti at Parihaka. Accordingly, he and his party, which included the above chiefs and two members of Parliament, set off for Parihaka the next day. Upon arrival, they found that Poharama and Eruera Kīngi of Te Ātiawa had preceded them there. In addition, there were representatives of Ngāti Maru, Taranaki Iwi, Ngā Ruahine and Ngāti Ruanui, more than five hundred people in total. An 'immense stack' of food had been piled up in front of the village and its distribution among the guests took up the whole of the first day and the following morning. In the afternoon the speeches began:

> Te Whiti commenced the business of the meeting by stating that the questions for consideration of the people assembled were three in

number, namely – the Government, The King, and the Prophets, all of whom, he said, had got into confusion and disorder, and the garments of each must be unravelled and a better state of things established. He said he belonged to the Government and to the King, but the ruling of both was bad, and as to the Prophets, he most emphatically condemned them, and said they had all been guilty of perverting the truth. One he referred to personally, Tamati Teito, who he said was an idiot (porewarewa).[35]

Let us examine this important address further. Firstly, as reported by Parris, Te Whiti distinguished three forms of leadership: government, Kīngitanga and prophetic, the latter including the leadership of Te Ito. While he recognised the first two as legitimate, although their actions had been wrong, he made it absolutely clear that he did not recognise the legitimacy of Te Ito's prophetic leadership. Te Whiti, as a political figure, 'belonged to' the government and the Māori King, but not to the prophets. Secondly, as reported by Parris, Te Whiti described Te Ito as an 'idiot (porewarewa)'. While there is no doubt that Te Whiti was publicly challenging the mana of Te Ito, he was doing so because the latter was an influential prophet, not because he was an 'idiot'. It is unclear whether Parris knew that 'pōrewarewa' was a term generally used to refer to tohunga and prophets at this time.[36] However, he certainly did know this in March the following year when he reported (with his own translation) a closely related speech by King Tāwhiao: 'Tawhiao stated to the meeting, "Moku te ra nei, kua kore rawa he ritenga mo nga porewarewa", the interpretation of which is "The present time is mine to decide what shall be done, no *tohungas* (seers or prophets) shall interfere."'[37] Te Whiti, like Tāwhiao, was not rejecting the interference or misguidance of 'idiots'; both leaders were publicly declaring the beginning of a new time (rā) in which they, as political leaders who transcended tribal divisions, would no longer accept or recognise the guidance of tohunga and prophets. As we shall see, Te Whiti reiterated this point at his important hui marking a new era at Parihaka, in June 1872.

Te Ito's Response

While Te Ito had certainly not been dismissed as an 'idiot', his mana had been openly challenged by a leader of great influence. His response was to reassert his mana as a Te Ātiawa leader.[38] He did so by inviting leaders to two hui at Mataitawa, one in October 1870 and another on 14 March the following year. The October hui in 1870 was of national interest; in addition to an account in the *Taranaki Herald*, it was reported in Auckland's *Daily Southern Cross* and Wellington's *Evening Post*.[39] The guests, numbering around two hundred, included Te Ātiawa from Waitara, a group of Te Ātiawa who were still living inland, representatives from Taranaki Iwi and about thirty of Tītokowaru's people.[40] They were presented with 'an abundance of food of all kinds, bread, flour, pork, fowls, fern-root, honey and several Maori delicacies', including the 'sweet-scented food' that had been offered at the Parihaka hui in March 1870.

The first day was spent welcoming guests and feasting. On the second day, the main Te Ātiawa speakers were Te Ito, Mahau and Te Tahana. Te Ito opened the discussions by speaking 'strongly in favour of peace' and repudiating his confrontational speech at his Māhoetahi hui exactly two years before: holding up his gun, he proclaimed that it was now broken.[41] The *Taranaki Herald* summarised Te Ito's 'highly figurative' address as follows:

> Tamati Te Ito stated, as far as we can understand, that he intended to exert himself to preserve peace and order in his own district, but objected to any interference from other tribes, as he considered that Taranaki should attend to its own affairs, Ngati Ruanui to its immediate concerns, and Ngati Awa (to which tribe Tamati and his people belong) were to manage their own affairs without meddling from other tribes. This was no doubt intended for a hint to Te Whiti and the Pariaka's.[42]

If this report is accurate, Te Ito appears to have been asserting his chiefly independence from the Parihaka leaders by proposing a return to the tribalism which, ironically, his Kaingārara movement had sought to transcend in the late 1850s. This was high-level politics from the 'pōrewarewa'. Te Ito knew well that the pull of ancestral loyalty was a significant challenge for Tohu and Te Whiti as they sought to build a unified community at Parihaka, so he was proposing an alternative future of tribally based independence.

Te Ito followed up this challenge with a second hui. On 13 March 1871 Parris received a letter inviting him to attend a large hui at Mataitawa. The Commissioner set off from town the next day accompanied by some twenty members of Te Ātiawa, including Te Tahana, Major Stapp, and an unspecified number of newspaper staff who were keen to attend the event. The *Taranaki Herald* reported:

> The place where the meeting was held is situated on the brow of a hill with the bush at the back, and was enclosed by a Maori fence. On entering the enclosure to the left was Hapurona and his followers, and to the right was Titokowaru and about forty of his men, all armed; whilst in the centre was Tamati Te Ito and his people.[43]

Te Ito knew how to stage dramatic spectacles, and the optics here sent a clear message: the prophet had brought together two great military leaders, Hapurona of Te Ātiawa and Tītokowaru of Ngā Ruahine, with a view to charting a new course for unity and peace. With this hui, Te Ito appears to have been positioning himself and his vision as an alternative to that of Te Whiti and Tohu at Parihaka. At least, this is how the press saw it, writing in the disparaging style it usually adopted for descriptions of Te Ito and Te Whiti: 'There are two self-styled Maori prophets in this district, who try to out vie each other in their revelations, and at regular intervals summon the chiefs and delegates from other tribes to attend their meetings. Their names are Tamati Te Ito of Mataitawa, and Te Whiti of Pariaka.'[44]

This hui was to be a further declaration of peace by Te Ito, this time including the presentation of Tītokowaru to Parris. One of the Ngā Ruahine group called to the Civil Commissioner, 'Parris, we have brought this reptile [ngārara] to you.' He was referring to Tītokowaru, but Te Ito must have enjoyed the word play and oblique reference to himself and his movement. Tītokowaru, who was living in the inland ranges, later followed this up, expressing concern that he was still being hunted and asking Parris for a date when things would finally be settled in relation to his status – a question Parris avoided answering.[45]

Te Ito opened the discussions after lunch with a long speech, 'quoting scripture as a prophet'. In calling for peace, he told the gathering that God had floated over his land and waters for six days and on the seventh day he rested. Te Ātiawa had also floated over their land for six days and now that the seventh day had come, it was time to rest. Presumably, Te Ito was alluding to the fact that the years of war, during which his people had been forced to live transient lives, had now ended. Other speeches followed, but apart from Tītokowaru's exchange with Parris, none of them were recorded. As Parris's party left in the late afternoon, Tāmati Te Ito was dividing the stack of food amongst his guests; the parcels included dried shark, bush honey, pork, corn, flour and bread.[46] As before, Te Ito did not directly criticise the Parihaka leaders. Rather, as a strong, visible display of peace, Te Ito's hui was in accord with their efforts while being, at the same time, an assertion of independent mana on behalf of, or in fellowship with, Te Ito's Te Ātiawa people. Significantly, he appears to have been publicly supported by his uncle, Te Tahana.

Te Ito at Parihaka

This would be the last of Te Ito's Mataitawa hui. Six months later he was addressing 800 people – men, women and children – at Parihaka, standing alongside Te Whiti:

> Te Whiti formally opened the meeting with an address of welcome to all, Tamati Te Ito followed, and the talk became general. Te Whiti said he was a 'great mountain' and he wanted all the little ones to decrease; that he was the supreme head, and he alone. A discussion then followed in which Mr. Parris, Tamati Te Ito and others joined. The subject matter of Te Whiti's discourse was to assert that he was an inspired being; and on the part of others to show that they did not believe in his pretensions.[47]

As subsequent events would show, Te Ito had now joined Tohu and Te Whiti and their Parihaka community, his mana publicly acknowledged by its leaders.

What had happened between March and September 1871? Had Poharama or Te Rangitāke convinced Te Ito to become a smaller mountain? Had Te Whiti or Tohu explicitly invited Te Ito to Parihaka? Unfortunately, we may never know. But it would have been obvious to Te Ito that the leaders of Parihaka had achieved what he had been unable to do in 1858 and 1859 – they had established a pan-tribal community in the heartland of Taranaki. As we have seen, Te Ito had received a firm offer of land for his Kaingārara settlement beside the Waitaha Stream, a little south of Wārea and Parihaka, but he had been unable to accept it due to a competing offer from Wiremu Kīngi Te Matakātea who was living further south at Te Umuroa. Following the massive destruction of homes, crops and mills by government troops in the early 1860s, a forested location inland from Wārea had been selected for the Parihaka settlement in the mid-1860s. In retrospect, therefore, the struggles of Te Ito and his Kaingārara council to found their prophet-led settlement appear to have been a prelude to the founding of Parihaka. Te Ito must have reflected on these struggles when he made the decision to join Tohu Kākahi and his co-leader Te Whiti-o-Rongomai.

Wiremu Kīngi Te Rangitāke, Te Ito's close companion before the war, had also become a strong supporter of Tohu and Te Whiti's community. When the Te Ātiawa leader formally came out of seclusion in February 1872, he travelled with Te Ito and Hapurona to Parihaka via New Plymouth. In New Plymouth their party was welcomed by Parris and the Native Secretary, Donald McLean, who assured Te Rangitāke that there were no longer any hostile feelings towards him. McLean added, 'Takahia nga huanui kua haerea e o matua' (Come and tread the paths along which your ancestors travelled). The old chief did not reply but sat with his people, including his wife and child, in deep contemplation.[48] Te Ito did reply to McLean, however, and in his brief address he referenced his Kaingārara movement of the 1850s:

Karangatia e Te Makarini. Ka tika – ka tika kia takahia. Ae, e tika ana kia takahia i te ra nei ano. Me takahi nga wahi tapu o mua – ka noa inaianei. Ko wai te kai hanga o te ra, o te aroha, o te tangi? Ko whai [*sic*] hoki te tupuna o te taha moana? – ko te Makarini. Karangatia mai, tenei te haere nei.

Welcome Mr. McLean. It is right – it is right to tread on [ancestral paths]. Yes, it is right to trample on things today. We must now whakanoa (make noa) sacred places (wāhi tapu). Who is the creator of the sun, of love, of weeping? And who is the ancestor of the seashore? – Mr. McLean. Welcome, this is the way forward.[49]

After a meeting with McLean Te Rangitāke travelled to Parihaka, where he lived with Te Ito throughout 1872: the two leaders, prophet and rangatira, now reunited.[50]

Te Ito had not only joined the Parihaka community but his pronouncements were also considered significant enough to be placed on record. On 18 June 1872, Te Ito responded to Te Whiti's address at the New Year (Puanga) hui held at Parihaka, and his speech was recorded in an official account that was probably authorised by the Parihaka leadership.[51] Parris, who attended the hui, wrote that there had been a greater interest than usual due to a widespread expectation that it would be 'a great event', and to a 'belief that there was to be some supernatural presentation in some shape or other, or some final decree'. He had been advised by Te Rangitāke not to argue with Te Whiti.

The event would, in fact, include a final decree. The translated record of the hui began as follows:

This is the day of the meeting of Te Whiti assembled at Parihaka. This is the day on which his spiritual talk ends. He now turns his attention to earth. All have seen, both great and small.

The food was laid in the enclosure as a sign of welcome to the people.

Te Whiti then stood up and said: We have assembled here today at my desire. I do not see either King, Prophet, or Queen in my presence; these are far from me. There is no one able to remit sins in my presence;

the striver is still striving in his place. This is my word – all strife is ended to-day; the thrones (emblems) of the King, Queen, Prophets, Chiefs and strong ones are ended. None of these things are in my presence. There is no day for remission of sins in my presence – one only absolver of sins on earth, I only.[52]

The translated record concluded with Te Ito's words from Scripture: 'Discontinue driving away the plebeians, lest they run away to Egypt or Canaan.'[53]

At this hui, Te Whiti was speaking as a high priest, a Christ-inspired figure. In his community, people of high mana such as monarchs, prophets and chiefs no longer had influence because they could not absolve sins. Only he, the 'great high priest' could do this.[54] Tāwhiao, Te Ito and Te Rangitāke were, in spiritual terms, distant from and far below Te Whiti and their God. Te Ito's concluding comments are enigmatic, but perhaps they were suggesting a parallel between the Jews oppressed by the Romans and Taranaki Māori oppressed by the colonial government.

Within days of this hui, Te Ito was visiting King Tāwhiao in Te Kūiti, possibly to convey to him Te Whiti's message announcing a new era. The Taranaki prophet possibly also spoke with the East Coast prophet, Te Kooti Arikirangi, who was visiting Te Kūiti at the time.[55] If so, Te Ito had personally made an extraordinary connection between the prophets, Te Whiti, Tohu and Te Kooti, and had strengthened the relationship between the prophets and the Māori King. We have already seen that his mission of tapu expulsion had also inspired the South Island prophet, Te Maihāroa. Parris wrote that when Te Ito returned from his visit, he brought the news that the King had become strongly influenced by Te Whiti and would probably seek pardon for his sins from him at Parihaka in September, when the largest hui ever held there would take place.[56] The unfulfilled expectation that Tāwhiao would recognise the higher authority of Te Whiti may have originated in a prophecy by Te Whiti himself. He is reported to have made a similar announcement six years later.[57]

The visit by Te Ito to Tāwhiao in 1872 highlights the contemporaneity or near-contemporaneity of seven prophets: Te Ito, Te Ua, Te Whiti, Tohu, Tītokowaru, Te Kooti and Te Maihāroa. Rather than being a succession of prophets, they formed a cluster within the thirty-year period of 1850 to 1880. The notion that Māori prophets were linked in a mystical or spiritual line of descent was most strongly argued by Judith Binney, whose outstanding accounts of Te Kooti and his successor Rua Kēnana established her as a foremost scholar of these and other prophetic movements. She summarised their relationships as follows:

> These leaders claimed spiritual descent from one another, though some were direct rivals. Almost all were persecuted by governments or police. But the concerns of these leaders were for the well-being of Māori, faced with ill health and land loss for much of two centuries. The common identity the leaders forged for Māori was as Israelites, cutting across tribal divisions while acknowledging them historically. The mana of a leader was seen as a gift of God, held in trust for a generation, then transferred. Thus, the line of prophets was regularly renewed.[58]

In light of the evident clustering of prophets around Te Ito, this view, which is ultimately a Biblical one, needs to be revised. None of the nineteenth-century prophets mentioned above claimed a spiritual descent from an earlier prophet, and none saw their gift as something held in trust for the next generation. Rather, as Binney herself noted, they shared a condition of colonial persecution by land-hungry governments and sought to regain mana motuhake – independent control of their land and lives.[59] But they also shared a concern for the malignant influences of atua and the dangerous condition of tapu that resulted. Tāmati Te Ito was the first of the prophets to seek a political and ritual solution for such a concern.

The Invasion of Parihaka

The 1870s must have been relatively good years for Te Ito, although dark clouds would gather towards the end of the decade. He had to some extent restored his mana as a visionary and Te Ātiawa leader and he was also one of a number of respected leaders who lived under the guidance of Tohu Kākahi and Te Whiti-o-Rongomai at Parihaka. In September 1875, Charles Brown, who had replaced Robert Parris as the Civil Commissioner for New Plymouth after Parris's retirement, attended the monthly hui at Parihaka. He wrote: 'There were two meetings – one on Friday, and one on Saturday [18th] – at which Te Whiti spoke at considerable length. Tohu and Tamati Teito were the other principal Native speakers, very few others offering any remarks.'[60]

Now in his forties, Te Ito had taken a new name, 'Uoa', possibly reflecting his new status at Parihaka. He and his third wife, Hinearapiti, lived in a small house with their daughter Maiterangi and her husband Hōri Pokima, in the midst of a growing and extremely well-organised pan-tribal settlement.[61] People had come from across Taranaki and also from further afield – Auckland, Rotorua, Wairarapa, the King Country, the Chatham Islands – to the monthly hui, at which Te Ito would on occasion speak. There was now a permanent population of about 1,500, and the settlement had its own bank, police force and large bakery able to produce over 1,000 kits of bread for the monthly hui. Advanced agricultural machinery was in everyday use, hundreds of acres of crops were planted, and organised teams harvested seafood and forest foods. Despite the prosperity, there was also much sickness, including, at the time of Brown's visit, more than fifty cases of measles.[62]

The Waitangi Tribunal considered that the main features of the Parihaka vision included the establishment of a Māori territory between the Hangatahua River in the north and the Waingongoro River in the south, 'the provision of a base for all hapū from Mokau to Whanganui', 'economic and social development using Maori and Christian philosophies', and 'the reformation and re-establishment of the spiritual dimension of Maori existence'.[63] Te Ito must have felt that his Kaingārara vision of a healthy and independent pan-tribal community in which people 'from Mokau to Patea' could live in peace with God would indeed be realised, although now in a transformed sense. Ninety years later, this vision was upheld in part by the Waitangi Tribunal, which concluded:

> Parihaka was proof of that which governments past and present have sought to avoid admitting: that aboriginal autonomy works and is beneficial for both Maori and the country. It was only at Parihaka and similar enclaves throughout New Zealand that change was being made on Maori terms, and it was at those places that the greater strides in Maori progress were then being achieved. Elsewhere, the Maori population was rapidly declining, as though the will to survive had disappeared.[64]

Rather than recognising the extraordinary achievement that Parihaka represented, however, the government sent 1,500 armed troops to smash it. For the third time in twenty years Te Ito would see his peaceful settlement invaded, his house destroyed, his crops and livestock plundered.

Under pressure from settlers who wanted more land, and needing to pay off a large debt, the government began surveying the Waimate plains (upon which Parihaka is located) in July 1878, cutting out sections for sale. Before this there had been a tacit understanding, both within government and among Māori, that the confiscation of the plains should no longer be enforced and that the area would revert to being Māori land.[65] Māori leaders, including those at Parihaka, had not been warned or consulted about the surveys and while initially they offered no resistance, in March the following year Tohu and Te Whiti sent out groups of men to pack up the surveyors' equipment and peacefully escort them across the Waingongoro River, on the southern edge of the plains.[66] One of these surveyors was W.H. Skinner, Percy Smith's friend, with whom Te Ito would refuse to parley in 1906.[67]

In the face of a refusal by the government to enter into dialogue with them, the Parihaka leaders initiated a carefully organised and highly disciplined campaign, in which groups of men ploughed fields across Taranaki, beginning at Ōakura on 25 May 1879. There, leaders of high mana, including Wiremu Kīngi Te Matakātea, were among the first arrests. By August, about two hundred men had been arrested and imprisoned in Dunedin.[68] Then in June 1880, Native Minister John Bryce ordered 'six hundred heavily armed men disguised as "road-builders" to move onto the Waimate plains' in a scheme that was intended to 'crush the last bastion of independent Māori power in Taranaki behind the construction of infrastructure'.[69] When the road-builders tore down fences and cut wide tracks through Parihaka cultivations, Tohu and Te Whiti sent out boys and men to repair the fences and in some places to build new ones. By September, some 220 fencers had been arrested and sent to jails in Lyttelton and Dunedin.[70]

The crushing of Parihaka took place the following year. When it was learned that the Governor, Sir Arthur Gordon, a man who had opposed the use of force at Parihaka, was returning to New Zealand from Fiji earlier than anticipated, the Chief Justice, James Prendergast, moved with extraordinary speed as government administrator to issue a proclamation calling on the Parihaka leaders to accept government-allocated reserves or suffer the consequences. The proclamation was issued after a hurriedly organised meeting at 8 p.m. on 19 October. Bryce left at 4 a.m. the next morning, 'to assemble an armed march on Parihaka, as had long been his dream. He had decided to deliver the proclamation at the point of a bayonet and to take punitive action without waiting for a response.'[71]

On 5 November 1881 a heavily armed military force of over 1,500 invaded and occupied Parihaka, the Native Minister, John Bryce, 'at their head, mounted on a white charger, with sabre and in full military uniform'.[72] They were welcomed by children, dancing and skipping. Seated on the marae and surrounding Tohu and Te Whiti were around 2,500 adults; Tāmati Te Ito was among them. Their resistance remained steadfastly passive and non-violent, even when their leaders Tohu and Te Whiti were arrested and led away and their settlement was pillaged.[73]

In the days that followed, all people not originally from Parihaka were ordered to disperse or be arrested. Members of the Armed Constabulary entered the village and, moving among the assembled inhabitants, called out the names of those who were to be evicted. Their main focus initially was those who came from Whanganui.[74] Among those marched out on 11 November was Tāmati Te Ito. *The Lyttelton Times* correspondent reported the event as follows:

> The tactics pursued yesterday were continued again today, and more prisoners belonging to the Wanganui tribes were taken. Twenty-eight in all were captured, but with one exception they are all obscure natives whose names are unknown to the outside world; the exception referred to is Tamati Tito, the old prophet, the first and original, whose name is now probably nearly forgotten.[75]

Te Ito was initially taken with the other prisoners to Fort Rolleston, the military camp overlooking Parihaka. He was held there for about a week before being escorted to Paraiti, where he was reportedly 'liberated'.[76] His and Hinearapiti's house at Parihaka would have been demolished by the troops, along with those of their neighbours; the family's life there now brutally ended. It is on this sad note, also, that we must end our narrative of the life of Tāmati Te Ito Ngāmoke.

Final Thoughts

When Percy Smith and W.H. Skinner visited Te Ito at Paraiti in 1906 it had been twenty-five years – a full quarter of a century – since the prophet's arrest at Parihaka. For this last period of his life there are no records. Perhaps he made a new life for himself and his family at Paraiti, the place where this story began. Perhaps he later moved back to Mataitawa to cultivate some land that he and Hinearapiti had been awarded by the government – a small compensation for the destruction of their homes and gardens at Mataitawa in 1864 and the confiscation of all of their land there the following year. What is certain is that after his arrest at Parihaka, Te Ito withdrew from public life. If his name was 'nearly forgotten' in 1881, the public memory of his leadership and influence; indeed, of his very existence, would be completely erased by the end of the century.

However, the thirty or so years of Tāmati Te Ito's life that have been chronicled here were watershed years in the history of New Zealand.

They include what Vincent O'Malley has described as the 'defining conflict in New Zealand history', the Waikato War of 1863–64, the focus of his powerful book, *The Great War for New Zealand*.[77] But they also include the years before, during which the settlers, colonial officials and some Te Ātiawa leaders succeeded in marginalising and undermining the efforts of other leaders who sought to map out an alternative future with their land. This resulted in the Taranaki wars that preceded the Waikato conflict and the struggles that continued well after it, culminating in the invasion of Parihaka. Viewing these watershed years through the lens of Tāmati Te Ito's life brings into focus features that have gone unnoticed or that have been under-appreciated in standard histories of the period. Let us conclude by considering three of these.

Firstly, the significance of Te Ito's role as leader of the ope whakanoa in the early 1850s and as leader of the Kaingārara later in the decade needs to be more clearly understood and appreciated. Land was much more than just property or a commodity for the Kaingārara, which meant that their struggle to prevent its sale was not informed by the same economic logic as that of the settlers who sought to purchase it. For Te Ito and the Kaingārara, the land was a source of both life and death – it was a place of shared habitation where people and atua dwelled antagonistically. People's safe and free occupancy of the land absolutely required, therefore, the ritual control and eventual expulsion of atua. Te Ito's work was critical for people's very survival in a world that included demons. The sale of land was nothing less than a shrinking of this world, dangerous though it might have been. Rather than holding onto property, the Kaingārara saw themselves as holding onto life itself. The struggles over land between settlers and the Kaingārara (misunderstood as a 'land league') were not merely political or economic, they were also ontological: they were informed by different understandings about the nature of reality.

Secondly, viewing this critical period of colonial conflict in the context of Te Ito's work brings into sharper focus the collective and ontologically informed nature of the opposition to the Waitara sale, and the need for a reassessment of the origins of the Taranaki wars in light of this. On the basis of evidence presented in Chapter Six, it is clear that the influence of Tāmati Te Ito and the Kaingārara was critical to the way in which the Waitara dispute unfolded. As the authors of the Waitangi Tribunal's *Taranaki Report* rightly note, '[i]t was not Wiremu Kingi who brought the issue of Maori autonomy to a head. It was mainly the concerns of the central and southern hapū.'[78] But we can now take this a step further by recognising that the views of most of the southern leaders were also those of the Kaingārara, and that as Te Rangitāke's advisor in the lead-up to war, Te Ito must have strongly represented these views to the Te Ātiawa rangatira. Of course, we cannot know the exact extent or nature of Te Ito's influence, but it was significant and now needs to be factored into any future discussion of the origins of the Waitara conflict. Moreover, there can be little doubt that Te Rangitāke shared the Kaingārara vision of a land freed from the influence of atua kikokiko, where people might live collectively and peacefully.[79] Like the prior struggles over land, ontological differences were implicit in the origins of the Waitara conflict.

Finally, when the establishment of Parihaka is viewed in the light of Te Ito's activities, it becomes clear that this community was in many ways the realisation of a Kaingārara vision of a pan-tribal settlement, in which people could live in peace under prophetic guidance. Prior to the war, Te Ito and the Kaingārara were unable to reach agreement on where such a community might be established, but by the mid-1860s, in the context of warfare, confiscation, poverty and suffering, the earlier squabbles had lost their meaning. Tohu and Te Whiti had remained aloof from the Kaingārara but they were broadly supportive of its political ambitions. They now revived the hopes and dreams of Te Ito's former followers, providing a new kind of leadership. In so doing, they announced the beginning of a new era under the guidance of God's prophets, while recognising the earlier leadership of Te Ito who, as described by Te Whiti, was a 'pōrewarewa' (person inspired or possessed by an atua).

When government troops entered Parihaka on 5 November 1881, later to plunder, rape, and burn down the houses of Te Ito and his former followers, it was more than an assault on one community; it was also the brutal destruction of an alternative future that had had its beginnings in the vision of Tāmati Te Ito Ngāmoke some thirty years earlier. The invasion prevented the full realisation of that future and sent its original architect into obscurity. It can only be hoped, therefore, that New Zealand's once forgotten prophet will one day be remembered as Taranaki's first prophet, an influential leader of national significance.

Acknowledgements

This book has benefited from the guidance of many people since it began life as a Marsden Fund research proposal in 2016. I am grateful for the opportunity that the Marsden grant provided for several breaks from university teaching. I am also grateful to the many people who assisted with the proposal in its early stages at Victoria University, particularly Gwyn Williams from the research office. Paul Meredith, then Pou Hautū, Office of Deputy Vice-Chancellor Māori, and Peter Adds, Professor at Te Kawa a Māui, provided wise advice at our frequent meetings during the first year of research. I am especially grateful to Paul for his continued engagement with the project, especially his suggestions concerning Chapter One, which resulted in significant revisions. I am also very grateful to Paul Diamond, Curator Māori at the Alexander Turnbull Library, for his ongoing engagement with the research, providing me with valuable early contacts and sharing his deep knowledge of the Kaingārara letters.

In the first year of research, I met Dennis Ngāwhare-Pounamu, then Manager of Te Wānanga o Aotearoa and subsequently Pou Rārangi Kōrero at Heritage New Zealand and Lecturer at Te Kawa a Māui. This was the start of a close collaboration through email and frequent meetings in New Plymouth and Wellington, most enjoyably at the Kelburn Pub. Dennis accompanied me on my visits to Parihaka and I am deeply grateful for the knowledgeable guidance that he provided throughout. Thanks also, Dennis, for your powerful foreword to this book.

I am extremely grateful for the encouragement given to me by Ruakere Hond at Parihaka in the early stages of the research, and for the engagement with the project by members of the Parihaka community when I presented it at hui. I especially want to thank Ruakere for reading the final version of the book and for his advice on Chapter Eight.

Staff at Puke Ariki museum and library in New Plymouth were very helpful during the research phase of this project. I particularly want to thank Lucy Macfarlane, Curator Archives, for her assistance, and Kelvin Day, former Manager of Puke Ariki, for his early encouragement and more recent advice on the maps. I also want to thank Ron Lambert, former Director of the Taranaki Museum, for his historical insights during the early stages of the project and Rob Hooper, farmer and local historian at Lepperton, for his kindness in showing me Mataitawa and helping me understand its relation to the surrounding landscape.

This book owes its existence in large measure to a ground-breaking thesis by Penelope Goode, in which she provided the first translation of letters written to Te Ito by his followers, the Kaingārara. I am grateful to Penelope for her early encouragement and for her reading of Chapter Five, in which the letters are discussed. Thanks, too, for the permission to use her detailed map showing Kaingārara settlements. Also of central importance for this work have been reports that Revd Johann Riemenschneider sent to his Lutheran superiors in Germany. I am very grateful to Tanja Schubert-McArthur for her skilful translation of the often difficult passages used from these reports.

I also thank the staff at the Hocken Library, Alexander Turnbull Library, National Archives, and Kinder Library, particularly Nick Wotton, and the Methodist Church of New Zealand Archives, particularly Jo Smith.

It has been a real pleasure working with Bridget Williams Books while preparing this book for publication. My sincere thanks go to Bridget Williams and Tom Rennie for their commitment to and enthusiastic engagement with this project. Thanks also to Nancy Swarbrick, Katrina Duncan, Tim Nolan, Laura Koziol and Kayla Campbell for their knowledge, expertise and incredible attention to detail. A special thanks to Chloë Reweti for creating such a beautiful, powerful cover.

Finally, I thank my wife, Catherine, for her love, support and theological engagement; my son, Hugo, for keeping me honest; and my dog, Rufus, who sat beside me in the kitchen for many hours as I wrote – a true companion.

Jeffrey Sissons, Wellington, July 2023

Editorial Note

Macrons
Macrons to indicate the long vowel have been used in general terms, place names, personal names, and for organisations and entities that take them. However, macrons are not used in quotations or publication titles unless they are in the original source. Only the author's translations of quotations have macrons.

Weights and measures
Some imperial measures are mentioned in the book. The conversions below may assist readers:

Linear measure
1 inch = 2.5 centimetres
1 foot = 12 inches = 30 centimetres
1 yard = 3 feet = 0.9144 metre
1 mile = 1,760 yards = 1.609 kilometres

Square measure
1 acre = 4,840 square yards = 0.405 hectare

Weight
1 ton = 1.016 tonnes

Currency
Money is often expressed in British sterling. Approximate equivalents in modern New Zealand decimal currency are as follows:
1 shilling (1s) = 12 pence = 10 cents
1 pound (£1) = 20 shillings = 2 dollars
1 sovereign = 1 pound (£1) = 2 dollars
Please note that the real value of these sums has changed over time.

Notes

Chapter One | Origins

1. Stephenson Percy Smith, Diary 1906, Diaries 1840–1822, MS-1962-2001, Alexander Turnbull Library, Wellington (ATL); S. Percy Smith and James Cowan, 'Clairvoyance among the Maori', *Journal of the Polynesian Society*, 29, 3 (1920), p.151.
2. William Henry Skinner, Diary, 1906, Puke Ariki, New Plymouth.
3. Smith and Cowan, 'Clairvoyance among the Maori', p.151.
4. Te Aka Māori Dictionary, https://maoridictionary.co.nz (accessed 18 January 2023).
5. When Tāmati Te Ito married Mihi Watara in 1857 he was twenty-eight years old, according to the marriage certificate signed by Revd John Whiteley, the Wesleyan missionary who knew Te Ito well. He would, therefore, have been about seventy-seven years old in 1906. The record of his age at marriage is supported by a reference to Te Ito as a 'young man' in 1857 (*The Age*, Melbourne, 11 August 1857, p.5).
6. Native Land Court, Taranaki Minute Book (TMB) 13, p.306.
7. TMB 14, pp.175–76, 182.
8. TMB 17, p.270; Aroha Harris, 'Histories of the Native Reserves Made in the Bell Block, Tarurutangi, Hua, Cooke's Farm and Waiwhakaiho Purchases in Taranaki 1848–1859', Report for the Waitangi Tribunal, 1991, pp.6–8.
9. Marriage certificate, Tāmati Te Ito and Mihi Watara, 1857; death certificate of Te Oneroa Tapeka. Te Oneroa's death certificate estimates his age at death in 1918 as eighty, hence his year of birth as 1838. However, this date of 1838 is almost certainly too early because Te Ito would have been only nine years old at that time (assuming the age of twenty-eight recorded on his marriage certificate in 1857 is correct). It is more likely that Te Oneroa was born in the early 1840s, when Te Ito was in his mid-teens, and that Te Oneroa was therefore in his mid-seventies when he died.
10. TMB 3, pp.332–35; TMB 14, pp.175–76; Penelope Goode, 'The Kaingarara Letters: The Correspondence of Tamati Te Ito Ngamoke in the A.S. Atkinson Papers', MA thesis, University of Canterbury, Christchurch, 2001, Letter 68, 10 December 1859.
11. TMB 3, pp.281–83; *Nelson Examiner and New Zealand Chronicle*, 2 June 1860, p.2. Rāniera and Matiu were brothers, the sons of Te Tahana's older brother.
12. W.A. Chambers, *Samuel Ironside in New Zealand, 1839–1858*, Ray Richards, Auckland, 1982, p.79.
13. Bernard Wells, *The History of Taranaki: A Standard Work on the History of the Province*, Edmondson and Avery, New Plymouth, 1878, pp.90–91.
14. Revd John Whiteley to the Secretaries, 15 August 1844, in Methodist Missionary Society, Letters and other Material Relative to Australia, New Zealand and the South Seas, Micro-MS-Coll-03 Reel 20, ATL.
15. John George Cooke, 'Reminiscences', vol.1, p.118, qMS-0542, ATL; Wells, *The History of Taranaki*, Chapter XIV. Puketapu people were engaged in large-scale clearing and burning on land selected by George Cooke throughout 1844, despite Cooke's protests. George Clarke (Junior), Assistant Protector of Aborigines, remonstrated with them but was rebuffed. The Puketapu leaders stated they were

clearing his land with reluctance and would move if he could find alternative land not already claimed by others. See Leanne Boulton, 'Native Reserves, Assimilation and Self-Determination: Te Atiawa, the Crown and Settlers, North Taranaki, 1840–1875', MA thesis, University of Canterbury, Christchurch, 2004, p.67.
16 There is a record of a 'here' (captive) being baptised with the name 'Tāmati' (Thomas) at Ōtāwhao (Te Awamutu) on 26 March 1848. The baptism was performed by the Anglican missionary Robert Maunsell, who was visiting John Morgan's mission station there. However, this 'Tāmati' is listed as a 'child' so is unlikely to have been Te Ito, who would have been nineteen years old at this time. Tāmati Te Ito was a Wesleyan; however, the Methodist archives hold no record of his baptism by John Whiteley or any other Methodist missionary in the Waikato region.
17 Te Manutoheroa was one of Rāniera's tīpuna and was living with the family at Oropūriri at the time of his death in 1852. See *Taranaki Herald*, 18 August 1852, p.2.
18 Alan Riwaka, *Nga Hekenga o Te Atiawa, Waitangi Tribunal Report Wai 607, April 2000*, Te Atiawa Manawhenua Ki Te Tau Iho Trust, New Plymouth, 2000, pp.59–61.
19 Ibid., pp.110, 113, 118–19.
20 Rāniera Ngaere to Donald McLean, 17 February 1846, in Inward Letters in Maori, Donald McLean (Sir), Papers, MS-Group-1551, ATL. Official English translation.
21 McLean to Te Huia and Rāniera, 19 September 1844, in Diary and Letterbook, Donald McLean (Sir), Papers, ATL.
22 TMB 3, pp.281–83.
23 Tahana to McLean, 1 March 1847, in Inward Letters in Maori, Donald McLean (Sir), Papers, ATL.
24 Death certificate of Te Oneroa Tapeka.
25 Waitangi Tribunal, *The Taranaki Report: Kaupapa Tuatahi*, GP Publications, Wellington, 1996, p.43.
26 Ibid.
27 Ibid., p.46.
28 Ibid., p.47.
29 *Nelson Examiner and New Zealand Chronicle*, 17 June 1848, p.64.
30 Alan Riwaka, *Nga Hekenga o Te Atiawa*, p.161; Richard Taylor, Journal, vol. 5, p.226a, typescript, MS-Papers-0254, ATL; Tony Walzl, 'Ngatiawa Land and Political Engagement Issues, c.1819–1900', Report for Waitangi Tribunal, 2017, pp.240, 285.
31 Simon Holdaway, 'SH3, Stage 3, Bell Block, Archaeological Excavations at Te Oropuriri, Final Report', Auckland University, 2006.
32 Simon Holdaway and Rod Wallace, 'A Materialisation of Social Organisation: The 19th Century Occupation of Te Oropuriri, Taranaki', in Matthew Campbell, Simon Holdaway and Sarah Macready (eds), *Finding Our Recent Past: Historical Archaeology in New Zealand*, New Zealand Archaeological Association, Auckland, 2013, p.79. See also drawing by Ian Smith in his *Pākehā Settlements in a Māori World: New Zealand Archaeology, 1769–1860*, Bridget Williams Books, Wellington, 2019, p.257.
33 Although a supporter of the government, Te Tahana also seems to have played a significant role in protecting his relatives during the war years of the early 1860s, informing them of troop movements. Te Tahana was jailed for communicating with 'the enemy' by letter in February 1861. See *Nelson Examiner and New Zealand Chronicle*, 9 February 1861, p.6. As discussed in Chapter Seven, Te Tahana later intervened to prevent the imminent arrest of his nephew, Te Ito. At the time of his death, in September 1884, Te Tahana was described by the *Taranaki Herald* as 'the head chief of the Puketapu tribe'. As he lay on his deathbed, some two hundred people from Parihaka travelled north to honour and farewell him (*Taranaki Herald*, 4 September 1884, p.2).

34 Ann Parsonson, 'He Whenua Te Utu (The Payment Will Be Land)', PhD thesis, University of Canterbury, Christchurch, 1978, pp.241–43.
35 'Taranaki Land Claims, 1 March, 1847', in Letterbook 1846–47, Donald McLean (Sir), Papers, ATL.
36 Wells, *The History of Taranaki*, p.147; Waitangi Tribunal, *The Taranaki Report*, p.58; NZHistory.net, 'Fitzroy's Pole in New Plymouth', https://nzhistory.govt.nz/media/photo/fitzroys-pole-new-plymouth (accessed 18 January 2023).
37 Ann Parsonson, 'Nga Whenua Tautohetohe o Taranaki: Land and Conflict in Taranaki, 1839–1859, Revision of Report No. 1 to the Waitangi Tribunal', 1991, pp.82–83.
38 *Maori Messanger: Te Karere Maori*, 11 April 1850, p.2.
39 Henry Halse, Police Reports 2nd and 3rd January, 1852, in Papers Relating to Provincial Affairs, Taranaki Inspector of Police, 31 January 1852, Donald McLean (Sir), Papers, ATL.
40 Statistics of New Plymouth, New Zealand, www3.stats.govt.nz/historic_publications/statistics_new_plymouth-1853-1856/statistics_new_plymouth-1853-1856.html (accessed 18 January 2023).
41 Parsonson, 'He Whenua Te Utu', pp.262–64.
42 Tahana and Others to McLean, 6 January 1852, in Inward Letters in Maori, Donald McLean (Sir), Papers, ATL. Official English translation.
43 TMB 17, p.270.
44 Penelope Goode, 'The Kaingarara Letters: The Correspondence of Tamati Te Ito Ngamoke in the A.S. Atkinson Papers', MA thesis, University of Canterbury, Christchurch, 2001, Letter 23, 16 September 1858. Further support for this conclusion comes from a letter written to Te Ito from the Ngāti Ruanui settlement of Owhangai by Patoro Te Karapu, who referred to himself as Te Ito's 'matua'. He wrote: 'Son, listen here, I have a word for you. The horse belonging to your sisters has been taken away by Ngati Ruanui. It was taken as payment for their son who fell off that horse.' See Letter 15, 12 July 1858.
45 William Woon to the Secretaries, 6 October 1846, in Letters to the Secretaries, Wesleyan Methodist Missionary Society, MET 004, John Kinder Theological Library, Auckland.
46 Woon to the Secretaries, 30 April 1847, in Letters to the Secretaries, Wesleyan Methodist Missionary Society, John Kinder Theological Library.
47 The future prophet Te Ua Haumēne was probably serving as assistant monitor under Reina at this time. According to his own account, Te Ua served 'under a native named Tamati'. See *Daily Southern Cross*, 16 March 1866, p.4.
48 Woon to the Secretaries, 30 September 1846, in Letters to the Secretaries, Wesleyan Methodist Missionary Society, John Kinder Theological Library.
49 Diary and Notebook, 21 October 1845, in Donald McLean (Sir), Papers, ATL. Revd Richard Taylor referred to this movement as 'tikanga hou' in his journals (20 December 1845, 24 January 1846) but later used the disparaging term 'Warea Delusion' in his book, *The Past and Present in New Zealand: With Its Prospects for the Future*, William Macintosh, London, 1868, pp.41–43.
50 Taylor, Journal, vol. 3, 14 January 1846, ATL.
51 *Taranaki Herald*, 8 May 1858, p.2.
52 Goode, 'The Kaingarara Letters', Letter 23, 16 September 1858. English translation by Penelope Goode, revised by Jeffrey Sissons.
53 Elsdon Best, *Maori Religion and Mythology: Being an Account of Cosmogony, Anthropogeny, Religious Beliefs and Rites, Magic and Folk Lore of the Maori Folk of New Zealand*, Te Papa Press, Wellington, 2005 [1924], vol.2, pp.185–89. Jeffrey Sissons, *The Polynesian Iconoclasm: Religious Revolution and the Seasonality of Power*, Berghahn Books, Oxford, 2014, pp.2–3.

54   Tony Sole, *Ngāti Ruanui: A History*, Huia Publishers, Wellington, 2005, pp.215–16. English translation in Sole's book.
55   Halse to McLean, 8 November 1851, in Papers Relating to Provincial Affairs, Taranaki Inspector of Police, Donald McLean (Sir), Papers, ATL.
56   Te Tahana and others to Ngāti Ruanui, 1 November 1851, in Donald McLean (Sir), Inward Letters in Maori, Donald McLean (Sir), Papers, ATL. English translation by E Mā: Ngā Tuhituhinga ki a Makarini (National Library of New Zealand).
57   *Taranaki Herald*, 20 October 1852, p.3.
58   *Taranaki Herald*, 2 July 1991 (supplement), p.8.
59   S. Percy Smith, 'The Evils of Makutu or Witchcraft', *Journal of the Polynesian Society*, 30, 3 (1921), pp.176–77.
60   Whiteley to the Secretaries, 14 May 1841, in Methodist Missionary Society: Letters and other Material Relative to Australia, New Zealand and the South Seas, ATL.
61   Charles Creed to the Secretaries, 11 October 1841, in Methodist Missionary Society: Letters and other Material Relative to Australia, New Zealand and the South Seas, ATL.

Chapter Two | The Mounted Tohunga and His Horsemen

1   A.S. Thompson, *The Story of New Zealand: Past and Present, Savage and Civilized*, John Murray, London, 1859, p.219; Peter Oettli, *God's Messenger: J.F. Riemenschneider and Racial Conflict in 19th Century New Zealand*, Huia Publishers, Wellington, 2008, p.118; *Wellington Independent*, 5 November 1851; *Appendices to the Journals of the House of Representatives (AJHR)*, 1939, H-31, p.2.
2   Ian Church, *Heartland of Aotea: Maori and European in South Taranaki before the Taranaki Wars*, Hawera Historical Society, Hāwera, 1992, p.111.
3   Ann Parsonson, 'The Pursuit of Mana', in *The Oxford History of New Zealand*, Oxford University Press, Wellington, 1981, p.143.
4   Richard Taylor, Journal, vol. 7, 12 June 1850, MS-Papers-0254, Alexander Turnbull Library, Wellington (ATL).
5   P.H. Buck (Te Rangi Hīroa), 'Medicine amongst the Maoris, in Ancient and Modern Times: Thesis for the Degree of Doctor of Medicine', University of New Zealand, Dunedin, 1910, p.23.
6   Richard Taylor, *Te Ika a Maui, or New Zealand and Its Inhabitants*, A.H. and A.W. Reed, Wellington, 1974 [1855], p.65.
7   T.G. Hammond, *In the Beginning: The History of a Mission*, 2nd edn, The Methodist Literature and Colporteur Society, Auckland, 1940, p.59. Revd Richard Taylor visited Stannard at Waitōtara on 13 January 1851. See Richard Taylor, Diary, GNZMS 297.14, Auckland Public Library.
8   Taylor, Journal, vol. 7, 14 June 1851, ATL.
9   These wāhi tapu ceremonies would also later be performed in Northland. The CMS missionary Richard Davis recorded that in July 1857 he attended a large hui at which it was agreed that tapu should be removed from 'all their sacred places'. An ope whakanoa (tapu-removing party) was immediately formed and this is said by Davis to have visited places 'both far and near'. The atua were expelled by boiling food on a fire made from timber gathered from the wāhi tapu: this food was then eaten by the ope whakanoa. See Report to the CMS, 27 July 1857, Richard Davis, Letters and Journals, 1824–1863, MS-1211 (typescript), Hocken Library.
10   Taylor, Journal, vol. 7, 10 September 1851, and vol. 8, 30 October 1851, ATL.
11   S. Percy Smith, 'The Evils of Makutu, or Witchcraft', *Journal of the Polynesian Society*, 30, 3 (1921), pp.177–78.
12   Taylor, Journal, vol. 4, 2 October 1846, ATL.

13 S. Percy Smith, H.T. Whatahoro, Te Matorohanga and Nepia Pohuhu, *The Lore of the Whare Wananga or the Teachings of the Maori College on Religion, Cosmogony and History*, The Polynesian Society, New Plymouth, 1913, vol. 3, pp.124–25.
14 Elsdon Best, *The Maori*, vol. 1, The Polynesian Society, Wellington, 1923, p.106.
15 Ibid.
16 Taylor, Journal, vol. 8, 8 May 1852, ATL.
17 Henry Halse, Report, 31 January 1852, in Papers Relating to Provincial Affairs, Taranaki Inspector of Police, Donald McLean (Sir), Papers, MS-Group-1551, ATL.
18 See entry for 'Joseph Jenner Merrett' in Una Platts, *Nineteenth Century New Zealand Artists: A Guide & Handbook*, Avon Fine Prints, Christchurch, 1980. Joseph J. Merrett to Donald McLean [1852], MS-Papers-0032-0452, ATL.
19 The New Plymouth District Council has identified about 280 pā sites in Taranaki: see www.npdc.govt.nz/media/erfhootu/appendix-26-waahi-tapu-sites-and-archaeological-sutes.pdf (accessed 18 January 2023).
20 AJHR, 1869, A-13, p.15.
21 As we will see in the next chapter, Te Ito later returned to Australia in order to obtain funds to purchase a horse.
22 Fred Cahir and Ian Clark, 'The Maori Presence in Victoria, Australia, 1830–1900: A Preliminary Analysis of Australian Sources', *New Zealand Journal of History*, 48, 1 (2014), p.118; Philip Hart, *Maori and Mining in New Zealand and Beyond*, Te Aroha Mining District Working papers, No.17, Historical Research Unit, University of Waikato, 2016, pp.5–9.
23 Hart, *Maori and Mining in New Zealand and Beyond*, p.5.
24 Cahir and Clark, 'The Maori Presence in Victoria, Australia, 1830–1900', p.116.
25 Hart, *Maori and Mining in New Zealand and Beyond*, p.10.
26 Ibid., p.10, quoting James Cowan, *The New Zealand Wars: A History of the Maori Campaigns and the Pioneering Period*, p.366.
27 AJHR, 1869, A-13, p.15.
28 S. Percy Smith and James Cowan, 'Clairvoyance among the Maori', *Journal of the Polynesian Society*, 29, 3 (1920), pp.150–51.
29 Ibid., p.152.
30 Ibid., p.150.
31 Ann Parsonson, 'Nga Whenua Tautohetohe o Taranaki: Land and Conflict in Taranaki, 1839–1859, Revision of Report No. 1 to the Waitangi Tribunal', 1991, p.83.
32 Ibid., p.112.
33 Waitangi Tribunal, *The Taranaki Report: Kaupapa Tuatahi*, GP Publications, Wellington, 1996, p.49. The number of vendors was incorrectly given as 115 in the report. The correct number is 315; see Parsonson, 'Nga Whenua Tautohetohe', p.112.
34 Tāmati Ito to Donald McLean, 8 February 1854, in Inward Letters in Maori, Donald McLean (Sir), Papers, ATL. English translation by E Mā: Ngā Tuhituhinga ki a Makarini (National Library of New Zealand).
35 H. Hanson Turton, *Maori Deeds of Land Purchases in the North Island of New Zealand (Copied from the Originals): In Two Volumes. Volume Two, Te Hua Block, Grey and Bell District*, Government Printer, Wellington, 1877–1878; Aroha Harris, 'Histories of the Native Reserves Made in the Bell Block, Tarurutangi, Hua, Cooke's Farm and Waiwhakaiho Purchases in Taranaki 1848–1859', Report for the Waitangi Tribunal, 1991, p.6.
36 Harris, 'Histories of the Native Reserves Made in the Bell Block, Tarurutangi, Hua, Cooke's Farm and Waiwhakaiho Purchases in Taranaki 1848–1859', p.6; Taranaki Minute Book (TMB) 3, p.332.
37 Ann Parsonson, 'He Whenua Te Utu (The Payment will be Land)', PhD thesis, University of Canterbury, Christchurch, 1978, p.274.

38 *Taranaki Herald*, 10 May 1854, p.2 and 24 May 1854, p.2.
39 Smith and Cowan, 'Clairvoyance among the Maori', p.151.
40 Parsonson, 'He Whenua Te Utu', p.279.
41 *Otago Witness*, 14 October 1854, p.3.
42 Simon Holdaway, 'SH3, Stage 3, Bell Block, Archaeological Excavations at Te Oropuriri, Final Report', Auckland University, Auckland, 2006, p.25; Simon Holdaway and Rod Wallace, 'A Materialisation of Social Organisation: The 19th Century Occupation of Te Oropuriri, Taranaki', in Matthew Campbell, Simon Holdaway and Sarah Macready (eds), *Finding Our Recent Past: Historical Archaeology in New Zealand*, New Zealand Archaeological Association, Auckland, 2013, pp.87–88.
43 This is considered more fully in the next chapter.
44 G.S. Cooper to McLean, 12 September 1852, in Series 1, Inward Letters, Donald McLean (Sir), Papers, ATL; also see G.S. Cooper to Colonial Secretary, 18 September 1852, Item 1852/2323, R23521743, Archives New Zealand (ANZ). George Sisson Cooper was appointed Inspector of Police in 1852 and in 1854 he was appointed Sub-Commissioner for the purchase of native lands in Taranaki.
45 James Belich notes, 'The connection between these most important political developments may be rather difficult to trace exactly, but the coincidence is certainly remarkable'. James Belich, *The New Zealand Wars and the Victorian Interpretation of Racial Conflict*, Auckland University Press, Auckland, 1989, p.146.
46 Taylor, Journal, vol. 5, 26 May 1853 and 9 May 1854, ATL; Church, *Heartland of Aotea*, p.117.
47 Keith Sinclair, 'Te Tikanga Pakeke: The Maori Anti-Selling Movement in Taranaki', in P. Munz (ed.), *The Feel of Truth: Essays in New Zealand History*, A.H. and A.W. Reed, Wellington, 1969, p.85, n.33.
48 Peter Oettli, 'The Taranaki Bible-Burying Incident – a Footnote', in *Turnbull Library Record*, 29 (1996), p.86.
49 Ibid. Taiporohēnui was later burned to the ground by General Chute's invading forces on 12 January 1866: see *Taranaki Herald*, 27 January 1866.
50 Ibid., p.87.
51 Ibid.
52 Taylor, Journal, vol. 5, 8 May 1854, ATL.
53 Quoted in Parsonson, 'Nga Whenua Tautohetohe', p.127. In fact, Cooper knew that such a compact was not new. Writing to the Colonial Secretary on 18 September 1852, he noted: 'on arriving at Manawapou, I found that a number of natives had assembled there from their inland cultivations, by whom I was informed that Ngatiruanui [sic] had made a solemn compact not to dispose of any land to government'. See Cooper to Colonial Secretary, 18 September 1852, 1852/2323, Item R23521743, ANZ.
54 *AJHR*, 1861, C-1, p.197.
55 Sinclair, 'Te Tikanga Pakeke'. Sinclair further notes (p.80) that the question of whether or not there was a 'land league' analogous to a coercive European union is important, because it was used by the government to explain Wiremu Kīngi Te Rangitāke's refusal to sell Waitara; Te Rangitāke was regarded by the government as an instrument of an unconstitutional form of 'tyranny'.
56 Sinclair pointed out that although McLean's 20 February reference to a 'land league' was more than two months before the Manawapou hui, 'within a few years it came to be believed, even by government officers such as McLean and Halse, that a league was established not before but at the Manawapou meeting'. Ibid., p.87.
57 Hammond, *In the Beginning*, p.59.
58 Ibid.

Chapter Three | From Tohunga to Prophet

1. S. Percy Smith and James Cowan, 'Clairvoyance among the Maori', *Journal of the Polynesian Society*, 29, 3 (1920), p.151. This horse must have been one that Rāwiri Waiaua purchased after the killing of Miriona in 1852 (Chapter One).
2. The date, 1858, might be a typo, a misreading by Smith of '1855' in his notes, a lapse of memory on the part of Te Ito, or perhaps Smith had misheard Te Ito.
3. Gray horses become whiter with age, and so there is no conflict between Smith and Wells here. Bernard Wells, *The History of Taranaki: A Standard Work on the History of the Province*, Edmondson and Avery, New Plymouth, 1878, pp.90–91.
4. James Belich, 'Riwha Tītokowaru', and Judith Binney, 'Rua Kēnana Hepetipa', *The Dictionary of New Zealand Biography* in Te Ara – The Online Encyclopedia of New Zealand, https://teara.govt.nz/en/biographies/1t101/titokowaru-riwha (accessed 18 January 2023) and https://teara.govt.nz/en/biographies/3r32/rua-kenana-hepetipa (accessed 18 January 2023).
5. Margaret Orbell, Introduction to 'An Account of Waitaha Origins, by Wi Pōkuku', translated by M. Orbell, *Turnbull Library Record*, 29, (1996), p.9.
6. S. Percy Smith, *History and Traditions of the Maoris of the Taranaki Coast, North Island of New Zealand Prior to 1840*, The Polynesian Society, New Plymouth, 1910, p.148, n.11. Smith suggests the date of 'about 1855' for the event.
7. Peter Oettli, Transcripts of J.F. Riemenschneider Papers, 2009, Part 6, p.113, MS-Group-1829, Alexander Turnbull Library, Wellington (ATL).
8. Smith, *History and Traditions of the Maoris of the Taranaki Coast*, pp.220–21, and footnote on p.220. James Cowan says that Tītokowaru revived the war gods Tu and Uenuku, rather than Maru. *The New Zealand Wars: A History of the Maori Campaigns and the Pioneering Period*, R.E. Owen, Wellington, 1956, vol. 2, p.179.
9. Ibid., p.199.
10. Reverend T.G. Hammond, Letter to Percy Smith, 29 December 1891, in Deposited Papers, Stephenson Percy Smith, Polynesian Society Records, Series-0242, ATL.
11. Oettli, Transcripts of J.F. Riemenschneider Papers, 2009, Part 6, p.113, ATL.
12. Riemenschneider picked up 'dunklen Andeutungen' (dark hints).
13. Ibid.
14. Peter Oettli, *God's Messenger: J.F. Riemenschneider and Racial Conflict in 19th Century New Zealand*, Huia Publishers, Wellington, 2008, pp.149–50. The original German read: '[U]nd hatte dort unter jenem Volk seine Lehre und seine Wunder im höchsten Grade entwickelt und daßelbe dadurch wie bezaubert. Im Geheimen hatten diese während ihres Hierseins zum Kirchenbau mit derselben Sache auf unser Volk eingewirkt, zugleich aber bis nach ihrer Heimkehr Schweigen gegen mich anbefohlen aus Furcht.'
15. *Te Karere o Poneke*, 7 June 1858, p.2. English translation by Jeffrey Sissons.
16. *Wellington Independent*, 22 July 1857; see also *Lyttelton Times*, 8 August 1857.
17. Basil Keane, 'Taniwha – Taniwha Today', Te Ara – The Encyclopedia of New Zealand, p.8, https://teara.govt.nz/en/taniwha/page-8 (accessed 18 January 2023).
18. Oettli, Transcripts of J.F. Riemenschneider Papers, 2009, Part 6, p.218, ATL. The original German read 'einen bescheidenen Freund und treuen Anhänger ihres Herrn'.
19. Ibid. The original German read 'einen allwissenden und zürnenden Gott'.
20. Ibid., p.222. Riemenschneider reported this as follows: 'Höre, o Rimene. Du und wir alle wissen unter welchen Umständen wir stehen und was unser gegenwärtiger Raruraru gänzlich in Anspruch nehmende und unerläßig notwendige Beschäftigung ist. Aber sei dem wie ihm wolle, du siehst, wir halten uns dabei mehr denn zuvor zu Gott und seinem Hause.'

21 Ibid., pp.222–23.
22 John Whiteley, Report, 1857, Wesleyan Missionary Society Reports, New Plymouth Circuit, qMS-2181, ATL.
23 In Riemenschneider's words, 'der Erfüllung der göttlichen Ordnung emporzukommen'.
24 Oettli, Transcripts of J.F. Riemenschneider Papers, 2009, Part 6, p.327, ATL. The original German read: 'Solches hier noch dazwischen liegende Hindernis sei er da in Gottes Namen hinwegzuräumen, um ihnen den Weg zur Vollkommenheit frei und leicht zu machen ... Die Erfüllung werde und müsse erfolgen wenn Werk vollendet sein würde; ... Nur müsse und dürfe sich unter ihnen selbst Keiner vermessen und es dürfe Keiner gestattet werden, ihn und sein Werk bezweifeln oder gar drein zu reden.'
25 *Taranaki Herald*, 10 April 1858; Oettli, Transcripts of J.F. Riemenschneider Papers, 2009, Part 6, p.271, ATL. As Riemenschneider put it, 'das große Werk ihrer Erlösung aus der Gewalt finsterer'.
26 Henry Halse to Donald McLean, 14 September 1857, in Inward Letters in Maori, Donald McLean (Sir), Papers, MS-Group-1551, ATL.
27 Whiteley, Report, 1857, Wesleyan Missionary Society Reports, New Plymouth Circuit, ATL.
28 *Lyttelton Times*, 15 August 1857.
29 *Lyttelton Times*, 8 and 15 August 1857; Oettli, Transcripts of J.F. Riemenschneider Papers, 2009, Part 6, p.218, ATL; *Appendices to the Journals of the House of Representatives (AJHR)*, 1869, A-13, p.15; *Te Karere o Poneke*, 7 June 1858, p.2.
30 *Wanganui Chronicle*, 20 March 1862, p.3.
31 *Taranaki Herald*, 20 June 1857.
32 Ian Church, *Heartland of Aotea: Maori and European in South Taranaki before the Taranaki Wars*, Hawera Historical Society, Hāwera, 1992, p.130; Richard Taylor, Journal, vol. 6, 4 and 5 January 1857, MS-Papers-0254, ATL.
33 Taylor, Journal, vol. 6, 4 January 1857, ATL.
34 Taylor, Journal, vol. 6, 28 March 1857, ATL. Ian Church, 'Ōraukawa, Tāmati Hōne', *The Dictionary of New Zealand Biography* in Te Ara – The Encyclopedia of New Zealand, https://teara.govt.nz/en/biographies/1o4/oraukawa-tamati-hone (accessed 18 January 2023).
35 Taylor, Journal, vol. 5, 30 May 1854, ATL.
36 Oettli, Transcripts of J.F. Riemenschneider Papers, 2009, Part 6, pp.221–22, ATL.
37 See for example, *Wellington Independent*, 22 July 1857; *Lyttelton Times*, 8 August and 15 August 1857; *Otago Witness*, 10 October 1857; *Maori Messenger: Te Karere Maori*, 30 November 1857.
38 Index of letters received, MA 1857/208, Archives New Zealand (ANZ); Halse to McLean, 15 June 1857, Inward Letters, Donald McLean (Sir), Papers, ATL.
39 *Taranaki Herald*, 20 June 1857, p.2.
40 S. Percy Smith, Diary, 1906, Diaries 1840–1822, MS-1962-2001, ATL.
41 See *Maori Messenger: Te Karere Maori*, 30 November 1857, p.3 (Māori version).
42 *Taranaki Herald*, 20 June 1857, p.2.
43 Marriage certificate, Tāmati Te Ito and Mihi Watara, 15 June 1857.
44 Te Papa, 'The Difference between Puanga and Matariki', www.tepapa.govt.nz/discover-collections/read-watch-play/maori/matariki-maori-new-year/what-matariki/difference-between-matariki-puanga (accessed 18 January 2023).
45 Patrick Kirch and Roger Green, *Hawaiki, Ancestral Polynesia: An Essay in Historical Anthropology*, Cambridge University Press, Cambridge, 2001, pp.261–63.
46 Jeffrey Sissons, *The Polynesian Iconoclasm: Religious Revolution and the Seasonality of Power*, Berghahn Books, Oxford, 2014. In this book, ritual practices intended to produce radical social change are termed 'rituopraxis'. Te Ito's fires were also examples of rituopraxis.

47 *Taranaki Herald*, 20 June 1857, p.2. On the morning of Te Ito's Paraiti fire, police inspector Henry Halse wrote to McLean to say that he was unable to attend the event: 'however, as the same ceremony is to be repeated over the district, opportunities for witnessing it will not be wanting'. See Halse to McLean, 15 June 1857, Inward Letters, Donald McLean (Sir), Papers, ATL.
48 Keith Sinclair, 'Te Tikanga Pakeke: The Maori Anti-Selling Movement in Taranaki' in P. Munz (ed.), *The Feel of Truth: Essays in New Zealand History*, A.H. and A.W. Reed, Wellington, 1969, p.88.
49 Penelope Goode, 'The Kaingarara Letters: The Correspondence of Tamati Te Ito Ngamoke in the A.S. Atkinson Papers', MA thesis, University of Canterbury, Christchurch, 2001, Letter 19, 25 August 1858.
50 Halse to McLean, 5 September 1857, Inward Letters, Donald McLean (Sir), Papers, ATL.
51 Halse to McLean, 14 September 1857, Inward Letters, Donald McLean (Sir), Papers, ATL.
52 *Lyttelton Times*, 8 August 1857.
53 Halse to McLean, 19 September 1857, Inward Letters, Donald McLean (Sir), Papers, ATL.
54 Halse to McLean, 12 October and 19 October 1857, Inward Letters, Donald McLean (Sir), Papers, ATL.
55 Oettli, Transcripts of J.F. Riemenschneider Papers, 2009, Part 6, p.218, ATL. Riemenschneider used the words 'Wüste' (desert), 'Steine und Knochen' (stones and bones) and 'Schatzgräber' (treasure-digger).
56 Ibid., p.219. Riemenschneider reported of his growing congregation, 'sie drängten sich fast mehr'.
57 Ibid. In Riemenschneider's words, 'verwirrten sprache ihres Babelwerks'.
58 Ibid., p.325. 'Verführer' (seducer); 'Engel des Lichts' (Angel of Light).
59 Ibid., p.114. Riemenschneider's original report read: 'Nur Erueti stand wie ein Felsen auf dem Felsen des freimüthigen Bekenntnisse Christi als des einigend Heilandes; und als er nichts ausrichten konnte und den an ihn gemachten Anforderungen nicht nachgeben konnte, zog er sich wochenlang gänzlich auf seine abgelegenen Aecker in die Einsamkeit zurück. Er sah nämlich daß Aperahama ihm keine Ruhe lassen würde, und daher aus Ehrerbietung und offenen Bruch zu vermeiden ging er aus dem Wege.'
60 Church, *Heartland of Aotea*, p.96; Taylor, Journal, vol. 10, 22 November 1857, ATL.
61 Oettli, Transcripts of J.F. Riemenschneider Papers, 2009, Part 6, p.327, ATL; Taylor, Journal, vol. 10, 22–23 November 1857, ATL.
62 Taylor, Journal, vol. 6, 22 November 1857, ATL. It is interesting to note that in addition to their participation in the fire ceremonies orchestrated by Te Ito, people living in southern Taranaki were still performing lizard-expelling ceremonies in wāhi tapu. Taylor wrote in this 22 November 1857 entry, 'I had a long talk about praying in wahi tapus. They endeavoured to justify their so doing and asked if it were not right to plant food in them and pray to God. Yes, I replied, but not to depend upon eating potatoes in them and prayer to expel the fancied spiritual inhabitants and ngarara from them ... they replied I did not know the power and malignity of these evil spirits, hence the many deaths amongst them.'
63 Richard Taylor, Journal, vol. 6, 23 November 1857, ATL.
64 *Te Karere o Poneke*, 7 June 1858, p.2.
65 Alan Taylor, *Maori Folk Art*, Century Hutchinson, Auckland, 1988, p.48.
66 John Houston, *Maori Life in Old Taranaki*, A.H. and A.W. Reed, Wellington, 1965, p.118.
67 *Wanganui Chronicle*, 17 April 1862, p.2.
68 Ibid., 20 March 1862, p.2.

69 Buddy Mikaere, *Te Maiharoa and the Promised Land*, Heinemann, Auckland, 1988, p.39. Margaret Orbell, Introduction to 'An Account of Waitaha Origins', footnote 12.
70 *Timaru Herald*, 9 November 1866, p.2; Mikaere, *Te Maiharoa and the Promised Land*, pp.39, 45.

Chapter Four | Mana Trouble

1 *Daily Southern Cross*, 16 March 1866, p.4. In this brief autobiography, Te Ua writes that as a former Waikato captive he returned to Taranaki about 1844, where he worked for Revd Skevington under a local teacher named Tāmati, probably Tāmati Reina. He wrote: 'I became assistant monitor in the Wesleyan connection, under a native named Tamati. Sometimes I had to conduct the services in the absence of the proper teachers.'
2 Te Ua was born about 1823 and was some six years older than Te Ito. He wrote in his brief autobiography that he was about three years old when he was taken captive by Waikato in 1826. This date of 1826 is from S. Percy Smith, *History and Traditions of the Maoris of the Taranaki Coast, North Island of New Zealand Prior to 1840*, The Polynesian Society, New Plymouth, 1910, pp.415–17.
3 Penelope Goode, 'The Kaingarara Letters: The Correspondence of Tamati Te Ito Ngamoke in the A.S. Atkinson Papers', MA thesis, University of Canterbury, Christchurch, 2001, Letter 216, undated, probably 1858. This lament is further discussed in Chapter Six.
4 'Pōrewarewa' is the term used by Te Ua to describe his state of spiritual possession in his autobiography.
5 L.F. Head, 'Te Ua and the Hauhau Faith, in Light of the Ua Gospel Notebook', MA thesis, University of Canterbury, Christchurch, 1983, pp.4, 28, 89, 170.
6 Ibid., pp.23–24, 57–58. English translation by Lyndsay Head, revised by Jeffrey Sissons.
7 Ngāti Ruanui chiefs to Robert Parris, 24 October 1857, in *Appendices to the Journals of the House of Representatives (AJHR)*, 1861, C-1, p.218. English translation by Jeffrey Sissons.
8 Tāmati Te Ito to Te Waitere Kātātore, 31 October 1857, in *AJHR*, 1861, C-1, pp.219–20. English translation given in this source; alternative suggestions by Jeffrey Sissons.
9 Henry Halse to Donald McLean, 9 November 1857, in Donald McLean (Sir), Papers, MS-Group-1551, ATL.
10 Keith Sinclair, 'Te Tikanga Pakeke: The Maori Anti-Selling Movement in Taranaki' in P. Munz (ed.), *The Feel of Truth: Essays in New Zealand History*, A.H. and A.W. Reed, Wellington, 1969, p.92.
11 James Belich, *Making Peoples: A History of the New Zealanders from Polynesian Settlement to the End of the Nineteenth Century*, Penguin, Auckland, 2007, Chapter 10, p.5.
12 Halse to McLean, 31 August 1857, in Donald McLean (Sir), Papers, ATL.
13 Robert Parris to McLean, 9 September 1857, in *AJHR*, 1861, C-1, pp.214–15.
14 Parris to McLean, 5 October 1857, in *AJHR*, 1861, C-1, p.216.
15 Parris to McLean, 18 November 1857, in *AJHR*, 1861, C-1, pp.220–21.
16 Parris to McLean, 9 September 1857, in *AJHR*, 1861, C-1, pp.214–15.
17 Parris to McLean, 27 August 1857, in *AJHR*, 1861, C-1, p.213.
18 Halse to McLean, 31 August 1857, in Inward Letters in Maori, Donald McLean (Sir), Papers, ATL.
19 Halse to McLean, 5 October 1857, in Donald McLean (Sir), Papers, ATL.
20 Peter Oettli, Transcripts of J.F. Riemenschneider Papers, 2009, Part 6, p.327, MS-Group-1829, ATL. Riemenschneider's words were: 'Dort ging er in einer

umfangreicheren Weise zu Werke, sammelte weit und breit zerstreute Zauber zusammen'.
21 Halse to McLean, 21 December 1857, in Donald McLean (Sir), Papers, ATL.
22 Oettli, Transcripts of J.F. Riemenschneider Papers, 2009, Part 6, p.328, ATL. 'Kriegsorakel und Siegesprophet'.
23 Ann Parsonson, 'He Whenua Te Utu (The Payment will be Land)', PhD thesis, University of Canterbury, Christchurch, 1978, pp.284–94.
24 Ibid., pp.294–95.
25 *Taranaki Herald*, 16 January 1858, p.3.
26 Halse to McLean, 28 January 1858, in Donald McLean (Sir), Papers, ATL.
27 Robert Parris, 'A Brief Narrative', in Guy Scholefield (ed.), *The Richmond–Atkinson Papers*, Government Printer, Wellington, 1960, vol. 2, p.618.
28 Oettli, Transcripts of J.F. Riemenschneider Papers, 2009, Part 6, p.329, ATL. Riemenschneider said, 'wollten sie ihn zur Vollendung zurückhaben, so mußten sie ihm schon gehorchen und folgen und ohne ihn glaubten sie nun einmal nicht fertig werden zu können'.
29 Ibid., p.329. 'Gott und der Wahrheit'.
30 Halse to McLean, 21 January 1858; Josiah Flight to McLean, 24 March 1858, in Inward Letters, Donald McLean (Sir), Papers, ATL; *Nelson Examiner and New Zealand Chronicle*, 23 January 1861, p.3; Parris, 'A Brief Narrative', p.618; Tony Sole, *Ngāti Ruanui: A History*, Huia Publishers, Wellington, 2005, pp.227–29.
31 Bernard Wells, *The History of Taranaki: A Standard Work on the History of the Province*, Edmondson and Avery, New Plymouth, 1878, p.162.
32 *Taranaki Herald*, 13 February 1858, p.2.
33 *Taranaki Herald*, 20 February 1858, p.2.
34 Halse to McLean, 9 November 1857, in Donald McLean (Sir), Papers, ATL.
35 *Taranaki Herald*, 27 March 1858.
36 Ibid.
37 Parsonson, 'He Whenua, He Utu', pp.244, 296; John Whiteley to McLean, 25 March 1858, in Inward Letters, Donald McLean (Sir), Papers, ATL.
38 Whiteley to McLean, 25 March 1858, in Donald McLean (Sir), Papers, ATL.
39 *Nelson Examiner and New Zealand Chronicle*, 23 January 1861, p.3.
40 Oettli, Transcripts of J.F. Riemenschneider Papers, 2009, Part 6, p.271, ATL. Riemenschneider's words were 'für das groß Werk ihrer Erlösung aus der Gewalt finsterer Zauberundä [sic] Todesmächte welches ihnen von Puketapu aus durch dressen großen Wundermann, Te Ito'.
41 *Taranaki Herald*, 10 April 1858.
42 Ibid.
43 Parris, 'A Brief Narrative', p.621; Henry Halse to Donald McLean, 5 June 1858, MA 1858/214, Archives New Zealand (ANZ).
44 Penelope Goode, 'The Kaingarara Letters: The Correspondence of Tamati Te Ito Ngamoke in the A.S. Atkinson Papers', MA thesis, University of Canterbury, Christchurch, 2001, Letter 9, 18 October 1857.
45 Goode, 'The Kaingarara Letters', Letter 11, 20 June 1858; Letter 12, 24 June 1858; Letter 224, 24 June 1858.
46 Goode, 'The Kaingarara Letters', Letter 12, 24 June 1858. Interestingly, Te Ito is here explicitly referred to as 'the lizard eater' or 'the reptile eater'. English translation by Penelope Goode, with alternative suggestions by Jeffrey Sissons.
47 Goode, 'The Kaingarara Letters', Letter 224, 24 June 1858. English translation by Penelope Goode, revised by Jeffrey Sissons.
48 Richard Taylor, Journal, vol. 10, 22 November 1857, MS-Papers-0254, ATL.
49 Goode, 'The Kaingarara Letters', Letter 68, 10 December 1859.

50 Goode, 'The Kaingarara Letters', Letter 17, 31 July 1858.
51 Ibid. English translation by Penelope Goode.
52 Goode, 'The Kaingarara Letters', Letter 68, 10 December 1859. Goode comments in a footnote to her translation (footnote 255) that the reference to Te Rangitāke's Women's Council may have been intended as an insult or there may indeed have been a council of women who were seeking to promote peace.
53 Goode, 'The Kaingarara Letters', Letter 18, 24 August 1858; Letter 67, 6 December 1859; Letter 72, 17 December 1859; Letter 79, 21 January 1860.
54 Ann Parsonson, 'Nga Whenua Tautohetohe o Taranaki: Land and Conflict in Taranaki, 1839–1859, Revision of Report No. 1 to the Waitangi Tribunal', 1991, p.165.
55 *AJHR*, 1860, E-3a, pp.5–6. Official English translation.
56 Sole, *Ngāti Ruanui*, pp.236–37.

Chapter Five | Living with Atua: The Kaingārara Letters

1   Ngati Ruanui chiefs to Robert Parris, 24 October 1857, in *Appendices to the Journals of the House of Representatives (AJHR)*, 1861, C-1, p.218.
2   The best discussion is by Anne Salmond, 'Tribal Words, Tribal Worlds: The Translatability of Tapu and Mana', in M. Marshall and J. Caughy (eds), *Culture, Kin and Cognition in Oceania: Essays in Honour of Ward H. Goodenough*, American Anthropological Association, Washington, 1989, pp.74–75; see also, F. Alan and Louise Hanson, *Counterpoint in Maori Culture*, Routledge and Kegan Paul, London, 1983, pp.50–52; Elsdon Best, *The Maori*, Government Printer, Wellington, 1924, vol. 2, p.251.
3   John Nicholas, *Narrative of Voyage to New Zealand*, James Black and Son, London, 1817, vol. 1, p.166. Nicholas may, however, have misunderstood what he had been told, crediting himself with too much agency; if Ruatara was sick at the time of his visit then the atua may have already begun its attack.
4   Elsdon Best, *The Maori*, Government Printer, Wellington, 1924, vol. 2, p.251.
5   Richard Taylor, *Te Ika a Maui, or New Zealand and its Inhabitants*, Wertheim and Macintosh, London, 1855, p.55.
6   *AJHR*, 1860, F-3, no.3, p.90.
7   Taylor, *Te Ika a Maui*, p.64.
8   Prytz Johansen, *The Maori and his Religion in its Non-ritualistic Aspects*, Ejnar Munksgaard, Copenhagen, 1958, p.197.
9   William Goldie, 'Maori Medical Lore: Notes on the Causes of Disease and Treatment of the Sick among the Maori People of New Zealand, As Believed and Practised in Former Times, Together with Some Account of Various Ancient Rites Connected with the Same', *Transactions of the New Zealand Institute*, vol. 37, p.4.
10 S. Percy Smith, H.T. Whatahoro, Te Matorohanga and Nepia Pohuhu, *The Lore of the Whare Wananga or the Teachings of the Maori College on Religion, Cosmogony and History*, The Polynesian Society, New Plymouth, 1913, vol. 3, p.12.
11 *Taranaki Herald*, 23 April 1864, p.2.
12 Paul Diamond, Curator Māori at the Alexander Turnbull Library, describes some of the letters as bearing the physical scars of the warfare in which they were plundered (personal communication).
13 See: Atkinson, Arthur Samuel, 1833–1902: Maori Letters from Taranaki, https://natlib.govt.nz/records/22797907.
14 Penelope Goode, 'The Kaingarara Letters: The Correspondence of Tamati Te Ito Ngamoke in the A.S. Atkinson Papers 1857–1863', MA thesis, University of Canterbury, Christchurch, 2001.

15 *Wellington Independent*, 22 July 1857.
16 Goode, 'The Kaingarara Letters', 'Note on the Texts'.
17 *Maori Messenger: Te Karere Maori*, 31 January 1858, pp.3–6.
18 Te Ito is addressed in three different ways in these letters: Tāmati Te Ito, Tāmati Te Ito Ngāmoke, and Tāmati Ngāmoke. Te Ito's marriage certificate gives his name as Tāmati Te Ito, omitting the Ngāmoke. It is not clear when he first took the name Ngāmoke, but its use may have accompanied his change of status in 1856–57.
19 Goode, 'The Kaingarara Letters', Letter 9. The letter numbers used here, and in the notes which follow, match those used by Penelope Goode in her MA thesis. English translation by Penelope Goode.
20 Goode, 'The Kaingarara Letters', Letter 25, Apera to Tamati Ngamoke and Wiremu Kingi, 2 October 1858.
21 Goode, 'The Kaingarara Letters', Letter 223, Hapurona Pukerima to Tamati Te Ito, (undated). English translation by Penelope Goode, revised by Jeffrey Sissons.
22 Goode, 'The Kaingarara Letters', Letter 23, Tamati Reina Ngawhare (tou papa kuare) to Tamati Te Ito, 16 September 1858. English translation by Penelope Goode.
23 Jeffrey Sissons, 'Personhood as History: Maori Conversion in Light of the Polynesian Iconoclasm', *Journal of the Polynesian Society*, 124, 2 (2015), pp.129–46.
24 John Skevington to The Secretaries, 19 April 1842, in Letters to the Secretaries, Wesleyan Methodist Missionary Society, Archives Group MET 004, John Kinder Theological Library, Auckland; L.M. Rogers (ed.), *The Early Journals of Henry Williams*, Pegasus Press, Christchurch, 1961; Herbert William Williams, *Dictionary of the Maori Language*, Government Printer, Wellington, 1971.
25 Henry Williams, Journal, 12 December 1839, in Rogers (ed.), *The Early Journals of Henry Williams*.
26 Timothy Yates, *The Conversion of Maori: Years of Religious and Social Change, 1814–1842*, William B. Eerdmans Publishing Company, Michigan, 2013, p.111.
27 Bronwyn Elsmore, *Mana from Heaven: A Century of Maori Prophets in New Zealand*, Moana Press, Tauranga, 1989, p.128.
28 Goode, 'The Kaingarara Letters', Letter 216, Horopapera to Tamati Te Ito Ngamoke (undated); Lyndsay Head, 'The Gospel of Te Ua Haumene', *Journal of the Polynesian Society*, 101, 1 (1992), p.9, n.15.
29 Goode, 'The Kaingarara Letters', Letter 31, Te Warihi to Tamati Te Ito, 15 October 1858. English translation by Penelope Goode.
30 Goode, 'The Kaingarara Letters', Letter 39, Te Warihi to Tamati Te Ito, 4 November 1858.
31 Goode, 'The Kaingarara Letters', Letter 12, Ropata Totoinumia to Tamati Te Ito, 17 November 1858. English translation by Penelope Goode.
32 Goode, 'The Kaingarara Letters', Letter 13, Wiremu Te Tata to Tamati Te Ito, 25 June 1858.
33 Goode, 'The Kaingarara Letters', Letter 12, Ropata Totoinumia to Tamati Te Ito, 17 November 1858. English translation by Penelope Goode, revised by Jeffrey Sissons.
34 Best, *The Maori*, vol. 2, pp.400–1.
35 Goode, 'The Kaingarara Letters', Letter 14, Poharama to Tamati Te Ito, 8 July, 1858.
36 Goode, 'The Kaingarara Letters', Letter 48, Te Watarauihi to Tamati Te Ito, 21 December 1858. English translation by Penelope Goode, revised by Jeffrey Sissons.
37 E.S. Handy, *Polynesian Religion*, Bernice P. Bishop Museum Bulletin 34, Bishop Museum, Honolulu, 1927, p.282.
38 Goode, 'The Kaingarara Letters', Letter 39, Te Warihi to Tamati Te Ito, 4 November 1848.
39 Goode, 'The Kaingarara Letters', Letter 42, Te Warihi to Tamati Te Ito, 18 November 1858.

40 Goode, 'The Kaingarara Letters', Letter 217, Te Kepa to Tamati Te Ito, 19 December 1858. English translation by Penelope Goode; Tony Sole, *Ngāti Ruanui: A History*, Huia Publishers, Wellington, 2005, p.24.
41 Goode, 'The Kaingarara Letters', Letter 49, Panapa Poa to Tamati Te Ito, 27 December 1858.
42 Goode, 'The Kaingarara Letters', Letter 35, Ihaia Te Karawa to Tamati Te Ito Ngamoke, 25 October 1858. English translation by Penelope Goode, revised by Jeffrey Sissons.
43 Henry Halse to Donald McLean, 23 November 1858, ATL.
44 E. Shortland, *Traditions and Superstitions of the New Zealanders*, Longman Brown, Green Longmans and Roberts, London, 1856, p.121.

Chapter Six | Prophet and Rangatira

1 Penelope Goode, 'The Kaingarara Letters: The Correspondence of Tamati Te Ito Ngamoke in the A.S. Atkinson Papers', MA thesis, University of Canterbury, Christchurch, 2001, Letter 216 (undated). English translation by Penelope Goode. A version of this lament was sent to Governor George Grey at the time of his departure from New Zealand in 1853. Goode, footnote 182 to Letter 216.
2 Goode, 'The Kaingarara Letters', Letter 9, 18 October 1857; Letter 11, 20 June 1858; Letter 64, 22 November 1859.
3 Goode, 'The Kaingarara Letters', Letter 18, 24 August 1858; Letter 20, 25 August 1858; Letter 21, 4 September 1858; Letter 23, 16 September 1858; Letter 27, 4 October 1858; Letter 30, 14 October 1858; Letter 43, 17 November 1858; Letter 47, 2 December 1858; Letter 79, 21 January 1860; Letter 188, 14 April 1863.
4 Goode, 'The Kaingarara Letters', Letter 67, 6 December 1859; Letter 72, 17 December 1859.
5 Goode, 'The Kaingarara Letters', Letter 64, 22 November 1859.
6 Angela Ballara, 'Introduction', *Te Kingitanga, The People of the Maori King Movement: Essays from the New Zealand Dictionary of Biography*, Auckland University Press, Auckland, 1996, p.8.
7 *Appendices to the Journals of the House of Representatives (AJHR)*, 1860, E-3a, p.5. Te Ito had moved from Te Whanga to Te Puata in September 1859. See Robert Parris to Donald McLean, 3 October 1859, in Inward Letters, Donald McLean (Sir), Papers, MS-Group-1551, Alexander Turnbull Library, Wellington (ATL).
8 Goode, 'The Kaingarara Letters', Letter 11, 20 June, 1858; Letter 64, 22 November, 1859; Letter 68, 10 December, 1859; Letter 69, 12 December, 1859.
9 Goode, 'The Kaingarara Letters', Letter 74, 29 December 1859. English translation by Penelope Goode, revised by Jeffrey Sissons.
10 Ann Parsonson, 'The Waitara Purchase, and the War in Taranaki', Report No.2 to the Waitangi Tribunal, July 1990, p.8; Waitangi Tribunal, *The Taranaki Report: Kaupapa Tuatahi*, GP Publications, Wellington, 1996, pp.69–70.
11 Ann Parsonson, 'The Waitara Purchase', p.9.
12 Bob may have been Ropata (Robert) Ngaromate, also known as Ropata Totoimua. He was referred to as Te Ito's 'teina' (younger sibling or younger cousin) in letters written to Te Ito. See Goode, 'The Kaingarara Letters', Letters 12, 64. The assessor, Wiremu Te Ngāhuru, referred to himself as a 'matua' (father or uncle) to both Te Ito and Ropata.
13 Parris to McLean, 7 November 1859, Inward Letters, Donald McLean (Sir), Papers, ATL.
14 Waitangi Tribunal, *The Taranaki Report*, pp.69–70; Ann Parsonson, 'He Whenua,

He Utu (The Payment Will Be Land), PhD thesis, University of Canterbury, Christchurch, 1978, pp.299-300.
15 Waitangi Tribunal, *The Taranaki Report*, p.70.
16 Waitangi Tribunal, *The Taranaki Report*, p.67. *AJHR*, 1860, E-3a, p.5; 1860, E-4, p.19; McLean to the Governor, 23 July 1860 in *AJHR*, 1860, E-3a, p.5. Governor's Despatch in *AJHR*, 1861, E-1, pp.16, 25; *AJHR* 1860, E-1a, p.18. Referring to the name, 'Kaingārara', Penelope Goode, 'The Kaingarara Letters', p.10, notes, 'Nineteenth century observers of the movement, however, do not use this term. They talk around it, calling it, for example, "a strange movement with regard to sacred places".'
17 C.W. Richmond, Memorandum, 26 June 1860, *AJHR*, 1860, E-1a, p.18.
18 McLean to the Governor, 23 July 1860, *AJHR*, 1860, E-3a, p.5.
19 Parris to McLean, 27 August 1857, *AJHR*, 1861, C-1, p.213.
20 *Taranaki Herald*, 12 March 1859, p.5.
21 Or, possibly, a finely woven flax cloak.
22 *Taranaki Herald*, 12 March 1859, p.5.
23 Ibid.; Parris to Chief Land Commissioner, 16 July 1860, *AJHR*, 1860, E-3a, p.2.
24 Parris wrote that the meeting was attended by 'all the leading men' of Waitara, Puketapu, Ngāmotu and some from southern Taranaki. *AJHR*, 1860, E-3a, p.2.
25 *AJHR*, 1860, E-3, p.4.
26 Waitangi Tribunal, *The Taranaki Report*, p.69.
27 Ibid., p.70.
28 *AJHR*, 1860, E-3, p.4.
29 Ibid.
30 *AJHR*, 1863, E-2, pp.4, 26.
31 *AJHR*, 1860, E-3, p.9.
32 *AJHR*, 1863, E-2, p.37. English translation published in the *AJHR* source.
33 *AJHR*, 1860, E-3, p.9.
34 Parsonson, 'The Waitara Purchase', pp.33-34; Waitangi Tribunal, *The Taranaki Report*, p.69.
35 Waitangi Tribunal, *The Taranaki Report*, p.72.
36 Ibid., p.73.
37 Goode, 'The Kaingarara Letters', Letter 78, 10 January 1860. English translation by Penelope Goode.
38 Waitangi Tribunal, *The Taranaki Report*, p.63.
39 Ibid., p.43.
40 *Taranaki Herald*, 10 March 1860, p.3; *Wellington Independent*, 8 January 1861, p.5.
41 *AJHR*, 1863, E-2, pp.10-11.
42 Ibid., pp.2-4.
43 Ibid., pp.3-4; *Taranaki Herald*, 10 March 1860, p.3.
44 Ibid.
45 *AJHR*, 1863, E-2, p.4.
46 Waitangi Tribunal, *The Taranaki Report*, p.89.
47 John Whiteley, Journal, 11 March 1860, qMS-2212-2213, ATL.
48 Bible (New International Version), Ezekiel, ch. 9.
49 Waitangi Tribunal, *The Taranaki Report*, p.72.
50 See for example, Georges Dumezil, *Mitra-Varuna: An Essay on Two Indo-European Representations of Sovereignty*, Zone Books, New York, 1988.
51 See Goode, 'The Kaingarara Letters', 'Introduction', pp.10-11, for a discussion of the name 'Kaingārara'.
52 Bronwyn Elsmore, *Mana from Heaven: A Century of Maori Prophets in New Zealand*, Moana Press, Tauranga, 1989, pp.95-106.

53 Goode, 'The Kaingarara Letters', 'Introduction', p.17.
54 *The Taranaki Report*, p.62, notes: 'The perceived illegality of combinations in restraint of trade and the imagining of a Taranaki land league in that category flowed from an ideology then in vogue in Britain that elevated individual rights to trade above all else.'
55 Ann Parsonson, 'The Waitara Purchase', p.27.
56 Henry Halse to McLean, 21 May 1859, Inward Letters, Donald McLean (Sir), Papers, ATL. Halse reiterated this claim in July, writing, 'W. Kingi has been persuaded by Te Ito to discountenance the peace making'. See Halse to McLean, 25 July 1859, Inward Letters, Donald McLean (Sir), Papers, ATL.
57 *Taranaki Herald*, 21 July 1860, p.3.

Chapter Seven | Mataitawa Years: 1860–1864

1 Ann Parsonson, 'The Waitara Purchase, and the War in Taranaki', Report No. 2 to the Waitangi Tribunal, July 1990, p.52.
2 Ibid.
3 G.H. Scholefield, *A Dictionary of New Zealand Biography*, Department of Internal Affairs, Wellington, 1940, p.354.
4 Penelope Goode, 'The Kaingarara Letters: The Correspondence of Tamati Te Ito Ngamoke in the A.S. Atkinson Papers', MA thesis, University of Canterbury, Christchurch, 2001, Letter 223 (undated); Letter 26, 3 October 1858; Letter 28, 8 October 1858.
5 Goode, 'The Kaingarara Letters', Letter 26, 3 October 1858; Letter 28, 8 October 1858.
6 James Cowan, *The New Zealand Wars: A History of the Maori Campaigns and the Pioneering Period*, R.E. Owen, Wellington, 1956, vol. 1, pp.164–66; Parsonson, 'The Waitara Purchase', pp.52–53.
7 John Whiteley, Journal, 20 March 1860, qMS-2212-2213, Alexander Turnbull Library, Wellington (ATL).
8 Cowan, *The New Zealand Wars*, vol. 1, pp.166, 465.
9 *Taranaki Herald*, 23 June 1860, p.3; Te Waitere Kātātore and Wiremu Tāmihana Poihaka to Hōri Pākeke and others, 2 November 1851, in Inward Letters, Donald McLean (Sir), Papers, MS-Group-1551, ATL. Tāmihana had only just managed to escape from the ambush in which Kātātore was killed in 1858.
10 Ann Parsonson, 'Te Rangitāke, Wiremu Kīngi', *The Dictionary of New Zealand Biography* in Te Ara – The Encyclopedia of New Zealand, https://teara.govt.nz/en/biographies/1t70/te-rangitake-wiremu-kingi (accessed 18 January 2023); *Appendices to the Journals of the House of Representatives*, (AJHR), 1873, G1, p.15; *Taranaki Herald*, 28 March 1863, p.4; Hazel Riseborough, 'Background Papers for the Taranaki Raupatu Claim', Waitangi Tribunal, 1989, p.80.
11 Goode, 'The Kaingarara Letters', Letter 188, 14 April 1863. This is discussed later in this chapter.
12 Peter Oettli, Transcripts of J.F. Riemenschneider Papers, 2009, Part 7, p.177, MS-Group-1829, ATL. Riemenschneider reported the question thus: 'ist nicht jenes Feuer dort drüben mein Dorf?'
13 Whiteley, Journal, 5 April 1860, ATL.
14 *AJHR*, 1863, I, E-2, p.4.
15 Whiteley, Journal, Sunday 8 April 1860, ATL.
16 *Nelson Examiner and New Zealand Chronicle*, 14 April 1860, p.3.
17 *Taranaki Herald*, 14 April 1860, p.4.
18 Cowan, *The New Zealand Wars*, vol. 1, p.523.

19 *AJHR*, 1861, E-1b, pp.16–17. The English is the official translation.
20 Goode, 'The Kaingarara Letters', Letter 13, 25 June 1858.
21 Heather Bauchop, 'The Wars and Iwi Losses, 1860–70: A Summary', Waitangi Tribunal Report, 143, June 1992, pp.12–14.
22 Tony Sole, *Ngāti Ruanui: A History*, Huia Publishers, Wellington, 2005, pp.235–36.
23 Bauchop, 'The Wars and Iwi Losses', p.44.
24 Ibid., p.22; see also map by Ian Smith showing the burnings in his *Pākehā Settlements in a Māori World*, Bridget Williams Books, Wellington, 2019, p.250.
25 Cowan, *The New Zealand Wars*, vol. 1, p.171.
26 See, for example, James Belich, *The New Zealand Wars and the Victorian Interpretation of Racial Conflict*, Auckland University Press, Auckland, 1989, pp.84–85; Vincent O'Malley, *The Great War for New Zealand: Waikato 1800–2000*, Bridget Williams Books, Wellington, 2016, p.114.
27 Waitangi Tribunal, *The Taranaki Report: Kaupapa Tuatahi*, GP Publications, Wellington, 1996, p.78.
28 Goode, 'The Kaingarara Letters', Letter 86, 14 June 1860.
29 *Taranaki Herald*, 25 August 1860.
30 Smith, *Pākehā Settlements in a Maori World*, pp.50–52.
31 *Taranaki Herald*, 14 July 1860, p.2.
32 John Gorst, *The Maori King: Or the Story of Our Quarrel with the Natives of New Zealand*, Macmillan, London, 1864, pp.144–46; *Taranaki Herald*, 1 September 1860.
33 *Taranaki Herald*, 8 December 1860.
34 *Taranaki Herald*, 1 September 1860.
35 Parsonson, 'The Waitara Purchase', p.53; James Belich, *The New Zealand Wars and the Victorian Interpretation of Racial Conflict*, Auckland University Press, Auckland, 1986, pp.102–3.
36 Gorst, *The Maori King*, p.163.
37 *Taranaki Herald*, 10 April 1861.
38 Parsonson, 'The Waitara Purchase', p.57.
39 *AJHR*, 1861, E-1b, p.5.
40 Wellington Carrington to Donald McLean, 8 May 1861, in Inward Letters, Donald McLean (Sir), Papers, ATL.
41 *Taranaki Herald*, 18 January 1862, p.2.
42 *Taranaki Herald*, 6 September 1862.
43 *Taranaki Herald*, 20 September 1862, p.2.
44 Ibid.
45 Atkinson was editor of the paper at this time: see Frances Porter, 'Atkinson, Arthur Samuel', *The Dictionary of New Zealand Biography*, in Te Ara – the Encyclopedia of New Zealand, https://teara.govt.nz/en/biographies/2a15/atkinson-arthur-samuel (accessed 21 June 2022).
46 Goode, 'The Kaingarara Letters', Letter 188, 14 April 1863. English translation by Penelope Goode.
47 F.D. Bell to McLean, April 1863, in *AJHR*, 1863, E-2, pp.5–6; George Grey to the Duke of Newcastle, 6 May 1863, in *AJHR*, 1863, E-2, p.21.
48 *AJHR*, 1863, E-2, p.2.
49 Waitangi Tribunal, *The Taranaki Report*, p.89.
50 *AJHR*, 1863, E-02, p.21.
51 Waitangi Tribunal, *The Taranaki Report*, p.91.
52 Bauchop, 'The Wars and Iwi Losses', p.60.
53 Lyndsay Head, 'Te Ua Haumēne', *The Dictionary of New Zealand Biography*,

in Te Ara – The Encyclopedia of New Zealand, https://teara.govt.nz/en/biographies/1t79/te-ua-haumene (accessed 18 January 2023).
54 Ian Church, 'Te Matakātea, Wiremu Kīngi Moki', *The Dictionary of New Zealand Biography*, in Te Ara – The Encyclopedia of New Zealand, https://teara.govt.nz/en/biographies/1t50/te-matakatea-wiremu-kingi-moki (accessed 18 January 2023).
55 *Daily Southern Cross*, 16 March 1866, p.4.
56 Waitangi Tribunal, *The Taranaki Report*, p.93.
57 *Otago Daily Times*, 18 September 1863, p.6.
58 Ibid.
59 Taranaki Minute Book (TMB), 14, pp.175–76, 182.
60 *The Press*, 16 September 1863, p.3.
61 Waitangi Tribunal, *The Taranaki Report*, p.94.
62 Matiu was living with Te Ito, while his brother remained as an assessor in New Plymouth. They were Te Ito's cousins. In March 1861, Matiu took a letter from Mataitawa to his brother reporting casualties. This relationship appears to have been the basis of a regular channel of communication. See *Taranaki Herald*, 12 March 1861, p.1.
63 *Taranaki Herald*, 15 October 1864, p.2; Waitangi Tribunal, *The Taranaki Report*, p.94.
64 The *Daily Southern Cross*, 13 October 1864, p.4, wrote, scathingly, that there was 'something of the burlesque' in this extravagant operation, that placed the troops 'in false and ridiculous positions'; *Taranaki Herald*, 15 October 1864, p.2.
65 *Taranaki Herald*, 15 October 1864, p.2.
66 *Taranaki Herald*, 22 October 1864, p.4.
67 Te Ito's land at Mataitawa was confiscated in 1865, and Manutahi subsequently became a military settlement. One of the military officers who took up a government offer of land was Lieutenant Colonel Maxwell Lepper. In 1878 the name of the settlement at Manutahi was changed to Lepperton. See Peter Wilson, *Even the Dogs have Forgotten How to Bark: The Events and People of Lepperton, Sentry Hill and Waiongona*, P.T. and L.M. Wilson, New Plymouth, 2012; *Taranaki Herald*, 5 April 1878. Such changes of name were expressions of colonial power.

Chapter Eight | A Gun Broken: The Path to Parihaka

1 *Taranaki Daily News*, 26 March 1928, p.6 (supplement).
2 *Appendices to the Journals of the House of Representatives (AJHR)*, 1868, A-13, p.5; *AJHR*, 1869, A-13, p.15.
3 *AJHR*, 1868, A-8, p.16.
4 *Taranaki Herald*, 27 June 1868.
5 *AJHR*, 1868, A-13, p.5.
6 *Taranaki Herald*, 27 June 1868.
7 Hazel Riseborough, 'Background Papers for the Taranaki Raupatu Claim', Waitangi Tribunal, p.34.
8 Ibid., p.46.
9 Ibid., pp.54, 64.
10 *Otago Witness*, 7 November 1868.
11 *Taranaki Herald*, 12 September 1868, p.2 and 28 November 1868, p.3. Most curiously, in March 1868, a Puketapu prophet named Horopapera asked his relatives to gather at Oropūriri. According to Wi Te Ahoaho, a former Waiwhakaiho River ferryman, he was inspired by the atua Maru, whose image Te Ito destroyed in 1855. Te Ahoaho wrote: 'The prophet of Maru (Horopapera) said at 8 o'clock this morning

the fire will descend and destroy the Pakehas, their houses and the town also. Let all the Maoris go inland to the bush and leave the Pakehas only to be destroyed by the fire of Maru. Two Maori Assessors, their women and children, knelt down to that Maori god, Te Tahana Papawaka and Te Kipa Wunu … [later] the foolish people assembled at the office of Mr. Parris in the town to talk about the god and the falseness of Horopapera. Mr. Parris called out to Horopapera, "You must leave off this foolish work". He agreed and said "it is ended, it is finished".' *Taranaki Herald*, 21 March 1868, p.2. It is possible, therefore, that Te Ito had restated the earlier prophecy of Horopapera, but it is also possible that Te Ahoaho had used a pseudonym and that the prophet named Horopapera was, in fact, Tāmati Te Ito.

12   *AJHR*, 1869, A-13, p.15.
13   Ibid.
14   *AJHR*, 1869, A-10, pp.40–41.
15   Ibid.
16   *AJHR*, 1864, E-3, p.17.
17   Ibid.; *Taranaki Herald*, 17 October 1868. This meeting house was one of at least two Te Ātiawa houses standing at the time. A second meeting house, which had been built by Rāniera at Oropūriri, was approximately 18 metres long and 7 metres wide. See Simon Holdaway and Rod Wallace, 'A Materialisation of Social Organisation: The 19th Century Occupation of Te Oropuriri, Taranaki', in Matthew Campbell, Simon Holdaway and Sarah Macready (eds), *Finding Our Recent Past: Historical Archaeology in New Zealand*, New Zealand Archaeological Association, Auckland, 2013, p.91.
18   The following account of the hui at Māhoetahi and its immediate aftermath is drawn mainly from two independent sources: a letter from Robert Parris to J.C. Richmond dated 21 October 1868 in *AJHR*, 1869, A-10, pp.41–42, and a report in the *Taranaki Herald*, 17 October 1868, possibly by a Māori writer. A third source, an account written in a derogatory tone by the same unnamed 'correspondent' that reported Te Ito's prophecy, has also been consulted: *Otago Witness*, 7 November 1868.
19   *Taranaki Herald*, 17 October 1868.
20   Ibid.
21   Ibid.
22   *AJHR*, 1869, A-10, p.42.
23   Ibid.
24   *Taranaki Herald*, 17 October 1868.
25   Ailsa Smith, 'Ko Tohu Te Matua: The Story of Tohu Kakahi of Parihaka', MA thesis, University of Canterbury, Christchurch, 1990, pp.61–63.
26   Dr Ruakere Hond, pers. comm., 12 May 2023.
27   *AJHR*, 1869, A-13, p.22.
28   Ibid., p.31. Like many others of Taranaki Iwi, Te Whiti returned to Wārea from the south in the early 1840s. Here he was taught by the local Ngā Mahanga missionary, Minirapa Rangihatuake, and later by Revd Riemenschneider. In 1862, he joined Wiremu Kīngi Te Matakātea in the rescue of the passengers and crew from the steamer *Lord Worsley*, and he and Tohu were with Te Ua's followers when they mounted the disastrous attack on Sentry Hill in 1864. Subsequently, they pursued a course of non-violent resistance, moving to Parihaka (formerly known as Repanga) in the mid-1860s. See Danny Keenan, 'Te Whiti-o-Rongomai III, Erueti', *The Dictionary of New Zealand Biography*, in Te Ara – The Encyclopedia of New Zealand, https://teara.govt.nz/en/biographies/2t34/te-whiti-o-rongomai-iii-erueti (accessed 18 January 2023).
29   *AJHR*, 1869, A-10, p.46.
30   Ibid.

31 *Taranaki Herald*, 20 October 1875.
32 *AJHR*, 1869, A-10, p.42.
33 Ibid., p.47. Some two weeks after the return to Te Puata, their missionary, Revd John Whiteley, who had made frequent visits there, was murdered at the north Taranaki settlement of Pukearuhe (White Cliffs).
34 *AJHR*, 1870, A-16, p.18.
35 Ibid.
36 Peter Buck (Te Rangi Hīroa) described 'pōrewarewa' as 'oracles' and people 'possessed' by a god in his doctoral thesis, 'Medicine amongst the Maoris, in Ancient and Modern Times: Thesis for the Degree of Doctor of Medicine', University of New Zealand, Dunedin, 1910, pp.51–52; Te Ua referred to himself as pōrewarewa 'under mesmeric influence' in his brief biography, *Daily Southern Cross*, 16 March 1866, p.4.
37 Parris to McLean, *AJHR*, 1871, F-6b, p.14.
38 Te Ito was officially recognised as a leading Puketapu chief, along with Te Tahana, Mahau and Tāmihana, in 1870. See *AJHR*, 1870, A-11, p.7.
39 *Taranaki Herald*, 29 October 1870; *Daily Southern Cross*, 31 October 1870; *Evening Post*, 5 November 1870.
40 Between 200 and 300 according to the *Daily Southern Cross*, but between 150 and 200 according to the *Taranaki Herald*.
41 *Daily Southern Cross*, 31 October 1870.
42 *Taranaki Herald*, 29 October 1870.
43 *Taranaki Herald*, 18 March 1871, p.2.
44 Ibid. The 'h' of Parihaka is silent in the Taranaki dialect, hence it is written here as 'Pariaka'.
45 *Taranaki Herald*, 18 March 1871.
46 Ibid.
47 *Taranaki Herald*, 30 September 1871, p.2.
48 *Taranaki Herald*, 24 February 1872, p.2; *Waka Maori*, 3 April 1872, p.58.
49 *Waka Maori*, 3 April 1872, p.58. English translation by Jeffrey Sissons.
50 *AJHR*, 1872, F-3a, p.24.
51 Ibid., pp.24–25.
52 Ibid., p.24.
53 Ibid., p.25.
54 Bible (New International Version), Hebrews 4:14 – Chapter 5:3.
55 *AJHR*, 1872, F-3, p.13.
56 Ibid.
57 *Taranaki Herald*, 28 November 1878.
58 Judith Binney, 'Maori Prophetic Movements – Nga Poropīti', *Te Ara – The Encyclopedia of New Zealand*, https://teara.govt.nz/en/maori-prophetic-movements-nga-poropiti (accessed 18 January 2023).
59 Ibid.
60 *AJHR*, 1876, G-1, p.1.
61 Taranaki Minute Book (TMB), 14, pp.175–76, 182.
62 Waitangi Tribunal, *The Taranaki Report: Kaupapa Tuatahi*, GP Publications, Wellington, 1996, p.213; Charles Brown to Under Secretary, Native Department, in *AJHR*, 1876, G-1, p.1.
63 Ibid., p.224.
64 Ibid., p.214.
65 Ibid., p.214–15.
66 Ibid., p.221.
67 Danny Keenan, *Te Whiti o Rongomai and the Resistance of Parihaka*, Huia, Wellington, 2015, p.120.

68. Waitangi Tribunal, *The Taranaki Report*, p.226.
69. Rachel Buchanan, *Ko Taranaki Te Maunga*, Bridget Williams Books, Wellington, 2018, p.50.
70. Ibid., p.51; Waitangi Tribunal, *The Taranaki Report*, p.202.
71. Waitangi Tribunal, *The Taranaki Report*, p.205.
72. Ibid., p.206.
73. Ibid., pp.236–37.
74. Keenan, *Te Whiti o Rongomai*, p.174; Waitangi Tribunal, *The Taranaki Report*, p.237.
75. *Lyttelton Times*, 14 November 1881, p.5; see also *Christchurch Star*, 14 November 1881, p.3; *Wanganui Chronicle*, 14 November 1881, p.2; *Auckland Star*, 12 November 1881, p.3.
76. Ibid.; *Otago Daily Times*, 21 November 1881, p.2.
77. Vincent O'Malley, *The Great War for New Zealand: Waikato 1800–2000*, Bridget Williams Books, Wellington, 2016, p.9.
78. Waitangi Tribunal, *The Taranaki Report*, p.60.
79. See Chapter Four and the discussion of Te Rangitāke urging his forces to complete Te Ito's work of cleansing.

Index

Acts and Regulations
   New Zealand Constitution Act 1852 33
   New Zealand Settlements Act 1863 136
adultery 87, 100, 103
agriculture 83, 90
alliances 14, 21, 30, 52, 65, 68, 74, 78, 99, 104, 114–15
   future 78
   independent Taranaki 99
   Kaingārara 114–15
   pan-tribal 21
   of tribal rūnanga 114
ambushes 33, 68, 130, 132
ammunition 11, 69
ancestors 23, 29, 42, 138, 148–49
ancestral relationships 78, 146
Anglican missionaries 24, 44, 49, 51–53, 117, 119 see also missionaries
Aotea canoe 39–40, 93–94, 141 see also canoes
Āperahama (Ngā Mahanga chief) 41, 53
Armed Constabulary 154 see also police
Arowhenua (South Canterbury) 58–59
arrests 4, 139, 153–55
   of Te Ito 67, 140
   of Te Whiti-o-Rongomai and Tohu Kākahi 154
   of Wiremu Kīngi Te Matakātea 153
assessors 11, 51, 64, 140
Atkinson, Arthur 82, 128, 134
atua 20, 22, 24, 37, 40, 42–43, 48, 55, 57, 61–62, 78–83, 87–97, 156–57
   ancestral spirits and demons 2
   destroying fires 55
   expelling malevolent 97, 102
   guardian 37, 62, 65
   kikokiko (malicious ancestral spirits) 49, 66, 81–85, 88–89, 96–97, 102, 114–15, 124, 157
   malevolent 11, 45, 87, 97
   ngārara (lizard gods) 23, 56
   rejecting ancestral 20
   whakapakoko (god image) 42–43, 55
Auckland 143, 152
Austral Islands 50

Ballara, Angela 100–1
baptisms 5, 12–13, 35, 87–88, 112
barracks see police barracks
Bates, Lieutenant Henry 109–10, 119
   Bates's report 111
battles
   Kōhia 117
   Māhoetahi 125, 138
   Sentry Hill 133
   Waireka 121
Belich, James 65, 113
Bell, Francis Dillon 111, 129–30
Bell Block 1, 10–11, 119–20
Best, Elsdon 23–24, 80–81
Bible 24, 46, 51, 53, 112, 151
Binney, Judith 151
blockhouses 126, 139
blocks 30, 91, 107
   Hua 31–32, 35
   Pekapeka 109, 111, 131
   Puketapu 31
   Tarurutangi 32
   Te Kuikui 110
   Waitaha 75
   Waiwhakaiho 30
boats
   HMS *Niger* 109, 121–22
   Lord Worsley 131
   Louisa 8
   Wikitoria 6–7
   see also canoes; see also waka
bones 17
bonfires 45–58, 70
boundaries
   established by the Kaingārara council 91
   for line fishing 91
   of the fishing canoes 92
   of gardens 48
   of the Maraeaute block 75
   of tapu areas 90
   Taranaki's northern 77
   of Te Ātiawa 16, 30
   tribal 37, 83
boundary stones 48
bread 35, 145, 147, 152

British regiments 117, 121, 125
Brown, Charles 152
Browne, Governor Thomas Gore 76, 105–6, 111, 122, 126, 139
Bryce, John 154
Buck, Peter 20
Bulkeley, Captain 109
bullock carts 70
burial of New Testament 34–37
burnings 39, 45–58, 70, 72, 78, 85–87, 109–10, 118–21, 132, 137
  ceremonial 46
  of settlements by government forces 122
  of settler houses by Te Ito 39, 119, 121, 123, 124, 132

Cameron, General Duncan 129
'Camp Waitara' 120
canoes 8, 39–40, 92–94
  Aotea 39–40, 93, 141
  Maru 93
  see also waka
Carrington, Frederic 109
Carrington, O. 110, 111
Carrington, Wellington (brother of Frederic) 126
carts 46, 70, 134
carved poles (pou whenua) 10
carvings 46, 48, 55
Catholic God 42, 55
Catholic priests 55
cattle 67, 121–22, 132
ceremonial bonfires 45–58, 70
ceremonies 20–26, 34–36, 39, 45–46, 50–54, 56–59, 62, 65, 67, 88, 96
  cleansing 2
  flag-raising 127
  kai ngārara 46, 51, 58
  lizard-eating 52
  protective 53
  superstitious 142
  tapu-removal 26
  Testament-burying 36
chants (karakia) 28, 40, 42, 48, 54, 81, 127
Chatham Islands 152
Chief Justice (James Prendergast) 154
chiefs 5, 15, 17, 20, 26, 36, 87, 146, 150
  see also leaders
Christianity 40–41, 44, 50, 52, 55, 57
  abandoned by Tītokowaru 40
  benefits of 105

burning of an image of Maru at Pātea after embracing 41
conversions in the 1840s 5, 81, 88
and the Kaingārara movement 45, 53, 58, 73, 75, 83, 108, 122
and the prospect of Māori and Pākehā living peacefully together 115
Christian 15, 24, 34, 37, 44, 51, 53, 80, 88, 115
  baptisms 2, 20, 88
  ceremonies 50
  communities 2
  faith 87, 112
  gatherings in the south 12
  and God 17, 24, 43–44, 81
  leaders 21
  missionaries 24, 44, 49, 51–53, 80, 117, 119
  philosophies 152
  prayers 46, 51
  sins 88
  supporters 115
church construction 12, 41
Church Missionary Society 8, 42, 71, 88
church services 12, 26, 44, 46, 112, 127
churches 42, 48, 52–53, 121–22
CMS *see* Church Missionary Society
colonial 4, 9, 80, 97
  forces 82, 97, 117, 121
  government 2, 25, 81, 99, 150
  invasion 114
  officials 156
  persecution of Māori prophets 151
  racism 120
  relations 27
compensation 103–4, 120, 155
Compensation Court 137
conversions (Christian) 50, 81
Cook Islands 50
Cook Strait 6
Cooper, George Sisson 30, 32–33, 35–36
correspondence *see* letters
courts 67, 76, 100, 137
Cowan, James 117, 122
Creed, Charles 17
crops 32, 41, 118, 120, 122, 128, 148, 152–53
Crown Grants 136

Daily Southern Cross 145
death 12, 15, 17–18, 19, 29, 32, 40, 43, 48, 51, 54, 56, 77, 80–81

certificates 4, 12
rates of Māori 19–20, 25, 55, 117
demons 2, 20, 43–44, 58, 81, 97, 156
devils 44, 54
diaries 49, 51, 56
Dictionary of the Maori Language (Williams) 88
disease 19, 25, 56
disputed lands 10, 29, 32, 75, 106
doctrines 13, 41
Domett, Alfred 129
Dunedin (Ōtākou) 154
dwellings 9, 27, 106, 116 *see also* houses

Eaglehawk (near Bendigo) 27
elders 11, 15, 55, 62, 64, 76, 89, 93, 95, 98
Elsmore, Bronwyn 88, 113
emissaries 24, 58, 100
encampments 17, 112
epidemics 2, 18–19 *see also* disease
Erueti (pro-Kīngitanga chief) 100–1
ethnographers 23, 80
Europeans 15, 34–35, 40, 81, 127, 130 *see also* Pākehā
Evening Post 145
evil 11, 23, 40, 49, 100, 125, 130–31

families (Māori) 16, 19, 30, 98, 108, 118, 120, 141 *see also* whānau
families (settler) 135–37, 139
farms 3, 5, 29–30, 70, 123–24, 135–36
feasting 46, 50, 145
fences 57, 119, 154
Fenton, Judge F.D. 81
feuds 33, 38
field guns 134 *see also* guns; *see also* muskets
fires 2, 22, 46, 52, 58, 61, 66–67, 70–71, 95–96, 98, 118–19, 124
  ceremonies 45–47, 49–50, 54, 55–56, 57–58
  Kaingārara (Taranaki) 45–55, 58–59
  Kaingārara (Whanganui) 55–58, 60
  Kaingārara movement 70, 124
  Kaitoke ceremony 58
  military 78
  prophets 39, 56, 60, 66, 70, 119
  tapu 46, 61, 70
  Te Ito 2, 45, 55, 60, 67, 70, 118
fishing 40, 54, 83, 90–92, 95, 112
  boundaries 91
  canoes 92–93

  from waka (canoes) 94
  hooks 134
  during the lamprey season 90
  nets 134
  parties 54
  transgressions 91
FitzRoy, William 9
flagpoles 14–15, 25, 71, 73, 100–1, 125, 127
flags 15, 71, 73, 101, 125, 127
flour mills 122
food 17, 21–22, 39, 46, 68, 70, 96, 142–43, 145, 147, 149
  baskets 20
  cooking 58, 87
  forest 152
  growing 17
  plantations 128
  supplies 69
Fort Rolleston 155
fortifications 33, 125, 134
furniture 109, 119

gardens 9, 29, 48, 85, 135, 155
garments 20, 53, 86–87, 116, 144
God/gods 13, 15, 20, 22, 42, 44–45, 54, 60–61, 80–81, 106, 115, 147, 150–52 *see also* atua
god image (atua whakapakoko) 40, 42, 55
Gold, Colonel Charles 109, 117–18, 122, 133
gold mining (New Zealand) 30
goldrush (Victoria) 26–27
Goode, Penelope 83–84, 113
Gordon, Arthur 154
Gospel 11, 113 *see also* Bible
government 7, 9, 30, 32, 61–62, 64, 68–69, 74, 78, 79, 91, 109–10, 129–32, 138, 143–44, 153
  administrators 154
  claims 130
  colonial 2, 25, 99, 150
  forces 124
  incursions 132
  land-hungry 151
  newspapers 107
  officers 36, 65, 104, 114
  spies 126
  surveyors 1, 108–9
governors 10, 120
  Arthur Gordon 154

governors (*cont.*)
   George Grey 7, 9, 77, 104–7, 109, 111, 115, 120–22, 129
   Thomas Gore Browne 126, 139
   William FitzRoy 9
greenstone 46
Grey, Governor George 7, 9, 77, 104–7, 109, 111, 115, 120–22, 129
guns 11, 33, 70, 134, 139, 145 *see also* rifles, *see also* muskets

haka 132
Hakopa (assessor) 11
Halse, Henry 10–11, 15, 25, 51–53, 55–56, 59, 64, 66–67, 96, 114
Hammond, Revd T.G. 21, 37, 39–40
Hangatahua River 152
hapū *see* iwi/hapū
Hapurona Pukerimu (known as Tianara Hapurona or General Hapurona) 86, 116–17, 122, 124–26, 146, 148
Haupōkia (Ngāti Maniapoto leader) 17
Hāwera 34, 55
healers 23, 113
Heke, Hōne 14
Heke Niho Puta (migration) 6
Hikurangi Pā 23
Hinearapiti (Te Ito's wife) 133, 152, 155
history 1, 4, 38, 113, 155
History of Taranaki (Wells) 38
Holdaway, Simon 9
Holy Communion 44, 48
Holy Scriptures 35–36 *see also* Bible
Holy Spirit 13
homes *see* houses
Horopūriri *see* Oropūriri
horses 8, 10–11, 26, 28, 38–39, 100, 104, 121–22 *see also* white horses
hospitals 103
houses 9, 29, 43, 46, 107
   burning of 49–50, 78, 110–11, 118–19, 120–24, 132, 137
   forced to abandon 112, 139
   plundering abandoned 121, 134
   Te Ito's house 152–53, 155, 157
Houston, John 55
Hua block 31–32, 35
hui 35–37, 51, 73, 76, 100, 127, 137–39, 141–47, 149–50
   large 66, 146, 150
   Māhoetahi 145
   Mataitawa 145, 146

mediation 78
monthly 152
pan-tribal 35
Parihaka 142, 145
Taiporohēnui 51
Huihana (Te Ito's wife) 4, 5, 7, 8
Hurirapa Pā 99, 110–11

Ikamoana Pā 68–71
illness 89, 124, 131
images of atua 40, 42, 50
independence 2, 19, 25, 59, 75, 145–46
   of indigenous people 99
   movement 34
   political 15–16, 28, 75, 97
   religious 16
Inglewood 135
invasion 109, 111–12, 114–18, 120, 122–23, 129, 131, 133, 148, 151, 156, 158
   colonial 114
   military 3, 4, 55, 78, 115, 120 *see also* war
Ironside, Revd Samuel 5
iwi/hapū 5, 7, 41, 88, 97, 101, 125, 152
   Ngā Mahanga 41
   Ngā Rauru 122
   Ngā Ruahine 8, 53, 97, 114
   Ngāti Maniapoto 7
   Ngāti Maru 143
   Ngāti Matakore 7
   Ngāti Ruanui 102, 114, 127
   Ōtaraua 68
   Puketapu 4, 8, 16, 29, 65–66, 138
   Taranaki Iwi 33–34, 36, 41, 51–54, 69–72, 74, 100, 102, 114, 116, 121–22, 130–32, 141, 143, 145
   Te Ātiawa 4–6, 8, 16, 29–30, 32, 65–66, 69, 71, 97, 99–100, 102, 114, 132, 141–43, 145–47

kahawai 92–93
kai ngārara ceremonies 46, 51, 58
kai ngārara fires 45–46, 55
Kaihīhī 35
Kaingārara movement 1–3, 52–54, 58, 60–62, 64–66, 73–82, 84, 97, 99–101, 103–5, 113–14, 121–24, 131, 156–57
   alliances 114–15
   allies 113
   chiefs 62, 121
   councils 75, 91, 148

courts 83, 118
doctrine 41–42
followers 37, 45, 88, 92, 97, 108, 117
and 'land league' 36, 65–66, 104–7, 113–15, 156
leaders 62, 64, 66, 69, 73, 77, 79, 82, 84, 89–91, 95, 100–3, 106
letters 79–97, 113, 129, 134
origin of the name 39–41
prophets of 2, 64
school 54, 66, 100, 131
settlement 83, 148
supporters 12, 51, 65, 79, 116, 131
vision 152, 157
Kaipakopako Pā 65, 68, 118
Kaitoke 57–58
Kāpiti 5, 17
karaka trees 70
karakia (chants) 28, 40, 42, 48, 54, 81, 127
Karutahi (atua) 43, 83, 137
Kātātore, Waitere 7, 9–10, 14, 32–33, 38, 61–62, 64–69, 71, 74, 76, 79
death of 71
murder ordered by Īhāia Te Kirikūmara 68
offer of land 91
Ketemarae 13, 62, 127
Keteonetea Pā 62, 93–94
King, William 110, 115, 122, 134, 143 see also Te Rangitāke, Wiremu Kīngi
King movement 71, 99–100 see also Kīngitanga
Kīngi, Eruera 143
Kīngitanga 99, 101, 103, 127, 131, 144
Te Ito's relations with 100, 125
and the Waitara conflict 157
see also King movement
King's flag 100–1
kokiro (ceremony for tapu-removal) 88
Kōmene (southern Taranaki leader) 73, 75, 76
Kuikui Pā 99, 109–11

lamprey (fish) 90
land 17–18, 25, 46, 51, 54, 78, 82, 114, 131, 153
cleansing of 55
confiscated 135, 138, 140
disputed 10, 29, 32, 75, 106
Puketapu 68
reserve 30
Te Ātiawa 30, 49, 119, 133

tribal 135
land confiscation 133, 136, 153, 155, 157
Mataitawa district 140
settlers 135, 138
southern Taranaki 135
Te Ito 138, 140
'land league' 36, 65–66, 104–7, 113–15, 156
land sales 7, 10, 14, 16, 25, 29, 35, 51, 54, 66, 68–69, 76
Bell Block 1, 10–11, 119–20
Hua block 31–32, 35
Kātātore's offer 91
Pekapeka (Waitara) block 109, 111, 131
and the Puketapu conflict 29
Waiwhakaiho block 30
language 27, 53, 138
laws 25, 81, 108, 126
leaders 28, 30, 37, 39, 41, 44, 65–66, 75–76, 78–80, 94, 101–2, 114, 125–26, 143–45, 148–49, 151, 156
prophetic 39, 105, 151
southern Taranaki 26, 65, 75, 114, 157
see also chiefs
leadership 6, 7, 68–69, 75–77, 118, 121, 128, 132, 142, 144, 155, 157
Lepperton 3, 135
letters 11–12, 14–15, 60, 62, 64–65, 73, 75–77, 79–97, 100–3, 105, 106, 114–17, 128–30
lizards 2, 16, 23–24, 43, 46, 56–57, 62, 80–81, 91 see also ngārara
Lord Worsley (mail steamer) 131
Louisa (Rāwiri Waiaua's boat) 8
Lutheran mission 34
Lyttelton Times 155

Mahau (native assessor) 137–40, 142–43, 145
mahi kikokiko 97, 101–2
Māhoetahi 125, 138, 140, 142, 145
Maiterangi (Te Ito's daughter) 4, 133, 152
mākutu (sorcery) 16, 22, 83–85, 88
mana 14, 17, 29, 39–40, 60, 64, 66, 68, 113, 115, 144–45, 148, 151–52
leaders 75, 145, 151
prophets 144, 151
Te Ito 76, 144, 152
Manawapou hui 36
Maniapoto, Rewi 27, 101–2, 118

Manutahi Pā 118, 134, 139
Māori 2, 19, 28, 33, 39, 45, 115, 120, 130, 137, 151–52
  and communities 3, 6, 20, 37, 46, 57, 73, 92, 96, 132, 135, 150, 157
  and government 153
  and land 27, 131, 151, 153
  miners 27
Maori Life in Old Taranaki (Houston) 55
maps
  Northern Taranaki (1862) 3
  Kaingārara presence in Taranaki (1857–64) 47
  Houses and farmsteads destroyed (1860–61) 123
marae 50, 101, 154
marines 109–10 *see also* sailors
Marlborough Sounds 5–7
marriage certificates 50, 84
martial law 108
Maru (atua) 39–40, 42, 48–49, 55, 93–94
Mataitawa 3, 108, 111–12, 116–18, 121, 123–28, 132–36, 139, 145, 155
  abandoned by Te Ito and Tāmihana Poihaka 135
  chief Tāmihana Poihaka 143
  and the departure of Te Ito to visit his Ngāti Ruanui whānau from 126
  encampment 112
  hui 146
  lightly defended pā protecting 134
  military invasion of 3, 133–34
  settlement 132, 140
Matariki 50
Matiu (Te Ito's cousin) 5, 31–32
Matiu (Rāniera's brother) 134
mats 105
mauri (object containing life-force or mana) 29, 33–34
McLean, Donald 6–7, 9, 11, 13, 30–31, 51, 68, 71, 76–77, 104–5, 107, 126, 148–49
measles 19, 152 *see also* illness
meeting house 34, 35, 41, 138
meetings 7–10, 15, 32, 35–36, 66, 73, 105–7, 138–40, 142–44, 146–47, 149, 152 *see also* hui
Merrett, Joseph Jenner 25–26
Methodist Church *see* Wesleyan (Methodist) Church
miasmas 19–20

Mihi Watara (Te Ito's wife) 50, 85, 101, 133
military 27, 126, 154
  aggression 132
  alliance 114
  campaigns 8, 135
  camps 155
  commanders 97
  defence 118
  intelligence 82
  leadership 68, 86, 146
  redoubt 129, 130
  reoccupation 131
  resistance 3, 114
  settlers 135–36
military invasion 3, 4, 55, 109, 111–12, 114–18, 120, 122–23, 129, 131, 133, 151, 156, 158
  Mataitawa 133–34
  Parihaka 4, 151–52, 156
  Waitara 3, 78, 109, 115
mills 35, 54, 148 *see also* flour mills
Miriama (Maiterangi) (Te Ito's mother) 4, 32
mission stations 21
missionaries 24, 44, 49, 51–53, 80, 117, 119
Mōkau 2, 76–77, 152
money 11, 26–27, 32, 38, 109, 119–20
Moturoa 142–43
movements 11, 13, 28, 44, 49, 52, 56, 99, 113, 147
  anti-land selling 113
  indigenous resistance 89
  King 71, 99–100
  land-holding 16, 28, 65
  prophetic 66, 151
  religious 113
  tikanga hou (new practices) 13
Murihiku (south Dunedin) 58
muskets 54, 117

native assessors 10, 67, 70, 137
Native Land Court 4, 133
Native Minister 111, 130
  C.W. Richmond 104–5, 136–40
  Francis Dillon Bell 111, 129–30
  John Bryce 154
Native Secretary *see* McLean, Donald
Naylor, William *see* Ngatai, Wiremu Nēra
Neirai (Te Ito's daughter) 101, 108

Nelson Examiner and New Zealand Chronicle 119
New Plymouth 1–2, 3, 5–10, 21, 25–26, 28–30, 33–34, 49, 51, 67–70, 82, 103, 121–22, 123, 125–66, 136–38, 140, 142–43, 148
New Testament 34–37
New Zealand Constitution Act 1852 33
New Zealand Settlements Act 1863 136
newspapers 49, 72, 126, 141, 146
  Daily Southern Cross 145
  Evening Post 145
  Lyttelton Times 155
  Nelson Examiner and New Zealand Chronicle 119
  Taranaki Herald 15, 70, 72, 82, 105, 115, 123–24, 127, 134, 137–38, 145–46
  Te Manuhiri Tuarangi 107
  Wanganui Chronicle 56
  Wellington Independent 43
Ngā Mahanga 34–35, 36, 37, 41
Ngā Rauru 122
Ngā Ruahine 8, 41, 48–49, 52–53, 62, 97, 100, 102, 135, 143, 146
Ngaere, Rāniera (Te Ito's cousin) 5–11, 14–15, 26, 31–33, 112, 134
ngārara 2, 16, 20, 22–23, 24, 37, 43, 58, 79, 80, 81, 91, 146
Ngāromate, Ropata (Te Ito's brother) 51, 143
Ngāruawāhia 100–2
Ngātai, Wiremu Nēra 88
Ngāti Maru 118, 134
Ngāti Ruanui 8, 12–21, 33–35, 39, 41–42, 62, 69, 71, 84, 86–87, 93, 100–1, 121–2, 125–26
Ngāwhare, Tāmati Reina (Te Ito's adoptive father) 12, 14–16, 25, 28, 34, 60, 62, 73, 87–88, 127
Nicholas, John 80
Niger, HMS 109, 121–22

Oettli, Peter 34, 36
Ōmatā 121–22
ontology (different realities) 156–57
ope whakanoa (tapu removal troop) 25–29, 33–34, 37, 39, 44, 102, 156
oral traditions 55
Ōraukawa, Tāmati Hōne 41, 48, 52
Oropūriri (Horopūriri) 6–9, 11, 14–15, 21, 31–33, 65, 112

Ōtākou (Dunedin) 154
Ōtaraua hapū 68

pā 2, 7, 9, 26, 29, 33, 37, 72, 75, 84, 87, 100–1, 116–17
  Hikurangi 23
  Hurirapa 99, 110–11
  Ikamoana 68–71
  Kaipakopako 65, 68, 118
  Keteonetea 62, 93–94, 99, 109–11
  Manutahi 134, 139
  Paraiti 45
  Taki Ruahine 55
  Taranaki 34
  Te Huiarapa 110
  Te Karaka 70
  Te Kōhia 116–17, 122
  Te Puata 99, 101, 103, 109, 111, 118–19, 143
  Te Whanga 84, 85, 89, 92, 95, 98, 99, 109, 111
  Wherohia 99, 109–11
Pākehā 15, 39, 105, 121 *see also* European
Pākehā settlements 2, 30
Pākeke, Hōri Kīngi 12
Parai, Hēmi 100
Paraiti 1, 4–11, 13–14, 18–19, 21, 25–27, 29–31, 33, 45, 49–50, 68, 70, 99, 155
Paramena (Te Ito's brother) 4, 13, 14, 101
parawai (bordered mat) 105
Parihaka 4, 53, 73, 77, 135, 141, 143–44, 146–57
  cultivations 154
  founding of the community 141, 148–49
  hui 142, 145
  leaders 142, 145, 147, 149, 153–54
  military invasion 4, 151–52, 156
  occupied by an armed military force 154
Parris, Robert 27, 62, 64–66, 68, 79, 103–7, 111–12, 115–16, 118, 124–25, 135–44, 146–50
Pataka, Hemi 143
Pātea 2, 41–42, 45, 48, 54–55, 67, 77
peace 114, 120, 125–26, 128, 131, 134, 139, 141–42, 145–47, 152, 157
  mission 142
  negotiations 134
  settlement 128, 153
Pekapeka block 109, 111, 131
Pelorus Sound 6
Pirimona 22

Pleiades cluster 50
Poharama Te Whiti 142–43, 148
Poihaka, Wiremu Tāmihana 118, 121, 123–28, 132–34
Pokima, Hōri 152
police 25–26, 42, 55, 151–52
police barracks 10, 14, 25, 26
political alliances 78 see also politics
political ambitions 71, 103, 157
political tensions 29
politics 30, 146
Pratt, General Thomas 125, 128
Prendergast, James 154
priests (Catholic) 55
priests (lizard-expelling) 16, 23, 40
priests (Polynesian) 50
prophecy 45, 72, 137, 150
prophets 23, 43, 89, 146–47, 151
   and horses 8, 10–11, 26, 28, 38–39, 100, 104, 121–22
   imposters 126
   of Kaingārara 2, 64
   leadership 131–32
   Parihaka 3
   and rangatira 98–115, 118, 149
   relations between 141, 144
   Riwha Tītokowaru 40, 135
   Rua Kēnana 39, 151
   Te Ito 1, 4, 30, 38, 40–42, 45–46, 60, 70, 84, 113–14, 122–24, 126–29, 154–60
   Te Kooti 39, 150–51
   Te Ua Haumēne 60–61, 88, 98, 131, 151
   Te Whiti-o-Rongomai 3, 53, 77, 141–54, 157
   Tohu Kākahi 141, 142, 151, 154
Puanga 50, 90, 149
Puketapu 5–6, 8–11, 16, 30, 33, 38, 43, 50, 68, 71–72, 138, 143
   assessors 15, 142
   block 31
   conflict over land sales 29
   forces 68
   hapū 4, 8, 16, 29, 65–66, 138
   land 31, 68
   leaders 7, 9–10, 61
   neighbours 10
   pā 138
   population 5
   settlements 5
   supporters 138
   whānau 124

Puketapu Feud 33, 38
Puketaua 35

Queen Charlotte Sound 6

rangatira 98–115, 118, 141, 149
   Kaingārara 99, 131
   and prophets 98–115, 118, 149
   Te Ātiawa 157
rangatiratanga 97
reserve land 30
Richmond, C.W. 104–5, 136–40
Riemenschneider, Revd Johann 34–35, 41–42, 43–45, 48–50, 53, 67–69, 71, 72, 115, 118
rifles 33 see also muskets
Rogan (Taranaki Land Purchase Commissioner) 118
Rua Kēnana 39, 151
Ruatara (Bay of Islands chief) 80

'sacred groves' 20, 22, 62
sailors 109–10
Satan 24, 44, 53
schools 54, 66, 75, 100, 131
ships see boats
Sinclair, Keith 36, 65, 113
Society Islands 50
South Island 39, 58–59, 150
South Taranaki 55, 88
Stannard, George 21–22, 37
Stapp, Major Charles 137
Sub-Protector of Aborigines see McLean, Donald
surveyors 1, 62, 79, 108–10, 153

Taiporohēnui hui 51
Taituha (Ngāti Ruanui chief) 84–85
Taki Ruahine Pā 55
Tamakaihou (waka) 8
Tāmati Te Ito Ngāmoke see Te Ito
Tāmihana, Wiremu see Te Waharoa, Wiremu Tāmihana
Tāne-nui-a-rangi (Great Tāne of the heavens) 23–24
taniwha 43, 62, 79
taonga 45–46, 73
tapu 2, 16–17, 20–22, 26, 28–29, 34, 37, 43–45, 49, 57–58, 60–61, 70–72, 78–83, 87–88, 97, 100–2
   bonfires 70
   clothing 46

dangerous 20, 82
defined 81
divine 35
heathen 34
influence of atua 88
items 2, 58, 67, 100
removal ceremonies 16, 26
sites 17–18
stones 37, 45, 48
tribal 87
uncontrolled 18
wāhi tapu (sacred places) 20–24, 37, 42–46, 49, 56, 149
Taranaki 1–2, 4–5, 7, 14–17, 20–21, 23, 25–27, 34–38, 43–45, 55–56, 59–61, 72, 101–2, 104–5, 124–26, 129–31, 152–54
art and material culture 55
atua 39–40
captives 5
ceremonies 58
coast 16, 54, 82
independence movement 2, 100, 108
leaders 7, 36, 51, 75
pre-Christian 16
tribes 21, 36, 69, 99, 102, 114, 121–22, 131, 133
unifying 16, 38, 52, 77
wars 3, 82, 99, 113–14, 140, 156
Taranaki Herald 15, 70, 72, 82, 105, 115, 123–24, 127, 134, 137–38, 145–46
Taranaki Institute 49
Taranaki Iwi 33–34, 36, 41, 51–54, 69–72, 74, 100, 102, 114, 116, 121–22, 130–32, 141, 143, 145
Taranaki Land Purchase Commissioner *see* Parris, Robert
Taranaki Report (Waitangi Tribunal) 104, 113, 122, 157
Tarurutangi block 32
Tātaraimaka 129–30
Tāwhiao, King 144, 150
Taylor, Alan 55
Taylor, Richard 8, 20–25, 48–49, 54–57, 75, 81, 107
Te Ātiawa 4–6, 8, 16, 29–30, 32, 65–66, 69, 71, 97, 99–100, 102, 114, 132, 141–43, 145–47
chief Wiremu Kīngi Te Rangitāke 120, 126, 142
communities 25
followers 101

forces 69
hapū 5
land 30, 49, 133
leaders 14, 17, 25, 113, 126, 133, 141, 145, 148, 152, 156
pā 86
rūnanga 102
settlements 99, 119
sovereignty 71
speakers 145
supporters 67, 141
and war 117
Te Hēnui 123
Te Ito
adoptive father 12, 14, 16, 73, 88
arrest of 4, 67, 140, 155
brothers 4, 13, 14, 51, 101
burning of his pā 78, 109
burning of settler houses 119–20, 123–24, 137
children 4, 12, 101, 108, 133, 152
and community at Mataitawa 3, 112, 118, 124, 126–27, 132–34
and community at Paraiti 4, 7–11, 25–26, 31, 33, 155
and community at Parihaka 3, 147–48, 149, 152, 155
correspondence with Kaingārara followers 82–97
cousins 5, 6, 31
fire ceremonies 45–47, 49–50, 54, 55–56, 57–58
Kaingārara leadership 2, 39, 52, 62, 64–65, 66, 73, 75, 77, 101–3, 105, 121, 123, 124, 128, 131, 156–57
Ngāti Ruanui relatives 4, 8, 12, 16, 30, 126–27
parents 4, 8, 12, 13, 32
prophetic status 39–45, 64, 71–72, 126, 144
Puketapu relatives 4–5, 8, 9, 14, 16, 21, 29, 38, 43, 50, 66, 124
relationship with Tāmihana Poihaka 118, 125, 126–27, 128, 132, 133, 134
relationship with Te Whiti-o-Rongomai 53, 141, 144, 145–46, 147–48, 149–51, 152, 157
relationship with Wiremu Kīngi Te Rangitāke 7, 17, 45, 85, 99, 108, 112–15, 118, 119–21, 122, 126, 148
Tamati Tito (known as) 28, 155
uncle 5, 7, 14, 30, 31, 137, 138, 147

Te Ito (*cont.*)
  vision of unity 2, 12, 16, 77–78, 108, 137, 146, 152–53, 158
  wedding 50
  whakanoa mission 2, 16, 20–21, 24, 25–26, 28, 33–34, 36–37, 39, 49, 53–54, 56, 67, 72, 156
  wives 4, 5, 7, 8, 50, 85, 101, 133, 152
Te Kaporoa 137
Te Karaka Pā 70, 103
Te Karawa, Īhāia 73–74, 95–96
Te Kekeu, Hōne Rōpiha Ngāmoke 84
Te Kepa 94
Te Kirikūmara, Īhāia 45, 67, 68–72, 74, 76–77, 99, 103–4, 114–15, 117, 142
Te Kohe, Piripi 58
Te Kōhia Pā 116–17, 122
Te Kooti 39, 150–51
Te Kuikui block 110
Te Kūiti 150
Te Maihāroa, Hipa 39, 58–59, 150–51
Te Manu Karaitoa (Te Ito's father) 4, 8, 12, 13
Te Manuhiri Tuarangi 107
Te Manutoheroa 5–6
Te Matakātea, Wiremu Kīngi 54, 69, 73, 75–76, 131, 143, 148, 153, 157
Te Mātorohanga, Moihi 23, 82
Te Ngāhuru, Tāmati Wiremu 51, 61, 64, 67, 70, 75–76, 78, 100, 124
Te Oneroa (Te Ito's son) 4, 12
Te Oropūriri (Horopūriri) 5, 112
Te Puata Pā 118
Te Rangitāke, Wiremu Kīngi 3, 7, 8, 9, 14, 17, 25, 36, 45, 66, 68, 71–72, 76–77, 99–107, 108, 109–15, 118, 119–20, 121–26, 128, 131–32, 141–43, 148–49, 150, 157
Te Rauparaha, Tāmihana 34–35
Te Rei Te Hanataua, 121
Te Tahana Papawaka (Te Ito's uncle) 5, 7, 9–11, 14–15, 30–32, 51, 105, 112, 137–40, 142, 145–47
Te-Tatau-o-te-po (ancient house of learning) 22
Te Teira 76–77, 103–11, 114–15, 118, 140, 143
Te Ua Haumēne 60–61, 88, 98, 131–32, 151
Te Umuroa 51, 62, 67, 72, 74, 76, 98, 100, 131, 148

becomes a significant centre of political independence 75
chief Wiremu Kīngi Te Matakātea 54, 69
large Taranaki Iwi kāinga 54
leader Wiremu Kīngi Te Matakātea 121
Te Waharoa, Wiremu Tāmihana 120–21, 125–26
Te Warihi (Kaingārara leader) 89
Te Watarauihi 75, 93
Te Whanga 84, 89, 98, 99
Te Wherowhero 104
Te Whiti-o-Rongomai 3, 53, 77, 141–54, 157
Te Whiwhi, Mātene 33–34
Te Kāhui 16, 22
teachers 12–13, 22, 35, 37
Testament-burying ceremony 34–37
tikanga (policy or plan) 65, 113
tikanga hou (new practices) movement 13
timber 116, 135
Tīraurau, Tāmati 68
Tītokowaru, Riwha 39–40, 135–36, 140, 145–47, 151
Tohu Kākahi, 77, 141–43, 146, 148, 150–54, 157
tohunga 11, 16, 20, 22–23, 26, 28, 32, 37–41, 49–59, 80–82, 91, 93, 144
  local 56, 83, 90
  matakite (seer) 26, 39, 60, 144
  pre-Christian 97
  and prophets 144
  specialising in expelling ngārara 16
Toma Whakapo 101–2
Totoinumia, Ropata 73–75, 90–91
tradition 14, 22, 23, 55, 92
transformation 39, 65, 82
  political 41
  from tohunga to prophet 39, 65, 82
translation of Māori into English 72, 77, 83–84, 113, 144
trawling for kahawai 92–93
Treaty of Waitangi 131
trees 56, 70, 94, 139
tribal 1–3, 7, 26, 34–35, 37, 66, 69–70, 83, 87, 99–100, 144–46, 148, 151–52
  affiliations 7
  boundaries 37, 83
  courts 99
  divisions 144, 151
  elders 55

history 1
lands 135
rūnanga 66, 114
systems 106
tribes 2, 8, 14, 27, 29, 36, 41, 66–67, 69, 122, 138, 145–46
  better-armed 5
  Taranaki 21, 36, 69, 99, 102, 114, 121–22, 131, 133
  Waikato 29
  Wanganui 155
  see also iwi/hapū
troops 2, 21, 26, 109–10, 112, 117, 122, 125, 130, 133, 140
  armed 153
  government 157
truce 125, 131
tūāhu (shrines, praying stones) 22, 40, 48, 81
tukutuku panels 42
Tully, John 27
Turton, Revd Henry 8, 10

unification 12, 46, 55, 61
  God's work of 61
  political 46, 55
  spiritually inspired 12
Urenui 72, 103, 143
utu 77, 119, 122

vendors of land 30–31
Victorian goldrush 26–27

wāhi tapu (sacred places) 20–24, 37, 42–46, 49, 56, 62, 149
  ceremonies 20–21, 26, 37, 46
  rites 24
Waiaua, Rāwiri 9–11, 15, 32–33, 38, 61
Waiheke 48–49
Waikanae 6–8
Waikato 5, 17, 26, 34, 81, 99–100, 123–25, 131
  atua 43, 83
  chiefs 17
  conflict 156
  emissary 100
  fighters 124
  forces 5, 125, 127, 138
  invaders 54
  supporters 101
  war 124, 156
  warriors 124

Waikato King 100, 104
Waingongoro River 152
Waiongana River 9, 99, 104, 109–10, 133, 139
Wairarapa 152
Waitaha 73–75, 90
Waitaha land offer 75
Waitaha Stream 148
Waitangi Tribunal 30, 104, 107, 113, 122, 130, 132, 152–53, 157
Waitara 3, 7, 73, 76, 96–97, 99–100, 105–6, 109, 111–16, 118–19, 124–26, 129–31, 133, 138–39, 143
  chief Te Teira 103, 107
  community 103
  dispute 157
  land 76–77, 103, 106–8, 114, 122, 126
  leaders 99, 104, 106
  military invasion of 3, 78, 109, 115
  rūnanga 76
  sale 107, 142, 156
Waitara River 8, 70, 118, 125, 132, 134
Waitōtara mission station 21
Waiwhakaiho block 30
Waiwhakaiho River 9–10
waka 8, 94, 141
  Aotea 39–40, 93–94, 141
  fishing 94
  Tamakaihou 8
  see also canoes
Wallace, Rod 9
Wanganui Chronicle 56
war 40, 110, 115, 117, 120, 122, 124–25, 127–32, 134, 141–42, 147–48, 157
  captives 5, 17
  and the Kaingārara movement 113–15
  leaders 27
  oracles 68
  parties 121
  Taranaki 131
  Waikato 124, 156
Wārea 13, 34–35, 41, 45, 48–49, 51–54, 62, 84, 122, 143, 148
warfare 10, 17, 24, 70, 157 see also war
Warre, Colonel 133–34
warriors 116, 122, 124
weapons 14, 139
Wellington Independent 43
Wells, Bernard 38
Weriweri 48–49
Wesleyan (Methodist) Church 32, 88
  church buildings 17, 32, 71

Wesleyan (Methodist) Church (*cont.*)
    ministers 12
    missionaries 5, 7, 12
    teachers 12
Wesleyan Missionary Society 45
Wetai, Āperahama 73
wētā 62, 79, 91 *see also* ngārara
whakanoa (tapu removal) 2, 21, 28, 46, 49, 53–54, 87–88, 149
whakapakoko rākau (images of gods) 40, 42–43
Whanga *see* Te Whanga
Whanganui 8, 13, 21, 46, 56, 58, 88, 127, 152, 154
Whanganui River 21, 23, 56–57
whānau 108, 111, 124, 126 *see also* families (Māori)
Wherohia Pā 99, 109–11
Whiro (older brother of Tāne) 23–24
white horses 38–39 *see also* horses
Whiteley, Revd John 5, 9, 17, 44, 71–72, 107, 112, 117–19
whooping cough 19
Williams, Henry 88
Williams, William 88
Winitana Tupotahi 27
women 75–76, 108
Woon, Revd William 12–13, 15
worship 32, 40, 46, 121